# Health for Life

*Authors*
**Julius B. Richmond**
John D. MacArthur Professor of
  Health Policy
Director, Division of Health Policy
  Research and Education
Harvard University
Advisor on Child Health Policy
Children's Hospital of Boston
Boston, Massachusetts

**Elenore T. Pounds**
Health Education Writer
Downers Grove, Illinois

*Physical Fitness Author*
**Charles B. Corbin**
Professor, Department of Health
  and Physical Education
Arizona State University
Tempe, Arizona

Scott, Foresman and Company
Editorial Offices: Glenview, Illinois

Regional Offices: Sunnyvale, California •
Tucker, Georgia • Glenview, Illinois •
Oakland, New Jersey • Dallas, Texas

## Authors

Julius B. Richmond, M.D., is the John D. MacArthur Professor of Health Policy and the Director of the Division of Health Policy Research and Education at Harvard University. He also is Advisor on Child Health Policy at the Children's Hospital of Boston. Dr. Richmond served as Surgeon General for the U.S. Public Health Service and as Assistant Secretary for Health from 1977–1981. Trained as a pediatrician, Dr. Richmond joined the faculty of the Harvard Medical School in 1971. He was professor of child psychiatry and human development before being appointed Surgeon General.

Elenore T. Pounds, M.A., is a health education writer and lecturer. A former elementary teacher, she served as directing editor of the Health and Personal Development Program. She is co-author of *Health and Growth, You and Your Health,* and other health publications.

Charles B. Corbin, Ph.D., is professor and coordinator of graduate studies in the Department of Health and Physical Education at Arizona State University. A former elementary physical education teacher, he previously served as professor and head of graduate studies in the Department of Health, Physical Education, and Recreation at Kansas State University. Dr. Corbin is the author of many research and professional publications, especially in the area of lifetime fitness.

ISBN: 0-673-29682-2

Copyright © 1990
Scott, Foresman and Company, Glenview, Illinois
All Rights Reserved. Printed in the United States of America.

1 2 3 4 5 6 7 8 9 10 VHJ 99 98 97 96 95 94 93 92 91 90

## Consultants

**Reading**
Robert A. Pavlik, Ed.D.
Professor and Chairperson
Reading–Language Arts Department
Cardinal Stritch College
Milwaukee, Wisconsin

**Medical**
Jerry Newton, M.D.
Director, Health Services
San Antonio Independent School District
Clinical Professor, Pediatrics
University of Texas Medical
School, San Antonio
San Antonio, Texas

**Design**
Design direction by Norman Perman
Graphic Designer and Art Consultant

Cover photograph by Michael Mauney

**Acknowledgments**
The dental health information contained in Chapter 8 is considered by the American Dental Association to be in accord with current scientific knowledge, 1986.

For further acknowledgments, see page 384.

## Content Specialists

### Dental Health
Mary Banas
Program Specialist
Bureau of Health Education and
Audiovisual Services
American Dental Association
Chicago, Illinois

### Drug Education
Chwee Lye Chng
Assistant Professor
Division of Health Education
North Texas State University
Denton, Texas

Merita Thompson
Professor
Department of Health Education
Eastern Kentucky University
Richmond, Kentucky

### Family Life Education
Linda Berne
Professor
Department of Health and
Physical Education
The University of North Carolina
Charlotte, North Carolina

### Nutrition
Jean Mayer
President
Tufts University
Medford, Massachusetts

### Safety and First Aid
Janice Sutkus
Technical Specialist
National Safety Council
Chicago, Illinois

## Reviewers and Contributors

Lourdes Alcorta-Rogover
Educational Consultant
Former Teacher
Miami, Florida

Ruth Ann Althaus
Professor of Public Health
Master of Public Health Program
Illinois Benedictine College
Lisle, Illinois

Matthew Bustamante
Bilingual/Cross-Cultural
Education Specialist
Bandini Elementary School
Montebello, California

Judi Coffey
Educational Consultant
Learning Disabilities Specialist
Jonesboro, Arkansas

Bryan Cooke
Professor
Department of Community Health
College of Health and Human
Services
University of Northern Colorado
Greeley, Colorado

Gail Daud
Teacher in Gifted Education
Spring Shadows Elementary School
Houston, Texas

Bo Fernhall
Director, Fitness and Cardiac
Rehabilitation
Department of Physical Education
Northern Illinois University
DeKalb, Illinois

Linda Froschauer
Teacher
Weston Public Schools
Weston, Connecticut

Rosalyn Gantt
Teacher
Midway Elementary School
Cincinnati, Ohio

Jon Hisgen
School Health Coordinator
Pewaukee Public Schools
Pewaukee, Wisconsin

Peter Loudis
Teacher of Gifted and Talented
Spring Branch Junior High School
Houston, Texas

Jeanne Mannings
Teacher
Adamsville Elementary School
Atlanta, Georgia

Wanda Nottingham-Brooks
Learning Disabilities Teacher
Morrisonville Junior and Senior
High School
Morrisonville, Illinois

Bert Pearlman
Director, Curriculum Research
and Evaluation
Office of the County
Superintendent of Schools
Santa Barbara, California

Candace Purdy
Health Teacher
Maine South High School
Park Ridge, Illinois

Joan Salmon
School Nurse
Greenwood School Corporation
Greenwood, Indiana

Jean Clark Shuemake
Teacher
Urban Park Elementary School
Dallas, Texas

Betty Smith
Teacher of Talented and Gifted
Kiest/Urban Park Elementary School
Dallas, Texas

David R. Stronck
Associate Professor of Health
Education
Department of Teacher Education
California State University, Hayward
Hayward, California

Terry Thompson
Teacher
Bowie Elementary School
Lubbock, Texas

Shirley Van Sickle
Health Teacher
DeVeaux Junior High School
Toledo, Ohio

3

# Chapter 1     Learning About Yourself  18

# Chapter 2

# Growing and Changing  48

**Chapter 3**        **Choosing Foods for Good Health**   74

# Chapter 4

## Becoming Physically Fit 104

# Chapter 5

## Safety and First Aid  140

# Chapter 7

## Fighting Against Disease  198

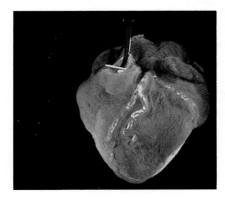

**Chapter 8**　　　　　**Daily Care for Good Health**　234

# Chapter 9

## Your Decisions as a Health Consumer 256

# Why Learn About Health

"When you have your health, you have just about everything." You might have heard this saying before. What does it mean to you? Most people agree that good health is one of the most important qualities a person could have. When you are healthy, you can enjoy life more fully, whether at school, work, or play. You not only feel and look your best, but you can think more clearly and get along better with others.

In the past, being healthy meant not being sick. Today, people are becoming aware of a more complete idea of health. This idea includes physical, mental, and social health. *Physical health* is the condition of your body. *Mental health* includes how you feel about yourself and how you handle problems. *Social health* involves the way you handle your relationships.

Good health is the responsibility of every person. Today more than ever, people can take control of their health. Because you are making more and more of your own health decisions, learning about health is very important. Decisions such as what to eat, whether or not to exercise, and how to treat others are part of daily life. To make the wisest decisions, you need sound, accurate information. Then you need to know how to use this information. Finally, you need to develop *skills for life*—skills that help you deal with events in your life in positive and healthful ways. Scott, Foresman's *Health for Life* provides all these tools, but it is up to you to use them. Make good health a part of your day and a part of your life, now and in the future.

# When You Read This Book

**1.** Read the question.

**3.** Find the answers.

**4.** Learn the health words.

**2.** Look at the pictures.

**sanitary landfill,** an area of land where garbage is buried in such a way as to minimize water pollution, air pollution, and the spread of disease.

**recycling,** changing a waste product so that it can be used again.

Glass can be recycled.

How is garbage buried at a sanitary landfill?

## 3 How Can People Dispose of Garbage More Safely?

Disposing of garbage is a major problem for many large cities. Garbage has to go somewhere. In the past, "somewhere" was usually a street, river, or open dump on the edge of town. These methods of garbage disposal were extremely unhealthy. The garbage attracted rats and other animals that carried diseases. The trash was often burned at the dump, but this burning caused much air pollution.

Today many communities dispose of garbage in ways that pollute as little as possible. One way is by using a **sanitary landfill.** Bulldozers smash the garbage together, as shown. Then a tractor covers the garbage with a layer of dirt. The next day, another layer of garbage is compacted and covered with dirt. This process is repeated with each day's garbage. Sanitary landfills reduce some kinds of pollution, but they must be checked constantly for leaks. Some landfills leak dangerous chemicals into the soil and groundwater. Another problem with sanitary landfills is that they use up a lot of land, and many communities are running out of land for them.

Another way to deal with the garbage problem is by **recycling**—changing waste products so they can be used again. The glass bottles in the picture, for example, will be separated according to their color. The glass will be crushed, melted, and made into new bottles. Paper, aluminum, and rubber are some other materials that can be recycled.

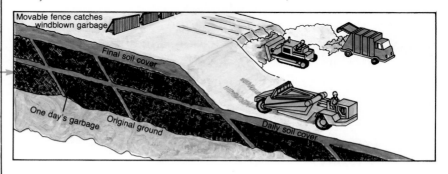

Movable fence catches windblown garbage

Final soil cover

One day's garbage

Original ground

Daily soil cover

298

Some communities burn garbage in large furnaces called incinerators. Trucks empty the garbage into a huge pit, like the one shown. A crane lifts the garbage and drops it down a chute that leads to an incinerator. Many incinerators have scrubbers or other devices to remove many of the materials from the smoke.

Disposing of wastes without polluting improves the quality of life in a community. Clean water, air, and land provide what a community needs for good health.

**Think Back** • *Study on your own with Study Guide page 335.*
1. What are the advantages and disadvantages of using sanitary landfills to dispose of garbage?
2. How does recycling and incineration help communities deal with garbage disposal?

*Did You Know?*
Some hospitals and large apartment buildings in Sweden use one of the most advanced garbage-disposal systems in the world. Trash is dumped into chutes and is sucked through a vacuum-powered pipeline to a central incinerator. The heat from the burning garbage generates electricity, warms buildings, and melts ice on roads during the winter.

Some communities burn garbage in large incinerators.

**5.** Use what you learned.

299

# 1

# Learning About Yourself

The people in the picture have a goal. Can you guess what it is? For two days, the mountaineers have been climbing the slopes of Mt. Rainier. They are willing to put up with hardships such as blistering wind and exhaustion because their goal is important to them. You probably have goals too. They might not include climbing Mt. Rainier, but each of your goals is just as important to you.

This chapter discusses goals and how to reach them. The chapter will also help you understand more about yourself and your relationships with others. Useful suggestions will show how you can work to improve yourself throughout your lifetime.

## Health Watch Notebook

Think of a time when you accomplished a goal that was important to you. Write a paragraph in your notebook describing how it felt to achieve something that you had worked hard for.

1  What Is Self-Image?
2  How Can You Get Along Better with Others?
3  How Can You Deal with Stress?
4  How Can You Set and Reach Goals?

**self-image,** the way a person feels about himself or herself.

## 1  What Is Self-Image?

The young people here are ready to start a new year at school. Like you, they have some special hopes and plans. They want to do as well as they can in their schoolwork. Some want to succeed in other ways. For example, some students might want to join school clubs or sports teams. Others might want to write for the school paper. Still others, especially the newcomers, want to make new friends.

A good **self-image** can help these people do many of the things they want to do. A good self-image can help you too. A self-image is the way a person feels about himself or herself. If you have a good self-image, you generally feel good about yourself.

## What Are Some Characteristics of a Person with a Good Self-Image?

If you have a good self-image, you have confidence in what you can do. You are willing to try something new. You do not avoid new activities just because you might not do well. You try not to let your mistakes get you down. Instead, you remember that everyone makes mistakes at times and that you can learn from mistakes.

If you have a good self-image, you also recognize that you are a very special person. In fact, you are unique. Nobody in all the world is just like you. Recognizing that you are unique helps you understand that all people are different. You are not just like others, and you do not expect others to be just like you. Accepting differences in people helps you get along with others better.

**On Your Own**
How might a person with a poor self-image feel about himself or herself? Write your ideas on a sheet of paper.

21

**attitude** (at′ə tüd), a way of thinking about a particular idea, situation, or person.

## How Can You Make Your Self-Image Better?

Your self-image does not have to stay the same. You can change it. If you have a poor self-image, you can work to make it good. If your self-image is already good, you can make it even better.

The following suggestions can help you improve your self-image. They are examples of good **attitudes**—ways of thinking—about yourself. You might recognize some of them as attitudes you already have. Others you might want to try to develop.

• Keep in mind that you are a special person. Nobody else has exactly the same combination of interests, abilities, problems, and feelings that you have. Nobody can take your place in the world because nobody else is exactly like you. You are an important person.

• Think about what you can do well. Everyone has some strengths. These strengths are different in different people. You might be good in a certain subject in school. Perhaps you are good in a certain sport, in singing or playing an instrument, or in building models. One of your strengths might be getting along well with people and helping others when you can. What do you think the person in the picture is good at? What do you do well?

Being able to take care of animals is one of this girl's strengths.

22

• Recognize and accept your weaknesses, but do not think about them too much. If you think more about your strengths, you will have enough self-confidence to help overcome your weaknesses, if you wish.

• Expect to make mistakes sometimes. You, like all people, will make mistakes throughout your life. When you make a mistake, learn from it. Try to figure out why you made the mistake so that you do not make the same one again. Understand that nobody is perfect. Making mistakes is part of life.

• Realize that you will not always get what you want. Everyone has disappointments. The way you react to those disappointments can either improve or hurt your self-image. For example, the two people shown here each worked very hard on a poster for a contest, but neither won a prize. They are both unhappy, but which person do you think is reacting in a way that is helpful to her self-image? Why do you think so?

**Think Back** • *Study on your own with Study Guide page 316.*

1. What is self-image?
2. What are three qualities of a person with a good self-image?
3. What attitudes can help make a self-image better?

Which student has the healthier attitude?

That does it! I'm just no good. If I were good, I would have won. I'm not going to enter any more stupid contests.

Oh well, I'll try again next time. I had fun making my poster and I know it's good. But now that I've seen the winning ones, I think I can do better another time.

# Health Activities Workshop

## Getting to Know Yourself

1. Like many people your age, you are probably beginning to ask some important questions about yourself. To answer some of these questions, write a newspaper article about yourself. Answer the questions below as you write your article. The picture shows an example of how your article might look.

- Who am I?
- What am I good at?
- What would I like to be better at?
- What do I care most about?
- What is a problem for me?
- Who are my friends?

2. In addition to or instead of the article in Activity 1, write a poem about yourself. The poem might describe your feelings right now, how you generally feel about things, or what you would like to do in the coming year.

## Daily News

An Interview with Joe Reyes, Famous Sixth-Grader

Who is Joe Reyes?
I am eleven. On December 17 I will be twelve. I like basketball and I play pretty well. I have black hair and brown eyes. I live in Santa Fe, New Mexico. I have two sisters, one older than I and one younger. I also have an older brother.

Joe, what do you feel you are good at?
I like science and I do okay in it. I am good at baseball and basketball. I can cook. My brother and I take care of the yard. We do a pretty good job.

What would you like to be better at?
I would like to be better at keeping my temper. I would also like to be better at giving oral reports. I get nervous when I give oral reports and sometimes I don't do well. I wish I could draw as well as my friend David.

What do you care most about?
I really like to go hiking in the mountains with my scout troop. Sometimes we see a lot of trash that other people leave behind. I care a lot about not messing up the land. I wish other people did.
I care a lot about my family and my friends. My family has a dog named Shane. I care a lot about him, too.

3. Write down the names of three or four people you admire most. Then, after each name, list the qualities of the person that make you admire him or her. Underline the qualities on the lists that you would like to have. Put a star next to the qualities you think you already have.

4. Make a poster that shows you are a special person. You might want to use a photograph of yourself in the poster.

5. Many different people, organizations, and events have probably influenced your ideas and feelings to help form the person you are. On a sheet of paper, write as many of these sources as you can think of. Some sources might include your family, a scouting troop, and television shows.

What problems do you have?
Some kids I know are starting to smoke. They say I should do it. I don't think I should. I know it's bad for your body, and my folks would have a fit. I wish those kids would stop bothering me.

Who are your friends?
I don't have a lot of friends, but I a lucky. I have two very good friends, vid and Frank.
hen we tried out for baseball last mer, I didn't have a good glove. So 'd let me use his.
ank, David, and I usually play her after school. If it is raining, ay games inside. Sometimes we watch

d says maybe his family is going soon. I hope not. I don't like k about not having David around.

## 2 How Can You Get Along Better with Others?

The pictures on these two pages show different kinds of **relationships**—connections between persons or groups. You have different relationships with different people. You have one kind of relationship with your friends and another kind with your teacher. You have different relationships with different family members. Which picture shows a family relationship? a student–teacher relationship?

Building good relationships is an important part of having a good self-image. Getting along with other people helps you feel accepted and valued. Then you feel better about yourself.

### What Does Getting Along with Others Mean?

Getting along with others does not mean that you always agree with other people. You do not always have to do what other people do, especially if you think what they are doing is wrong. Getting along with others means that you listen to other people and try to understand how they feel. You do not always try to get other people to do what you want to do. Getting along with others also means that you treat them the way you would like them to treat you.

What four relationships do these pictures show?

Most people will treat you in some of the same ways you treat them. How do you want to be treated by other people? Do you want to be pushed around and made fun of, or do you want to be liked and treated with respect? If you want to be treated with respect, you have to treat others that way. What are some ways to show respect for members of your family? for friends? for other people you know?

## Why Are Friendships Important?

Friendships are very important relationships. You can talk with friends about problems. You can spend time together working on activities you enjoy. People become friends for different reasons. You and your friends probably share some of the same interests. You enjoy some of the same activities. You might have other friends who do not share many of your interests, but they might share some of your attitudes toward certain things.

You cannot be friends with everyone. However, getting along with people who are not your friends is also important. Most people have a few close friends they spend time with, but they are also friendly toward other people who are not their close friends.

***On Your Own***

Three months after Phil started at his new school, another new boy, Doug, joined his class. Phil remembered how lonely and shy he had felt on his first day in the new school three months before, so he sat with Doug during lunch. A few days later, one of Phil's friends was having trouble with a math lesson. Phil offered to help him after school.

Why is Phil the kind of person others might want for a friend? How might the way Phil treats other people affect his own self-image? Write your answers on a sheet of paper.

## What Can Help When You Are Angry?

Marie was almost ready for school. She went to her closet to get her favorite sweater. The sweater was not there. "Rita did it again!" she shouted. Marie slammed the closet door. She ran to the head of the stairs and called down. "Mom, Rita took my sweater again. Tell her to give it back."

"She's already gone, Marie. Wear something else."

Marie was furious. She thought, "It's just not fair. I never borrow Rita's clothes without asking first. Just wait till I see her this afternoon."

Feeling angry at times, even at people you care about, is part of life. Most people feel angry when they think they have been treated unfairly, or when they see someone else being treated unfairly. Learning to deal with your anger will help you get along better with other people. However, keeping angry feelings locked up inside yourself will make you feel unhappy. You need to get the feelings out in a healthy way.

The first step in dealing with anger is to admit that you are angry. Then you need to get rid of the angry feelings so that you can deal with the problem that made you angry. You are more likely to solve problems when you are not upset. Finally, you need to try to solve the problem that made you angry.

Marie walked to school to help work off her angry feelings.

Taking your mind off your feelings for a while can often help you get rid of anger. You might work on a hobby, visit a friend, listen to music, or read a book.

You could try being physically active to get rid of your anger. Ride your bike, take a walk, or do some other kind of physical activity. You work off your angry feelings as you exercise. After a while, you probably will be able to think more calmly about the situation that made you angry.

If you are very angry or if your angry feelings stay with you for a long time, you might want to talk about your feelings with someone you trust. You could talk with a family member, a friend, or a teacher. Talking about a problem can help you get your feelings into the open. Then you might be better able to deal with those feelings. The person you talk with might also suggest ways to solve the problem that made you angry. Look at the pictures to see how Marie dealt with her anger.

**Think Back** • *Study on your own with Study Guide page 316.*
1. How can a person get along better with others?
2. Why are friendships and family relationships important for health?
3. What are some helpful ways to deal with anger?

**On Your Own**
Write a list of some things that make you angry. Then explain how you could deal with that anger in healthy ways.

Marie talked with a friend and then with her sister about her feelings.

**stress,** the body's physical and mental reactions to demanding situations.

Science test
Tickets
Basketball
Messy room
Family moving

What is causing Steve's stress?

# 3 How Can You Deal with Stress?

Steve has a science test next Friday. He has promised to sell twenty tickets for the Boy Scout Jamboree, and so far he has not sold one. His friend Ryan keeps urging him to sign up for basketball at school. At the moment his room is a mess and his mother is annoyed about it. On top of all this Steve knows his father is thinking of taking a new job in another town. His family might have to move.

How do you think Steve is feeling? He is worried about the test. He wishes he had never promised to sell so many tickets. He does not really want to play basketball, but he does not want to tell that to Ryan. Steve's messy room makes him feel uncomfortable now that he really looks at it. Also, he is concerned about the possibility of moving to another town.

These many troublesome feelings cause Steve to feel tense. His head hurts and his stomach is a little upset. He is experiencing **stress**—his body's reactions to the demands he is facing. Stress prepares the body to deal with difficult situations. Sometimes stress can be helpful. When a person is faced with danger, stress gets the body ready to face the danger or to get away from it quickly.

### What Causes Stress?

You might think that only upsetting or dangerous events cause stress, but this is not true. Even events you might think of as fun can cause stress. The people on the roller coaster are feeling stress. Getting ready to go on a vacation might cause stress. Any exciting event or situation, such as taking a test, watching an exciting sports event, or arguing with other family members can cause changes in your body that you feel as stress.

Change can also cause stress. Such changes include moving to a different town or school and changes in your family, such as a birth, death, divorce, or illness. Your body reacts to these changes by producing certain chemicals. Even being tired, thirsty, or hungry causes stress. Your body reacts to these situations by signaling you to sleep, drink, or eat.

## What Are Some Harmful Effects of Too Much Stress?

A certain amount of stress cannot be avoided and is not harmful to you. In fact, some amount of stress helps you do your best and is often pleasant. Too much stress, however, can harm your health. Stress affects different people in different ways. Some common effects of stress include headache, sleeplessness, and upset stomach. Feeling nervous, getting angry easily, losing an appetite, or eating too much are other effects of stress.

Sometimes people who are under too much stress begin to have problems with their friends and families. They might become short-tempered. They might have trouble with their schoolwork or jobs. These reactions to stress cause even more stress.

Some causes of stress are fun.

*Did You Know?*
Whether stress comes from something pleasant or from something unpleasant, the following physical changes occur:
• Special endocrine glands, the adrenals, send the chemical adrenaline into the blood.
• The pupils of the eyes get larger.
• Body temperature rises.
• Breathing becomes faster.
• More blood is sent to the brain, heart, and large muscles.
• The liver sends stored sugar into the blood.

## How Can You Deal with Problems That Cause Stress?

Remember how upset and tense Steve was? Perhaps you have felt like Steve at times. Most people feel upset by stress every now and then. You can deal with stress in several healthy ways.

The first step is to realize that you are upset. Think about the problems that are bothering you. Then answer these questions.

- Which problems can I do something about now?
- Which problems can wait a while?
- Which problems cannot be changed?

Instead of just worrying and feeling under stress, you are now ready to take action.

When several problems are bothering you, working on one at a time can be helpful. Pick one problem to work on and do something about it right away. Ignore the other troubles for a while. Look back at Steve's problems. What is one thing he can do something about right away?

He should probably clean his room first. If he does that, he can get rid of two problems—the mess in his room and his mother's anger. Also, the physical work of cleaning his room can help get rid of some of his upset feelings.

Which problem could Steve work on next? After he cleans his room, he might start selling the Jamboree tickets to his neighbors. Selling the tickets will probably be less stressful than worrying about them.

Steve's worry list is getting shorter. Now he can deal with the problem of basketball. Steve can decide to tell Ryan how he feels, instead of putting it off and worrying about it. He can call Ryan and politely tell him that he really does not want to spend his free time playing basketball. Thus, Steve can change this stressful situation by making a decision and then acting on it.

Steve might not be able to get rid of all his nervousness about the science test. However, he can study a little bit each day to prepare himself for it. Each time he studies, he can review what he studied last. Then he can study a little more. Studying and reviewing a little at a time can be more helpful than trying to study everything at the last minute. Just knowing that he is working to prepare himself for the test might help lessen Steve's stress.

Steve has one problem he really cannot change. If his father takes the job in a different town, the family will move. Steve can try to stop thinking about the move so much. He can also try to change his feelings about it. He can remind himself that he will be able to make new friends, explore new places, and do different things in a new town. He can also write to his present friends from time to time.

In dealing with problems, keep in mind that all problems cannot be solved. Some, like Steve's moving, must be accepted. When you are able to accept problems, they often seem less important. What other kinds of problems might need to be accepted?

## How Can You Learn to Relax?

One way to help get rid of stress is to relax. You can teach yourself to relax in several ways.

The picture shows a simple exercise that will help you relax. Sit or lie in a comfortable position. Breathe out as completely as you can. Then breathe in through your nose as deeply as you can. Hold your breath while you count to four in your mind. Next, breathe out through your mouth while you count to eight in your mind. Do this exercise three or four times. You will be surprised how much calmer you will feel. Your heart will slow down and you should feel relaxed. This exercise is very helpful because you can do it almost anywhere.

Playing sports or doing any other kind of physical exercise you enjoy can help you relax. Working on a hobby is also a way to relax. Some people listen to music when they want to relax and get their minds off their problems. Getting your mind off a problem is not the same as avoiding a problem. Taking time off from thinking about a problem can often help you deal with it in a helpful way later.

Sometimes you cannot deal with a problem on your own. You might want to ask for help at such a time. Talk about your feelings with someone you trust. Sharing your feelings will often help you feel more relaxed. Also, a friend or family member might suggest ways to deal with your problem.

Breathing exercises can help you relax.

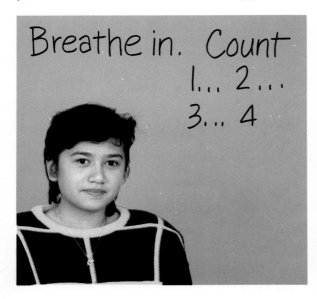

34

## How Can Making Decisions Help You Deal with Stress?

Dealing with stress often includes making a decision. You need to decide how to deal with the situation that is causing stress. Then you need to carry out your decision. Many people have trouble making decisions and then carrying them out.

You can follow five steps to help yourself make decisions and then follow through on them.

**Step 1. Realize that a decision is needed.** If you are feeling stress, you need to do something about it.

**Step 2. List the possible choices.** Think of all the ways to deal with the problem that is bothering you. Remember that some problems, such as Steve's worry about moving, cannot be solved and must instead be accepted. You might want to list accepting the problem as a possible choice of dealing with it.

**Step 3. List the possible results of each choice.** You might think of several ways to deal with your problem. Now think about the good and bad results that might happen from each choice. For each choice, ask yourself if it fits the guidelines on the right. You can eliminate choices that do not fit the guidelines.

**Step 4. Decide which choice is best.** After you think about the possible results of each choice, you will probably find that one choice stands out as the best one to follow.

**Step 5. Judge your decision.** After you decide which choice is best, try it. Then judge your choice to see if it worked. Sometimes your choice will not work out the way you want it to. If your first choice for dealing with a problem does not help, try another choice. Remember that you might just have to accept the problem since things often do not work out exactly as you would like.

| **Guidelines for Responsible Choices** |
| --- |
| • The choice should be safe and promote health. |
| • The choice should be legal and follow the rules of school and community. |
| • The choice would be acceptable to parents and other family members. |
| • The choice shows respect for self and others. |

**Think Back** • *Study on your own with Study Guide page 317.*

1. What causes stress?
2. How might stress affect the body? a person's actions?
3. What are some ways to deal with stress?
4. What are five steps for making a decision?

**goal** (gōl), something a person wants to do or achieve.

## 4 How Can You Set and Reach Goals?

Michael wanted to invite three of his friends to his home for lunch on Saturday afternoon. Before he invited his friends, he asked his mother if they could come over and use the kitchen. Michael told her he would shop for the food. He also told her he and his friends would do all the cooking, and they would clean up the kitchen after lunch. His mother agreed.

Michael and his friends had a great time. Michael's mother was happy too. Michael had set a **goal** for himself and reached it. A goal is something a person wants and is willing to work for. Michael worked to reach his goal of having his friends over for a lunch that they made. He felt good about himself.

People have different goals. Some people have goals about schoolwork or sports. Some have goals that involve hobbies, jobs, pets, or other people. Some goals might take a long time to reach. They are long-term goals. Others might be short-term goals. They take a short time to reach. For example, doing well on a certain test is a short-term goal. Improving grades in general is a long-term goal.

Michael set a goal, worked for it, and reached it.

## What Kinds of Goals Should You Set for Yourself?

People who are good at setting and reaching goals make sure several things are true about the goals.

First, a goal must be good for the person who sets it—you. How was Michael's goal good for him?

Second, the goal should be reachable in ways that are not harmful to others. For example, a person might set a goal of completing a coin collection. The person might decide to take coins from a friend's collection without the friend knowing about it. In reaching his or her goal, the person is harming someone else. What would be a responsible way for the person to reach the goal of completing a coin collection?

Finally, the goal should be realistic. A realistic goal is not too hard and not too easy. A realistic goal takes hard work and, sometimes, a little luck. A goal that is too easy takes no work at all. A goal that is too hard might be impossible to reach and require a great amount of luck. Each student shown here has set a goal of completing a science project in two weeks. Which student has set a goal that is too easy? Which student has set a goal that might be too hard? Which one has set a realistic goal?

Whose goal is the most realistic?

I'm really interested in volcanoes. If I read more about them, I could make a volcano model and a big chart about recent eruptions.

I'll use the same project I made for the science fair in the school I went to last year.

I don't know anything about lasers, but I'll hurry and learn all about them for my project.

## How Can Knowing Your Abilities Help You Set Goals?

The first step in setting a goal is deciding what you want to work toward. To make this decision, you need to think about your abilities—the things you do well.

Knowing what your abilities are can help you decide what to work toward. For example, a person who is good in art might decide to make a drawing for a student art show. A person who is a fast runner might decide to try to make the school track team. Both of these people have set realistic goals. They have abilities that will help them reach their goals.

Think about what you do well. You might be good at math, science, reading, or some other subject. You might be good at more than one subject. You might do well in a sport or in several sports. You might have a good singing voice or play the piano well. Perhaps you are good at caring for pets or farm animals. You might have responsibilities at home that you perform well, such as taking care of the yard or helping to care for younger children. You might have the ability to talk with, listen to, and help other people. What abilities do each of the people shown on these two pages have?

*On Your Own*
Think of some goals you might like to reach. List your ideas on a sheet of paper. Now think about your abilities. Think of as many of your abilities as you can. List your abilities on another sheet of paper. Compare your lists. Which of your abilities might help you reach some of your goals?

What abilities do these people have?

Knowing you are good at something gives you self-confidence. If you know you have an ability, you know you have a good chance of reaching your goal by working toward it. After you have reached a few goals, you will have even more self-confidence. You might then decide to try new activities. If you try new activities, you might find you have abilities you did not even know about. For example, suppose you have been playing ping-pong for a couple of years and are good at it. You might decide to try tennis. After a while, you might find that you could do fairly well at tennis too. Then you might set a goal of playing in a local tournament.

No two people have exactly the same abilities, so no two people are likely to set exactly the same goals in life. You do not have to set exactly the same goals as your friends. You and your friends might have some goals in common, but you will probably have many others that are different.

## How Can You Reach Your Goals?

Once you choose a goal to work toward, you can make a plan telling how you will reach your goal. Your plan should include a list of all the tasks you will have to do to reach your goal. List the tasks in order from first to last. Also list any problems you think you might have in reaching your goal. Then list ways to solve the problems. Think about any help you might need from other people.

Suppose, for example, that your goal is to memorize the part of a character for your school play. Your plan will include several tasks. First, you will need to read the part over several times. Then you will need to figure out how much of the part you need to learn each week in order to have the whole part memorized in time for the rehearsals of the play. You will have to study the part over and over. You might ask someone to watch the script and correct you when you make mistakes.

Once you make your plan, you can begin working on the tasks you listed. Check your progress from time to time. This step is important in reaching any goal you set. When you see that your plan is working, you will be encouraged to keep trying.

Sometimes when you check your progress, you might find that your plan is not working. Then you can change your plan and work toward your goal in a different way. After you have carried out your plan, you might want to ask yourself these questions.

- Did I reach my goal?
- Was my goal good for me and not harmful to others?
- Was my goal realistic—not too hard, not too easy?
- What did I do well in working toward my goal?
- What could I have done better?
- What did I do in working toward this goal that could help me reach future goals?

You might not reach every goal you set. However, you should not feel too badly about failing once in a while. Everybody has disappointments, but most people will reach many of their goals. You are a special person with abilities that can help you reach many goals.

## What Can Help If You Become Discouraged About a Goal?

As you work toward a goal, you might become tired or discouraged. Most people have these feelings at times. The chart shows several ways to keep working toward your goal in spite of these feelings.

Think about goals you have reached in the past. Kim wanted to learn to play the clarinet. When she got tired of practicing, she thought about how much she enjoyed playing the piano. Her years of practicing piano had been worth the work.

Think about how good you will feel if you succeed. Jim wanted to write a poem good enough to be published in the school newspaper. He thought about how proud he would be to have his friends and family see his poem in the papers.

Divide the goal into smaller parts. Calvin wanted to earn enough money to buy a new twelve-speed bicycle. He knew he would have to work for a long time to get enough money. He set smaller goals of how much money he wanted to earn each month.

Promise yourself a reward for working toward your goal for a certain amount of time. Carla decided to clean up her room. She promised herself she would stop after an hour and listen to music for fifteen minutes.

Set special times to work on your goal. Janet wanted to make a new dress. She decided to work on the dress every night between 7:30 and 8:30.

**Think Back** • *Study on your own with Study Guide page 317.*

1. What three things should be true about your goals?
2. What is a realistic goal?
3. How can setting goals build self-confidence?
4. What should a plan for reaching a goal include?
5. What can help if a person becomes discouraged about a goal?

# Health Activities Workshop

## Thinking More About Goals

1. Write a report about a real person who is famous for having set and reached a goal. Such a person might be a scientist, a doctor, an athlete, or an inventor. You can find information about such people in books, encyclopedias, magazines, or newspapers.

2. The picture shows that a young person has just reached a goal of being able to buy a bicycle. Describe what the person might have done to reach that goal.

3. Interview a person you know who has set and reached an important goal. The person could be either young or an adult. Ask the person these questions.

- What goals have you reached?
- How did you feel when you reached your goals?
- What new goals are you working toward?

## Looking at Careers

4. "What would you like to be when you grow up?" You have probably heard this question before. Perhaps you have asked it to yourself. Working at a particular career is a major goal and accomplishment in many people's lives. However, deciding on a career and planning how to train for it can be confusing. A **counselor** can help young people make such decisions.

A counselor at a high school might help students try to match their abilities and interests with possible career choices. Often the counselor helps students meet with people who are in various fields of work. These people tell students about their work. To be effective, a counselor keeps up with information about jobs of many kinds and the training needed for each kind of job. A counselor usually has four to six years of college education.

Imagine that you are a counselor. Ask a classmate to act as a student who is meeting with you to discuss career choices. Conduct an interview with the student to find out what possible careers might interest him or her.

For more information write to the American Association for Counseling and Development, 5999 Stevenson Ave., Alexandria, VA 22304.

5. Sometimes people have emotional problems that remain troublesome for a long time, such as not being able to deal with stress. Often, friends, family, or a family physician can help solve these problems. In some cases, a **psychiatrist** might be the most helpful.

A psychiatrist is a medical doctor (M.D.) who has additional training in preventing, finding the cause of, and treating emotional problems. Many people think a psychiatrist is concerned only with people who have serious mental illnesses. This is not true. Today, psychiatrists work to build people's self-confidence and improve self-images. They try to prevent people's problems from growing into serious ones.

A psychiatrist first checks to see that disease, injury, or infection is not the cause of a person's problems. Then the psychiatrist works with the person to learn how he or she thinks, feels, and behaves. To be helpful, a psychiatrist needs to know how the person feels about himself or herself, and how the person gets along with others and treats others.

A career closely related to a psychiatrist's is that of a psychologist. Look in an encyclopedia or other library book to find how these careers are alike and how they are different.

For more information write to the American Psychological Association, Educational Affairs Office, 1200 17th Street NW, Washington, DC 20036.

### Jasmine Lin Solos with the Chicago Symphony

The curtain rises. On stage the world-famous Chicago Symphony Orchestra begins tuning. As the lights dim, a hush falls over the crowd. The conductor emerges from a side curtain and strides to center stage. Following him is the soloist, twelve-year-old Jasmine Lin. The crowd begins to applaud. As the conductor raises his arms, Jasmine takes up her violin. The music is about to begin.

How did Jasmine come to solo for such a famous symphony at such a young age? She entered a contest with hundreds of other young musicians—and won. Her prize was money for continued music lessons and the honor of playing with the Chicago Symphony Orchestra.

How do you think you would feel about performing in front of a large audience? Like Jasmine, you would probably feel nervous at first. However, once she began playing, Jasmine says she was able to concentrate on the music. She very much enjoyed playing with the orchestra and learning about music from the orchestra members and the conductor.

Encouraged by her success, Jasmine has set new goals. She plans to try to win other music contests. Practicing every day, she says, will help her meet her goals. Listening to others play violin, studying music, and playing duets with her friends also help Jasmine become a better musician.

Setting and meeting goals is something Jasmine does very well. Her advice: Whatever you choose to do, stick with it. Keep working on it every day. With determination, you will likely succeed and feel proud.

**Talk About It**
1. How did Jasmine Lin get a chance to play with the Chicago Symphony Orchestra?
2. What are some goals for yourself that you have set and met? What are some goals you would like to set now?

## Planning Your Study Time

Getting good grades is a goal set by many people your age. To reach this goal, you need time to study. You can plan your study time at home. Begin by answering the following questions about how you study now.

- Do you study every day?
- Do you study at the same time every day?
- Do you do other things while you study, such as watch television, eat, or listen to music?
- Do you take breaks from studying?

You now have enough information to decide whether or not you already plan your study time well. Here are some ideas that can help you improve your study habits.

- Study at the same time every day. You might want to do all your studying at once, or do some work before dinner and the rest right after dinner.
- Try to find a quiet, well-lighted place to study where you will not be bothered by others.
- Do not do anything else while you study.
- Take a break once in a while.
- Review your work in the morning for a few minutes before leaving for school.

You could share these ideas with your family. Other students in your family might want to try to improve their own study habits. Family members who are not students could become more aware of your need for good study habits, and they might be willing to help you work toward this goal.

## Reading at Home

*Participate in a Group* by Judith E. Greenberg and Helen H. Carey. Watts, 1983. Learn how to be a part of a group and how to get along with others.

*Secrets of a Small Brother* by Richard J. Margolis. Macmillan, 1984. Explore through poems the relationship of two brothers.

*Moods and Emotions* by Ruth Shannon Odor. Child's World, 1980. Discover the positive and negative feelings people have and ways to recognize those feelings in ourselves.

# Chapter 1 Review

## Reviewing Lesson Objectives

1. Describe the characteristics of a good self-image. List some attitudes that help improve self-image. (pages 20–23)
2. Explain some ways to build good relationships. Explain why having good relationships with family and friends is important. (pages 26–29)
3. Describe some causes and effects of stress. List some ways of dealing with stress. (pages 30–35)
4. Make a list of guidelines to follow that can help a person set and reach goals. Describe how setting goals can affect a person's self-confidence. (pages 36–41)

For further review, use Study Guide pages 316-317

Practice skills for life for Chapter 1 on pages 338-340

SKILLS FOR LIFE

## Checking Health Vocabulary

Number your paper from 1–5. Match each definition in Column I with the correct word in Column II.

### Column I

1. the body's physical and mental reactions to demanding situations
2. the way a person feels about himself or herself
3. a way of thinking about a particular idea, situation, or individual
4. a connection or condition that exists between two or more people
5. something a person wants to do or achieve

### Column II

a. attitude
b. goal
c. relationship
d. self-image
e. stress

Number your paper from 6–8. Next to each number write one or two sentences using that word to explain how a person could improve his or her self-image.

6. confidence
7. mistakes
8. unique

Number your paper from 9–16. Next to each number write a sentence about goals using the word or words.

9. short-term goal
10. long-term goal
11. realistic goal
12. abilities
13. plan
14. discouraged
15. reward
16. change

## Reviewing Health Ideas

Number your paper from 1–15. Next to each number write the word that best completes the sentence.

1. A person who feels good about himself or herself probably has a good _____ .
2. A person with a good self-image knows he or she can _____ from mistakes.
3. You are _____ , that is, nobody in the world is exactly like you.
4. Everyone has certain _____ and weaknesses.
5. A person has a different _____ with each member of his/her family.
6. A person who wants to be treated with respect should treat others with _____ .
7. Keeping _____ feelings locked up inside is not a healthy idea.
8. The first step in dealing with anger is to _____ that you are angry.
9. Stress prepares a person's body to _____ with difficult situations.
10. In dealing with problems, a person should realize that all problems cannot be _____ .
11. Learning to relax is one way to help get rid of _____ .
12. One exercise that could help a person relax involves _____ in and out deeply.
13. After making a major decision about something, a person should _____ the decision to see if it was really the best one.
14. A _____ goal is not too hard and not too easy.
15. Reaching goals helps build a person's _____ .

## Understanding Health Ideas

Number your paper from 16–27. Next to each number write the word or words that best answer the question.

16. What is a person's self-image?
17. Why should a person try to figure out why he or she made a certain mistake?
18. What is a relationship?
19. What do friends usually have in common?
20. After admitting that you are angry, what is the next step in dealing with anger in healthy ways?
21. What might a person do to get rid of angry feelings?
22. What is stress?
23. How can stress be helpful?
24. What is one harmful effect of stress?
25. What is the first step in the five-step decision-making process?
26. What are short-term goals?
27. What should be included in a plan for reaching a goal?

## Thinking Critically

Write the answers on your paper. Use complete sentences.

1. How would you describe a person with a good self-image?
2. Suppose a friend of yours is very angry about something. How could you help your friend deal with his or her anger?
3. Suppose two friends each invite you to sleep overnight at their houses for the same night. How would you deal with this problem? Use the five steps for making a decision discussed in the chapter.

# Growing and Changing

"Were my feet really ever that small?" You might ask this question if you saw the shoes you wore when you were a baby. You have grown and changed much since then. As the picture suggests, you will grow and change more.

This chapter discusses changes of growth you might be experiencing now or will likely experience in the next few years. You will explore what causes these changes and how you can deal with them as you continue to grow.

## ⌐ Health Watch Notebook ⌐

In your notebook, make a family tree, recording the heights of your relatives. Write a paragraph explaining how heredity affects growth.

1  How Are You Growing?
2  How Do Your Endocrine Glands Affect Your Growth?
3  How Does Heredity Affect Your Growth?
4  How Do Your Health Decisions Affect Your Growth?
5  How Might Your Emotions and Relationships Change As You Grow?
6  How Can You Deal With Growth and Change?

# 1 How Are You Growing?

The picture shows students making scenery for their class play. The picture also gives a clue about the different ways people grow. All the students shown are about the same age. However, they have grown in different ways and are not all the same size. Some students might have grown several inches during the last year. Others might have grown one inch (2.5 cm) last year but will grow two inches this year. Still others might grow only a half-inch over the next two years, then suddenly grow three inches the following year.

These different growth patterns mean that every classroom has students of different heights. You and your classmates have different growth patterns too. Your own growth pattern is just one of the many things that makes you special.

Each person has a different growth pattern.

Your body has been growing and changing since before you were born. Old photographs of you would show gains in height and weight over the years. Sometime between the ages of nine and fifteen, however, you will start to grow more quickly. This stage of rapid growth is called a **growth spurt.** It lasts about two to three years. During this time, you might grow as much as five inches (12.5 cm) in a year. You might also gain ten or fifteen pounds (7 kg) in a year. These few extra pounds are a part of growing and do not make a person overweight.

Individuals differ in the age when their growth spurts begin. Girls generally begin their growth spurts at an earlier age than boys. Most girls experience rapid gains in height and weight sometime between the ages of nine and thirteen. Most of this growth usually occurs at age twelve or thirteen. Boys usually begin their growth spurts between the ages of eleven and fifteen. Most of their growth occurs at age fourteen or fifteen. Because of the timing of the growth spurts, many nine- to eleven-year-old boys are shorter than girls their own age. The boys usually catch up later during their own growth spurts.

**growth spurt,** a period of rapid growth. A growth spurt usually begins between the ages of nine and fifteen.

51

## How Do Different Parts of Your Body Grow?

During the growth spurt, each part of your body grows rapidly toward its adult size. However, this growth does not take place evenly. Different parts of your body grow at different rates. They reach adult size at different times. For example, feet, hands, arms, and legs often grow fastest. They can reach their full adult size before the rest of the body.

The cartoon exaggerates uneven growth. This growth might make a person feel awkward. You might feel as though your legs or arms are too long for your body. Keep in mind that the rest of your body will catch up as your growth continues.

Your growth spurt might have begun in fourth grade, or it might not begin until high school. The timing of your growth spurt will not affect your adult size. However, knowing what to expect during the growth spurt can help you deal with the changes of growth.

**Think Back** • *Study on your own with Study Guide page 318.*

1. What happens to the body during the growth spurt?
2. How is the timing of the growth spurt usually different between girls and boys?
3. What is an example of uneven growth during the growth spurt?

Different body parts grow at different rates.

## Thinking About Growing

1. As you grow, your body proportions change. Different parts of the body become larger or smaller in comparison to the rest of the body. You can investigate this comparison. For each person shown below, measure the length of the head and compare it to the total body length. How does this comparison change as a person grows?

2. Write a poem about growth. The poem might describe what happens as a person grows, or it might describe some of your feelings about growing.

## Looking at Careers

3. You have read about some changes that occur during growth. The proper, healthy growth of people your age is a major concern of a **pediatrician.** A pediatrician is a physician who specializes in the care of young people—from infants to teenagers.

A person who wants to be a pediatrician, or any other kind of physician, must attend school for seven to nine years after high school. This education includes three or four years of college, four years of medical school, and at least one year that combines classroom instruction with actual medical practice in hospitals and clinics. Many physicians train for an additional three years to become specialists, such as pediatricians.

Make a list of various kinds of physicians, including pediatricians. You might want to look up "Physicians" in an encyclopedia to find a list. Write what each kind of physician does.

For more information write to the American Academy of Pediatrics, 141 Northwest Point Road, Elk Grove Village, IL 60007.

**Did You Know?**

A condition known as
pituitary dwarfism occurs
when the pituitary gland
produces too little growth
hormone. People with this
condition seldom grow taller
than thirty-five to forty
inches (90-100 cm).
Scientists have recently
learned how to produce
growth hormone in the
laboratory. The use of this
artificial growth hormone will
help to reduce the effects of
pituitary dwarfism. Up to
now, the supply of growth
hormone was limited
because it had to be taken
from pituitary glands.

## 2  How Do Your Endocrine Glands Affect Your Growth?

You have learned that your body grows rapidly during the growth spurt. What causes this rapid growth? Part of the answer lies within a few tiny organs in your body.

Your growth is directed by a team of organs—the **endocrine glands.** The endocrine glands make chemicals called **hormones.** The hormones are released into the blood and carried to cells throughout your body. The hormones control how some parts of your body work. For example, some hormones cause your body to grow in height and weight. Other hormones cause other changes of growth.

The **pituitary gland** affects your growth more than any other gland. The illustration shows that the pituitary gland is located at the base of your brain. It is about the size of a pea. This tiny gland produces many kinds of hormones. One of these is growth hormone, which directs bone and muscle growth. Your growth spurt begins when your pituitary gland starts making a certain amount of growth hormone. When the pituitary gland stops making so much of this hormone, your growth stops, and you have reached your adult height.

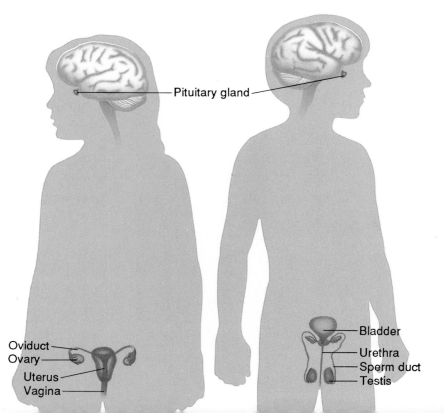

How do these endocrine glands affect growth?

The pituitary produces hormones that control the actions of many other glands. For example, the pituitary gland releases hormones that cause the reproductive glands to become more active. As the reproductive glands become more active, many important changes occur inside and outside the body.

Inside the body the testes in boys begin producing **sperm cells.** The ovaries in girls begin developing **egg cells.** The sperm and eggs are reproductive cells. The development of these cells gives a male or female the ability to reproduce, or have children.

As the testes and ovaries become more active, they begin making hormones of their own. These hormones cause the body to develop several adultlike features. For example, notice in the drawings how the body develops a more adultlike shape. Other changes include a deepening of the voice and the growth of body hair.

The time of life when these body changes take place is called **puberty.** Like the growth spurt, puberty begins at different ages for different people. Puberty usually begins in girls between the ages of eleven and fifteen. The changes of puberty usually begin in boys between the ages of twelve and sixteen.

**Think Back** • *Study on your own with Study Guide page 318.*

1. How does the pituitary gland affect growth?
2. What are the reproductive glands called in boys? in girls?
3. What changes occur as the reproductive glands become active?

**testes** (tes′tēz′) *sing.* **testis** (tes′ tis′) male reproductive glands.

**sperm** (spėrm) **cell,** the male reproductive cell.

**ovaries** (ō′vər ēz), female reproductive glands.

**egg cell,** the female reproductive cell.

**puberty** (pyü′bər tē), a period of time when the body develops more adultlike qualities, including the ability to reproduce.

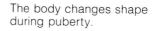
The body changes shape during puberty.

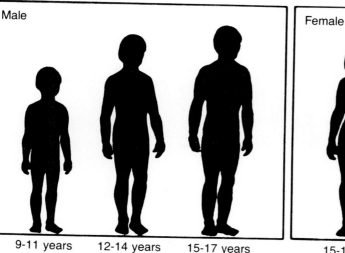

Male

9-11 years    12-14 years    15-17 years

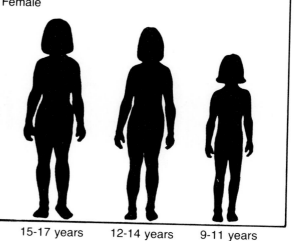

Female

15-17 years    12-14 years    9-11 years

## 3 How Does Heredity Affect Your Growth?

Chris noticed something interesting as his father and uncles were posing for a picture at the family reunion. They were all tall men. In fact, Chris was one of the tallest boys in his class. When he asked his father why most of the males in the family were tall, his father replied, "I guess it's our heredity."

What did Chris's father mean when he spoke about heredity? **Heredity** is defined as the passing on of certain traits from parents to their children. Some inherited traits are eye color, nose shape, the time the growth spurt begins, and adult height. Your mother and father shared in giving you inherited traits.

Shaded figures in Chris's family tree show the ancestors who were taller than the average height. Notice that this trait is more common on the father's side of the family. The trait of being tall was passed on from one generation to the next. Chances are that Chris will also be taller than the average adult male.

The trait of tallness has passed from one generation to the next.

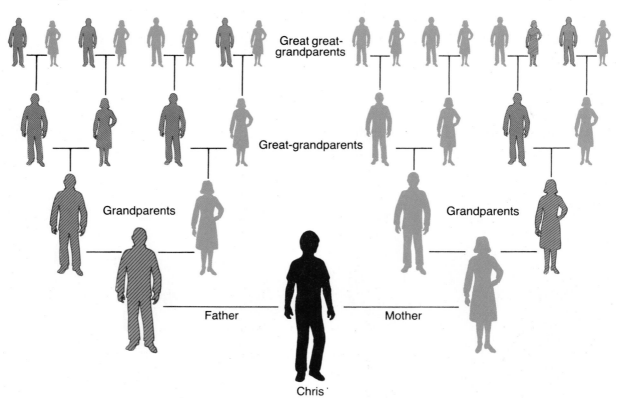

Great great-grandparents

Great-grandparents

Grandparents

Grandparents

Father

Mother

Chris

## What Determines Your Heredity?

The material that determines your heredity is found deep within the body cells. Almost every cell in your body has a central part called a nucleus. The nucleus controls the cell's activities.

Inside the nucleus are strands of matter called **chromosomes.** Each chromosome is made of a chemical substance known as **DNA.** The drawing shows that the structure of DNA looks like a spiraling ladder. The chemical structure of the DNA determines your inherited traits and your heredity. The portion of DNA that affects only one trait is a **gene.** The genes on your chromosomes are a combination of the genes from your mother and father.

**chromosome**
(krō′mə sōm), a strand of matter in the nucleus of a cell that contains the information for a person's heredity.

**DNA,** a chemical substance that makes up chromosomes and determines inherited traits.

**gene** (jēn), a small part of a chromosome that influences a specific inherited trait.

## How Do Chromosomes Pass from Parent to Child?

Almost every cell in your body has forty-six chromosomes. When a cell grows to a certain point, it divides, as shown in the pictures. First, the chromosomes make exact copies of themselves. The chromosomes thicken and the boundary of the nucleus begins to break down. Then, the chromosomes line up in the center of the cell. Next, the copies separate and move to opposite sides of the cell. Finally, the cell divides. Each new cell has forty-six chromosomes like those that were in the original cell.

A reproductive cell, however, grows and divides in a more complicated way than other cells. After the chromosomes make copies of themselves, the reproductive cell divides. Then, each of the two new cells divides again, resulting in four cells, as the drawing shows. This second division takes place without the chromosomes making copies of themselves. Therefore, each of the four sperm or egg cells has only twenty-three chromosomes.

When an egg and sperm cell unite, the twenty-three chromosomes in the sperm cell join the twenty-three chromosomes in the egg cell. The egg now contains forty-six chromosomes and is called a fertilized egg.

This fertilized egg divides and eventually develops into a baby whose cells have forty-six chromosomes. Half of the baby's chromosomes come from the mother, and half of the chromosomes come from the father. These chromosomes contain the information for the child's inherited traits.

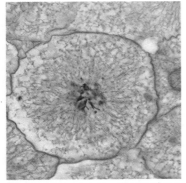
Chromosomes copy themselves and thicken.

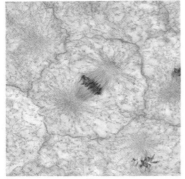
Chromosomes line up.

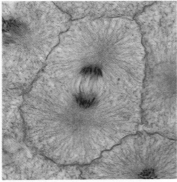
Chromosomes separate.

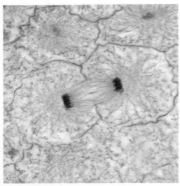
Cell divides.

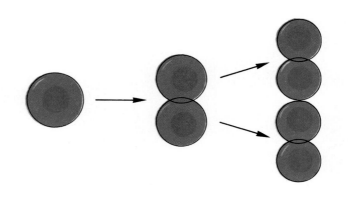

How is the division of a reproductive cell different from other cells?

## What Determines Whether a Person Is a Boy or a Girl?

The pictures below show the chromosomes from a boy and a girl. To make these pictures, chromosomes from the skin cells of two people were photographed under a microscope. Then, each picture was cut up, and the chromosomes were arranged into twenty-three pairs for each person. Notice the last pair in each picture. These chromosomes are the sex chromosomes. They determine the person's sex. In a female, both sex chromosomes are called X chromosomes. In a male, one sex chromosome is an X and the other is a Y.

An unfertilized egg cell or a sperm cell carries only one chromosome from each of the twenty-three pairs shown in the pictures. Therefore, each egg or sperm cell has only one sex chromosome. The sex chromosome in an egg cell is always an X. The sex chromosome in a sperm cell can be an X or a Y.

The drawing to the right shows what happens if a sperm with an X chromosome unites with an egg cell. The sex chromosomes of the offspring will be XX, and the baby will be a girl. If a sperm with a Y chromosome unites with an egg cell, the sex chromosomes will be XY. The baby will be a boy.

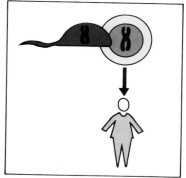

A fertilized egg with XX sex chromosomes will develop into a girl.

A fertilized egg with XY sex chromosomes will develop into a boy.

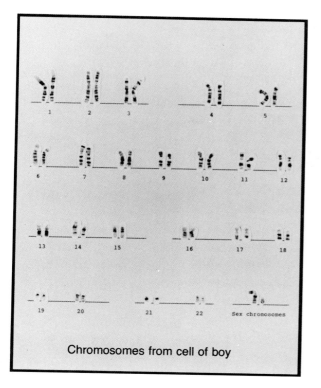

Chromosomes from cell of boy

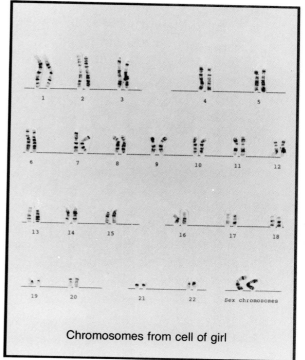

Chromosomes from cell of girl

## Why Do Individuals in a Family Differ?

Different sex chromosomes explain why some people in a family are male and some are female. Yet, even people of the same sex are very different from each other. Why do the sisters in the picture have different traits even though their chromosomes and genes came from the same parents?

The growth and division of reproductive cells gives each reproductive cell a different set of chromosomes. Every child in a family received forty-six chromosomes from the parents, but not the *same* forty-six chromosomes. Each child is likely to have different inherited traits because each child received different chromosomes with different DNA and genes.

## How Does Heredity Affect Growth Patterns?

Heredity affects growth patterns in three major ways. First, heredity determines when the growth spurt begins. Certain genes direct the pituitary gland to begin producing more growth hormone. Second, heredity influences how fast a person grows during the growth spurt. Third, heredity helps determine when the growth spurt stops. Genes direct the pituitary gland to stop producing so much growth hormone. At this point, a person has reached full adult height and weight. A person's weight will probably continue to change, but the height will stay the same throughout most of his or her adult life.

The series of pictures shows two brothers at various stages of growth. They have inherited some similar genes, but they did not inherit *all* the same genes. Different heredities gave each of them a different growth pattern. Notice how their heights differed as they grew.

Your growth pattern is part of the heredity that makes you a special person.

Different heredities gave these brothers different growth patterns.

**Think Back** • *Study on your own with Study Guide page 318.*

1. How do a sperm and an egg cell provide a person's inherited traits?
2. Why do children in a family have different inherited traits?
3. In what three ways does heredity affect growth patterns?

## Investigating Heredity and Growth

1. Use a life science text or an encyclopedia to find out how identical twins differ from fraternal twins.

2. The picture shows a famous painting by the French artist Pierre Renoir. What are some traits that the child seems to have inherited from her mother?

## Looking at Careers

3. A **geneticist** is a scientist who studies the inheritance and traits of living things. Some geneticists experiment with the genetic makeup of certain plants and animals to develop breeds, or types, that better serve human needs. For example, a plant geneticist might try to develop a type of corn that has better flavor or that can resist disease better. Other geneticists develop different breeds of farm animals, such as cattle or chickens, that grow more quickly or produce better meat. Medical geneticists work to prevent inherited diseases. They try to discover how certain substances affect human genes.

Like all scientists, a geneticist usually has at least seven years of college education.

Use an encyclopedia or a library book about genetics to find out how a plant geneticist develops different kinds of plants. What fruits and vegetables available today are the result of the work of geneticists?

For more information write to the American Society of Human Genetics, St. Christopher's Hospital for Children, 2600 N. Lawrence St., Philadelphia, PA 19133.

## 4 How Do Your Health Decisions Affect Your Growth?

Your heredity and your endocrine glands are not the only factors that affect your growth. Your health decisions have a strong influence on how you grow. You cannot control the actions of your heredity or your endocrine system. However, you can make decisions that influence your health and growth.

Your heredity sets limits for your growth. The pictures on these two pages show some of the health decisions that affect your growth within those limits. For example, the genes you inherit might set an upper boundary of five feet nine inches (about 175 cm) for your adult height. However, you might not reach this height if you have poor eating habits during your school years. Your body needs the right amounts and the right kinds of food to grow as it should. You can give your body the materials it needs for growth by eating a variety of foods. A good variety includes fruits and vegetables; dairy products; breads and cereals; and meat and fish. Eating too much of one kind of food does not give your body what it needs for proper growth.

Food and rest affect health and growth.

Heredity sets limits for weight, body shape, and muscle development. However, exercise gives you a great deal of control over these physical features. For example, if you exercise several times a week, your muscles are likely to become strong and firm. Strong muscles help you perform activities well without tiring easily. Strong muscles also help you hold your body correctly, giving you good posture. Muscles will develop only if you exercise them. Exercise helps you look and feel your best as you grow.

Your decisions about rest also affect how you grow. Most people your age need about nine to ten hours of sleep each night. While you sleep, your body uses energy from the food you eat to build new cells. Also, your body produces most of your growth hormone while you sleep.

Eating right, exercising, and getting enough sleep are wise decisions you can make to help you grow properly.

**Think Back** • *Study on your own with Study Guide page 319.*

1. If the upper limit of a girl's inherited adult height is five feet six inches (about 160 cm), will she definitely be that tall as an adult? Explain your answer.
2. What are three decisions you can make that affect your growth?

Exercise affects health and growth.

## 5 How Might Your Emotions and Relationships Change As You Grow?

Jan had never worried about her appearance before. This year, however, she has noticed some changes that make her feel uncomfortable about the way she looks. Her legs have grown three inches (7.5 cm) since last year. Her feet have grown much larger too, and she sometimes feels clumsy when she walks or runs. She wishes she was not so different from others in her class.

Jan's feelings about her growth show how physical changes can lead to emotional changes. Changes in height and weight might make you worry about your appearance. You might worry more about what others think of you. You might not be happy about the way you are growing because it makes you look different from your friends. Your worries could make you suddenly feel angry at times. Your mood might switch unexpectedly between happy and sad several times a day. Such emotional changes are bothersome, but they are a normal part of growing up.

Carla, Terri and Melissa are in the same class and have been close friends all year. They usually spend their Saturday mornings together.

One day Carla told her friends that her parents bought a piano and she wanted to learn how to play. Saturday morning was the only time she could take lessons.

Between lessons and practicing, Carla spent much less time with her friends.

Changing relationships is another normal part of growing up. Your relationships might change in two main ways as you grow. First, friendships with people your own age will likely become more and more important. Your relationship with your family can remain strong, but you might want to spend more time with your friends than ever before.

Second, some of your friendships might change as you develop new interests. The example pictured on these two pages shows one way new interests can change friendships and lead to new friendships.

**Think Back** • *Study on your own with Study Guide page 319.*

1. What emotional changes might occur as a person goes through the growth spurt and puberty?
2. In what two ways might relationships change as a person grows up?

**On Your Own**
If you were Melissa or Terri, would you have been angry with Carla after she decided to take piano lessons? Give a reason for your answer and explain in a paragraph. Think of a time when one of your friendships began, ended, or changed in some other way. Describe what caused the friendship to begin, end, or change.

Carla found out that Debbie, a girl from another class, was also taking piano lessons.

Debbie's family did not have a piano at home, so Carla often invited her over to practice. They quickly became good friends.

Carla, Terri, and Melissa still spend time together, but Carla's new interest in music has changed their friendships. Her new interest has also led to a new friendship.

## 6  How Can You Deal with Growth and Change?

As you grow and change, you will probably have many new, interesting, and exciting experiences. At times, however, the changes of growth can be troubling. You might feel uncomfortable about your appearance or feel afraid to make new friends. You can deal with these and other feelings in several ways.

Developing a good self-image is one way to help yourself enjoy your growth. If you have a good self-image, you will have greater confidence in yourself and feel good about yourself as you grow and change.

Accepting responsibility helps you develop a strong self-image. As you grow, you will have more freedoms and privileges. New responsibilities come with these privileges. For example, you become responsible for your own safety when you go places by yourself. If your family lets you visit friends after school, you become responsible for being home on time.

Other responsibilities might include watching a younger brother or sister or doing household chores. The boy shown here was babysitting for his younger sister. His friends wanted him to go with them to the park, but he said he would meet them later. He was responsible for his sister until their mother got home. He thought of his babysitting job as a chance to prove he was trustworthy. Accepting his responsibility made him feel proud and built greater confidence in himself.

Accepting responsibility helps build confidence.

Explaining how you feel is another helpful way to deal with concerns about growth. You might want to talk to someone about your feelings, as this girl is doing. A friend, parent, older sister or brother, or other relative can give the understanding and advice that you need. However, friends and relatives can help you only if you let them. Tell them how you feel and accept their help when they ask, "What's wrong?"

You and your friends will experience many of the same physical and emotional changes even though you will all grow in different ways and at different times. Having patience with the way you and others are growing will be helpful as you grow and change. If you feel as though your body is changing too quickly, remember that your growth will eventually slow down. If you are worried because your friends are changing faster than you, remember that you will have your growth spurt sooner or later. Your own pattern of growth and change is one of the things that makes you a special person.

Explaining how you feel helps you deal with concerns during growth.

## Think Back • *Study on your own with Study Guide page 319.*

1. How can accepting responsibility help a person feel good about himself or herself?
2. How can a person's family help him or her deal with the feelings of growth?
3. What does the phrase "having patience with your growth" mean?

## Identical Twins and Scientific Research

No two people grow in exactly the same way, but some people come very close. Identical twins, such as those shown here, have the same genes. Therefore, they have the same inherited traits. Besides looking alike, identical twins often share similar interests, abilities, and growth patterns.

Because identical twins have identical genes, they are very important as subjects in research studies. By observing twins, scientists can find out if a certain trait is caused mainly by heredity or by a person's surroundings. This type of research is especially valuable if twins have been raised in separate households.

Such a study is being conducted now by Dr. Thomas Bouchard at the University of Minnesota. His study involves thirty-three pairs of identical twins and fourteen pairs of nonidentical twins. Each of these twins has been raised apart. Dr. Bouchard has found that identical twins often show similar behavior even though they had different experiences and were brought up in different ways.

Twin studies are helping scientists find out more about the effects that heredity and environment have on personality, mental skills, and diseases such as cancer and heart disease.

### Talk About It
1. Why are identical twins important subjects in research studies?
2. How could twin research help determine what causes a certain trait?

## Using Photographs to Examine Your Growth

Photographs of yourself and family members can illustrate many of the topics discussed in this chapter. Compare school photographs of yourself taken over the past several years. Look for physical features that have changed a lot and those that have changed little.

Some pictures, like the one here, might show a family member when he or she was close to your age. You might ask an adult to help you find such a picture. Examine it closely. Notice any resemblance between yourself and the person in the photograph.

Ask adults in your family if they remember when they started their growth spurts. Ask them what changes they experienced. How did they handle the changes of growth?

## Reading at Home

*The Answer Book About You* by Mary Etling and Rose Wyler. Grosset and Dunlap, 1980. Find answers to some questions young people ask about their growth and development.

*How You Grow and Change* by Dorothy Baldwin and Claire Lister. Bookwright/Watts, 1984. Further explore the changes of growth.

# Chapter 2 Review

### Reviewing Lesson Objectives
1. List the physical changes that occur during the growth spurt. (pages 50-52)
2. Describe the physical changes caused by the hormones of the pituitary gland and reproductive glands. (pages 54-55)
3. Explain how heredity influences growth patterns and other inherited traits. (pages 56-61)
4. Give examples of health decisions that affect growth and describe the need to care for the body with adequate sleep, rest, and physical activity. (pages 64–65)
5. Describe situations that show how emotions and relationships change during growth. (pages 66-67)
6. Describe ways to build a positive self-image while growing and changing; describe the role that relationships with family and friends plays in this process. (pages 68–69)

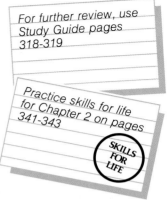

For further review, use Study Guide pages 318-319

Practice skills for life for Chapter 2 on pages 341-343

SKILLS FOR LIFE

### Checking Health Vocabulary
Number your paper from 1-13. Match each definition in Column I with the correct word or words in Column II.

*Column I*
1. the male reproductive glands
2. the female reproductive glands
3. a strand of matter in a cell's nucleus that contains DNA
4. the passing of traits from parents to children
5. the small part of a chromosome that affects only one trait
6. the endocrine gland that makes growth hormone
7. a female reproductive cell
8. a male reproductive cell
9. a general name for an organ that produces chemicals and releases them directly into the blood
10. the period of rapid growth usually between the ages of nine and fifteen
11. a chemical made by an endocrine gland
12. the period of time when the body develops the ability to reproduce
13. the substance that makes up chromosomes

*Column II*
a. chromosome
b. DNA
c. egg cell
d. endocrine gland
e. gene
f. growth spurt
g. heredity
h. hormone
i. ovaries
j. pituitary gland
k. puberty
l. sperm cell
m. testes

## Reviewing Health Ideas

Number your paper from 1-15. Next to each number write the word that best completes the sentence.

1. During the growth spurt the body grows more _____ than usual.
2. Girls usually experience their growth spurt _____ than boys.
3. During the growth spurt, growth takes place at _____ rates.
4. Growth is directed by a team of organs called the _____ glands.
5. The _____ gland affects growth more than any other gland.
6. A person's _____ can help him or her deal with changes by giving understanding and advice.
7. Eye color and nose shape are examples of inherited _____.
8. Before a body cell divides, the _____ copy themselves.
9. A _____ egg has 23 chromosomes from the egg cell and 23 chromosomes from the sperm cell.
10. If a sperm cell with an X chromosome unites with an egg cell, the offspring will be a _____.
11. Except for identical twins, every child in a family receives 46 chromosomes from the parents but not the _____ 46 chromosomes.
12. A person's heredity sets _____ for his or her growth.
13. Physical changes can lead to _____ changes.
14. People can have greater confidence in themselves if they develop a good _____.
15. _____ gives you control over your weight, body shape, and muscle development.

## Understanding Health Ideas

Number your paper from 16-25. Next to each number write the word or words that best answer the question.

16. Between what ages does the growth spurt usually start?
17. What parts of the body usually grow fastest during the growth spurt?
18. What endocrine gland releases hormones that cause the reproductive glands to become more active?
19. What is the period of time called when the body develops adultlike qualities and is able to reproduce?
20. What chemical substance determines a person's heredity?
21. How many chromosomes are in each reproductive cell?
22. How does heredity help determine when the growth spurt begins?
23. What kinds of foods make up a healthy variety of foods for proper growth?
24. How many hours of sleep do eleven- to twelve-year-olds generally need each night?
25. What can a person develop by accepting responsibility?

## Thinking Critically

Write the answers on your paper. Use complete sentences.

1. Identical twins have the same genes and, therefore, the same inherited traits. How then might identical twins grow in different ways?
2. Suppose a friend of yours is feeling uncomfortable about the changes of growth. What could you say to help your friend feel better?

# Chapter 3

# Choosing Foods for Good Health

Unless you have just eaten, the food in the picture might look tempting. In this case, however, looks are deceiving—the food in the picture is fake! This dish is an artistic creation of wax, plastic, rubber, and paint made in a Japanese factory. Restaurant owners in Japan often display these delicious-looking works of art in their windows. Such illustrated menus help tourists choose foods in restaurants.

To choose healthy foods you need to know more than just how food looks. This chapter provides information to help you choose the foods you need for a lifetime of good health.

## Health Watch Notebook

Think of a question you have about good nutrition. Find articles in newspapers or magazines to answer your question. Place the article in your notebook, and write a paragraph explaining how the information can be helpful to you and others.

1  Why Do You Need Food?
2  What Is a Healthy Diet?
3  How Does Food Processing Affect the Quality of Food?
4  How Can You Be a Wise Food Consumer?

74

nutrient (nü/trē ənt), a
substance found in food that
your body needs to stay
healthy.

# 1  Why Do You Need Food?

All the people in the picture are performing
activities that require a lot of energy. Where do
people get all that energy? They do not absorb it
from the sun. They do not soak it up from water.
They do not breathe it in from the air. People get
their energy from the food they eat.

Food contains certain substances—**nutrients**—that
your body needs to stay healthy. Some nutrients give
you energy to run, jump, walk, talk, write, and even
breathe. Other nutrients help build and repair your
body cells. Still others help keep the systems of your
body working properly. The six major kinds of
nutrients are carbohydrates, fats, proteins, vitamins,
minerals, and water. Your body needs some of each
kind every day.

Where do people get their
energy?

## How Do Carbohydrates Help You?

Sugar, starch, and fiber belong to the group of nutrients called **carbohydrates.** Sugar and starch provide most of the energy your body uses. **Fiber** provides almost no energy, but it does help the digestive system efficiently move food and wastes through your body.

The foods shown are some of the many sources of carbohydrates. Sugar, for example, is found naturally in milk, honey, and a variety of fruits and vegetables. The roots, stems, and seeds of various plants are good sources of starch. Carrots are roots that people eat. Potatoes are underground stems. Rice, corn, and peas are seeds. Other foods high in starch include macaroni, cereals, and bread. These foods are made from the seeds of such plants as wheat, rye, and oats.

Fiber is found in the seed coats of cereal grains such as wheat and rice. The tough or stringy parts of plants also contain fiber. Whole-grain bread, fruit skins, and celery stalks are good sources of fiber.

Most dieticians recommend that carbohydrates make up at least half of a person's daily diet. They advise people to limit foods that contain a lot of added sugar to avoid tooth decay and overweight.

**carbohydrates**
(kär′bō hī′drāts), a group of nutrients that supplies energy and includes sugar, starch, and fiber.

**fiber** (fī′bər), a carbohydrate that helps move food and wastes through the body.

Fiber sources

Starch sources

Sugar sources

**fats,** a group of nutrients that provides energy and carries certain vitamins through the body.

| Fat Content of some foods | |
|---|---|
| 100% | Oils, shortenings |
| 80% | Butter, mayonnaise |
| 60% | Peanuts, almonds and other nuts |
| 50% | Peanut butter, chocolate, bacon, |
| 30% | Cheese, roast beef, salad dressings |
| 10% | Sherbet, fish, chicken |
| 5% | Milk, bread |
| 1% | Most fruits and vegetables |

One way to limit fat in your diet

## Why Are Fats Important?

Like carbohydrates, **fats** are a group of nutrients that supply energy. Fats also help carry important vitamins to your body cells.

The chart shows the fat content of some foods. Notice that such spreads as butter and mayonnaise are 80 percent fat. Cooking oil is all fat. People need to eat some fat to stay healthy, but experts in nutrition recommend limiting the amount of fat in the diet. A fatty diet can lead to overweight and to such health problems as high blood pressure and heart disease later in life.

The boy in the picture is showing one way his family limits fat. He is removing the fatty skin from a piece of chicken. Another good practice is to limit the amount of fried foods that you eat. For example, baked, mashed, or boiled potatoes contain less fat than French fries or potato chips. Chocolate, ice cream, gravies, sauces, and salad dressings also contain large amounts of fat and should be limited in the diet.

## What Are Proteins?

As you grow, you become taller and heavier, partly because your body is building new cells. Your body also repairs damaged cells and replaces old cells that become worn out. **Proteins** are the group of nutrients your body needs to build, repair, and replace cells. Your muscles, skin, hair, and teeth are made mostly of proteins. This kind of nutrient also provides energy, though not as much as fats do.

Eating protein-rich foods is especially important at this time in your life. You are growing rapidly and your body needs protein to build new cells. Good sources of protein include dried beans and peas, eggs, fish, and other foods shown below. You need to include some protein-rich food in your diet each day.

Compare the foods in the picture with those in the chart on page 78. Notice that many foods high in protein are also high in fat. In fact, most animal sources of protein contain more fat than protein. To protect the heart and blood vessels, nutrition experts recommend that people choose vegetable sources as well as animal sources of protein.

**proteins** (prō′tēnz′), the group of nutrients that builds, repairs, and maintains body cells.

Some sources of protein

vitamins (vī′tə mənz), a group of nutrients needed in small amounts to keep the body working properly.

minerals, a group of nutrients needed to provide healthy teeth, bones, muscles, and blood cells.

## How Do Vitamins, Minerals, and Water Help You?

The Latin word *vita* means "life." It makes sense that the word *vitamin* comes from *vita,* since vitamins are essential for a healthy life. **Vitamins** do many things to keep your body working properly. The chart lists the functions of some of the thirteen vitamins scientists have discovered.

Notice that vitamins are found in many foods that are rich in other nutrients. Your body needs only a small amount of each vitamin. Therefore, eating many different foods should give you all the vitamins you need. You do not usually need vitamin pills if you eat a variety of foods.

Your body also needs eighteen different **minerals.** Like vitamins, minerals perform many functions to keep your body working properly. For example, the minerals calcium and phosphorus work together to help build strong teeth and bones. Milk is a good source of both of these minerals. Iron and copper help give you healthy red blood cells. Both iron and copper can be found in meats and grains. Additional sources of copper include fish, nuts, and raisins. Eating a variety of foods should give you all the minerals you need.

**Sources and Functions of Vitamins**

| Vitamin | Food sources | How it helps your body |
|---|---|---|
| A | Whole milk; egg yolk; butter; margarine; liver; green and yellow vegetables | Aids in preventing eye disorders<br>Helps form and maintain healthy skin, hair, and mucous membranes |
| B group<br>$B_1$<br>(Thiamin) | Meats, especially pork and liver; vegetables; nuts; milk; whole-grain breads and cereals | Helps release energy from foods<br>Helps nerves function<br>Keeps digestive tract healthy |
| $B_2$<br>(Riboflavin) | Meats, especially liver; eggs; cheese; green, leafy vegetables; whole-grain breads | Helps body use carbohydrates, fats, and proteins to release energy<br>Keeps skin, eyes, and nerves healthy |
| Niacin | Whole-grain breads and cereals; meat; fish; poultry; legumes | Helps produce energy from carbohydrates<br>Helps maintain all body tissues |
| C | Citrus fruits; berries; tomatoes; green, leafy vegetables; green peppers; potatoes | Helps heal wounds<br>Necessary for healthy teeth and gums<br>Helps resist infection |
| D | Milk; fish-liver oil; liver | Helps build strong teeth and bones |

The picture shows the most important nutrient. You could live for some weeks without food, but you can survive only a few days without water. Water carries other nutrients to your body cells and carries wastes away from the cells. Wastes are carried out of the body by the urinary system. Water in perspiration also helps cool your body.

The most familiar way to get water is to drink it from a glass. Experts recommend drinking 6–8 glasses of fluid each day. You also get this nutrient in other beverages, fruits, and soups. In fact, most foods contain a great deal of water.

**Think Back** • *Study on your own with Study Guide page 320.*

1. What does food contain that keeps the body healthy?
2. What are the six kinds of nutrients and what is a function of each?
3. How does fiber help your body?
4. How can you be sure you are getting vitamins and minerals you need in your diet?

Why is water an important nutrient?

## 2 What Is a Healthy Diet?

The variety of food in a modern supermarket was not available to people in the early 1900s. The fresh foods sold in grocery stores at that time came from local farmers. Today, thanks largely to air travel and refrigerated train cars, supermarkets sell a variety of fresh fruits and vegetables, such as those shown here, all year round. Not only are more different foods available now, but people know more about choosing foods to stay healthy. For example, nutrition experts have taught people a great deal about a healthy diet for infants and young people.

A healthy diet includes a variety of foods every day. No single kind of food has all the nutrients you need. Therefore, you need to eat a variety of foods to give your body a variety of nutrients.

### How Can You Make Sure You Get the Nutrients You Need?

Today a food guide is available that helps people choose foods for a healthy diet. The food guide on the next page includes the basic four food groups. What are they? How many servings are needed daily from each group? You can get all the nutrients you need by eating foods from the basic four food groups in the amounts suggested every day.

Today you can choose from a great variety of fresh foods.

| Food Group | Main Nutrients Provided |
|---|---|

**Vegetable-fruit**
Four servings a day

Carbohydrates
Vitamins A, C, and
  riboflavin ($B_2$)
Minerals, especially
  calcium and iron
Water

**Bread-cereal**
Four servings a day

Carbohydrates
Vitamins, especially the B
  group vitamins
Minerals, especially
  phosphorus and iron

**Milk-cheese**
Three servings a day
  for children
Four servings a day
  for teenagers
Two servings a day
  for adults

Fats
Proteins
Vitamins, especially D and
  riboflavin ($B_2$)
Minerals, especially
  calcium and phosphorus
Water

**Meat-poultry-fish-bean**
Two servings a day

Fats
Proteins
Vitamins, especially the B
  group vitamins
Minerals, especially
  phosphorus and iron

## How Can You Use the Food Guide?

The food guide on page 83 is a very flexible one. Different families can use it to plan very different daily menus. Yet each of the menus can provide enough foods from the basic four food groups. For example, one person might have cold cereal for breakfast, two slices of bread during lunch, and spaghetti for supper. These foods make up four servings from the bread-cereal group. Another person's four servings might come from eating hot cereal for breakfast, rice during lunch and supper, and blueberry muffins for a snack.

Variety is the key to healthy meals. Below is one example of a family's food choices for one day. Notice the variety of foods included. Has this family chosen enough foods from each of the four food groups? What changes might you or your family make in this menu to suit your own tastes?

Notice that you do not need to choose foods from each group as part of every meal. Just include the suggested servings in each group sometime during the day. You can do this in regular meals or in snacks.

**On Your Own**
Use the food guide shown on page 83 to plan meals and snacks for one day. Choose a variety of foods you would enjoy eating and that would give you the right kind and amount of nutrients.

## Amounts of Sugar in Sweet Foods

| Food | Serving size | Teaspoons of sugar |
|------|--------------|-------------------|
| Chocolate bar | 1 ounce | 7 |
| Chewing gum | 1 stick | ½ |
| Chocolate cake with icing | 1 piece | 15 |
| Angel food cake | 1 piece | 6 |
| Brownie | 1 piece | 3 |
| Ice Cream | ½ cup | 5-6 |
| Sherbet | ½ cup | 6-8 |
| Apple pie | 1 piece | 12 |
| Sweetened soda pop | 12 ounces | 6-9 |
| Maple syrup | 1 tablespoon | 2½ |

## What Kinds of Foods Do You Need to Limit?

Nutrition experts think people need to cut down on foods that contain a lot of sugar, fat, cholesterol, and salt. Frequently eating foods with large amounts of these substances can lead to health problems.

Too much sugar, for example, can cause tooth decay and help make a person overweight. Some foods contain added sugar for a sweeter taste. The chart shows the amount of sugar added to some common desserts and snack foods. You might be surprised by some of the information in the chart. For example, an average-sized chocolate bar contains seven teaspoonfuls of sugar. Most sweetened breakfast cereals are one half sugar.

Instead of eating a lot of these foods, people could try to eat more fresh fruits and vegetables. Fruits and vegetables contain small amounts of natural sugar, but they also provide many other nutrients needed for good health.

Many foods high in added sugar, such as chocolate and ice cream, are also high in fats. A diet that includes a lot of fats can eventually lead to overweight and diseases of the heart and blood vessels. People should try to limit such fatty foods as bacon, lunch meats, potato chips, and fried foods.

Too much **cholesterol** also can lead to diseases of the heart and blood vessels. This fatlike substance is made naturally in the body and is part of many foods that come from animals. Egg yolks and beef liver are some foods that contain high amounts of cholesterol. Some people should limit the amount of cholesterol in their diet. You might want to discuss this topic further with a doctor.

Salt contains minerals necessary for good health. Enough salt occurs naturally in most foods to satisfy your body's needs. However, many foods, such as bacon, soups, and potato chips, contain added salt. Many people add more salt to food while cooking. Then they add even more salt at the dinner table. Some studies show that too much salt in a person's diet might lead to high blood pressure. You can cut down on salt by not adding salt to foods during cooking or at the table. Also, you might want to look for low-salt products, similar to those shown, the next time you go shopping with your family.

**cholesterol** (kə les′tə rol′), a fatlike substance that is made naturally in the body and is present in foods from animal sources.

**Think Back** • *Study on your own with Study Guide page 320.*

1. What should a healthy diet include?
2. How can you be sure your meals provide all the nutrients you need?
3. What are the names of the basic four food groups?
4. What foods should people limit in their diets?

How many of these low-salt products have you seen?

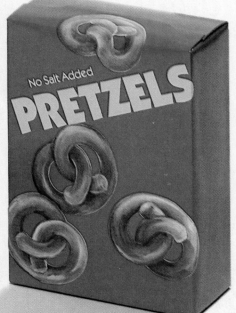

## Discovering More About Foods for Good Health

1. To add variety to meals, people often serve the same food in different ways. For example, potatoes might be baked, mashed, boiled, or served in soup. List some different ways that each of the following foods might be served: apples, carrots, ground beef, chicken. If you wish, list some other foods and the different ways each can be served.

2. Cut out pictures of food from magazines. Classify the pictures into each of the basic four food groups.

Then glue the pictures on posterboard and write the name of the correct food group under each set of pictures. Also write the number of servings from each group that you need to include in your diet each day.

3. Copy the following recipe for No-Bake Peanut Butter Logs and try making them at home if you can. Why do you think this snack is nutritious?

   1 cup powdered milk
   1/3 cup honey
   1 cup peanut butter
   2 tablespoons toasted wheat germ
   1/2 cup sesame seeds

Mix all the ingredients together in a bowl, except for the sesame seeds. Shape the mixture into tiny logs and roll them in sesame seeds, as shown. Place the logs on wax paper and refrigerate before eating.

4. Visit the library to find a cookbook of recipes from other countries. Use the cookbook to plan a dinner. The meal might include an appetizer, soup, salad, main course, and dessert. On a sheet of paper, list all the foods included in the meal. Then, classify the foods into the basic four food groups. Also include the name of the country where these foods are popular.

## Looking at Careers

5. Think of a person whose career deals with food. Many people would quickly think of a **chef.** Chefs prepare food in restaurants, hotels, schools, airports, hospitals, and factory cafeterias. Besides preparing the food, some chefs might plan the menu, direct the work of the kitchen staff, create new dishes, and buy food supplies.

Many chefs start their careers as kitchen helpers. They learn their skills on the job and eventually become assistant chefs and then chefs. They can also attend special classes at a college or cooking school.

Use a book about restaurants to find out the many different kinds of chefs employed in a large restaurant.

For more information write to the Culinary Institute of America, P.O. Box 53, Hyde Park, NY 12538.

6. In a hospital, the patients' meals are planned by a **dietitian.** A dietitian is an expert on how the body uses nutrients and what nutrients are necessary for good health. Dietitians use their knowledge to plan healthy and tasty meals that meet the special needs of patients in a hospital or nursing home. Dietitians might also work with chefs to plan meals for schools and restaurants.

To become a dietitian, a person must study food science and nutrition in college for four years. After college many dietitians enter an internship program that combines job experience with classroom work.

On a sheet of paper, describe what you might like about this career. What might you not like about it? You might want to keep a folder with information about many careers related to health. Include in this folder your likes and dislikes about the careers.

For more information write to the American Dietetic Association, 430 N. Michigan Ave., Chicago, IL 60611.

**food processing,** the changing of food before it is eaten.

A basic food, such as potatoes, comes in many forms.

How does this store compare with a modern supermarket?

## 3 How Does Food Processing Affect the Quality of Food?

Notice the old-fashioned grocery store in the picture. A hunded years ago most grocery stores were about the size of a large living room. Today, many large supermarkets cover an area the size of a football field!

Grocery stores are larger today partly because of the greater variety of foods available. People have discovered how to use basic foods to make new food products. Potatoes are a good example. Years ago people could buy only whole, raw potatoes. Today you can buy potatoes that have been cut, cooked, canned, frozen, and dried to make the products shown here.

Most items in a grocery store come from foods that have been changed in some way. The changing of food before it is eaten is called **food processing.** You process food at home whenever you wash, cut, mix, or cook it. Food processing also takes place at factories. Food might be dried, canned, frozen, partially cooked, or mixed with other substances before it reaches the supermarket. To make the healthiest food choices, you need to know how various processing methods affect the quality of food.

## How Do Drying and Freeze-Drying Affect Food?

Drying and freeze-drying are two methods of food processing that preserve foods, or keep foods from spoiling. Drying removes most of the water from foods. Without water, bacteria cannot grow on the food and spoil it. Raisins, dry cereals, pudding mixes, and macaroni are some dried foods. The process of freeze-drying removes water from food while the food is frozen.

Drying and freeze-drying reduce the size and weight of food. These processes make food easier to transport and store. Dried foods are especially convenient for space travel and backpacking. The hikers shown here enjoy the taste and nutrition of a freeze-dried fruit snack without worrying about the fruit spoiling or weighing down their backpacks.

Some freeze-dried foods are convenient as well as nutritious.

## How Do Canning and Freezing Affect Food?

Many people enjoy canning and freezing their own food, as shown below. Perhaps you have helped can tomatoes or freeze green beans and sweet peppers. Canning and freezing not only preserve food but also shorten the time needed to prepare the food before eating it.

*Canned food* refers to food in jars and bottles as well as in cans. The containers are sealed airtight to prevent bacteria from entering them. Freezing foods also prevents bacterial growth because bacteria cannot live at such low temperatures.

Most of the canned and frozen foods in a store were partially or completely cooked at a factory. The picture to the left shows part of the canning process at a factory. Here, fresh fruits and vegetables are washed, cut, canned, cooked, and labeled before leaving the factory. Such foods are convenient to use because they can be stored for a long time and they do not take long to prepare at home.

Workers separating sliced peaches at a food factory.

What are some advantages of canning your own food?

## How Nutritious Are Processed Foods?

Food processing methods are helpful because they preserve foods and make foods convenient to carry, store, and cook. However, foods lose some of their nutrients during processing. Also, many processed foods are high in salt. Most people think processed foods do not taste as good as fresh foods. For these reasons, many people choose fresh foods whenever possible.

The girl in the picture has a decision to make. She was asked to buy corn for supper, but she has to choose among canned, frozen, and fresh corn. She might make her choice based on the price and preparation time of each product. Which product should she choose if she wants the most nutrients?

Many people would pick the fresh corn-on-the-cob as the most nutritious—the best for health. Many fresh foods do have more nutrients than processed foods. However, fresh foods start to lose nutrients from the time they are picked. Therefore, the shorter the time between picking a food and eating it, the more nutritious that food is. Frozen foods keep almost all their nutrients unless they have been completely precooked. Precooking also removes nutrients from canned foods. In addition, some nutrients in canned foods leak out into the water that is packed in the can.

Now can you tell which product the girl should choose? If the corn-on-the-cob has been grown locally and has not been in the store very long, it is probably the most nutritious. The frozen corn would be the next most nutritious.

**On Your Own**
Frozen corn is more nutritious than canned corn, but it is also usually more expensive. Suppose a can of corn costs 49 cents and a bag of frozen corn costs 89 cents. Both products have the same amount of corn. Write a paragraph explaining which product you would buy and the reasons for your choice.

Which food item is the most nutritious?

## What Substances Are Added to Food During Processing?

You might have seen the words *fortified* or *enriched* on cartons of milk and packages of flour, bread, or cereal. A fortified or enriched food has nutrients added to it. Milk is fortified with vitamin D. Some breads are enriched with a variety of vitamins and minerals.

Any substance added to food for a particular purpose is an **additive.** Pepper and other spices are additives you might use at home to add flavor. Many processed foods contain additives to help preserve them. These additives are **preservatives.** Without preservatives, many foods would spoil before people could use them. Other additives add taste, color, texture, or nutrients to food. The chart shows some additives and tells why they are added to food.

People who work for the Food and Drug Administration (FDA) study and test additives to try to make sure they are safe to use. If the FDA finds an additive to be harmful, the FDA will limit or stop the use of that additive. Even though the additives used today are not thought to be harmful, many people prefer foods with few or no additives.

## Functions of Additives

| Type of additive | Why it is used | |
|---|---|---|
| Acids | To control sourness and prevent discoloration | |
| Colorings | To make food look more appetizing | |
| Emulsifiers | To keep substances mixed so product has a uniform texture | |
| Flavorings | To add or bring out flavor | |
| Nutrients | To improve nutritional value | |
| Preservatives | To prevent foods from spoiling | |

## How Can You Cook Foods in Nutritious Ways?

Cooking food is one way you and your family process food at home. The way you cook food affects the amount of fat, vitamins, and other nutrients that you get. For example, foods lose some of their nutrients when they are overcooked. Fresh vegetables that are cooked until soft have lost much of their vitamins. Vegetables should be cooked just enough to make them tender, yet firm. Another healthy idea is to eat some vegetables raw, since raw vegetables keep most of their nutrients.

Frying foods in butter, oil, or some other fat adds that fat to the foods. Frying in fat also takes some nutrients out. Baking, broiling, steaming, roasting, boiling, and stir-frying provide alternatives to frying. The baked chicken shown here has kept most of its nutrients. It is less fatty than fried chicken. The liquid in the pan came from the chicken itself, not from additional cooking fats.

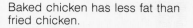

Baked chicken has less fat than fried chicken.

**Think Back** • *Study on your own with Study Guide page 321.*

1. What is the difference between processed potatoes and fresh potatoes?
2. How is food processing helpful?
3. Why do some people try to limit processed foods?
4. What are two nutritious ways to cook food?

## 4  How Can You Be a Wise Food Consumer?

Food labels have a lot of useful information

Lisa poured the milk and sat down to eat her breakfast cereal. She read the back and sides of the cereal box while she ate. Lisa suddenly raised her eyebrows in surprise. On the side panel she read that one serving of the cereal contains fifteen grams of sugar. She knew that fifteen grams is about the same as four teaspoons of sugar! Lisa made two decisions: to start eating unsweetened cereals and to read food labels more often.

Reading food labels is part of being a wise food consumer—someone who consumes, or uses, food. Most foods in a supermarket come in some sort of a container with a label. People often notice the variety of colors, designs, and product names on these labels. However, many people do not bother reading the rest of the information on labels. A wise food consumer reads and compares labels to find products with the best nutrition possible at the best price.

### What Can Food Labels Tell You?

Food labels are like maps. They can tell you a lot if you know how to read them. Notice the labels on the food containers below. Each label has a list of ingredients. The ingredients must be listed in order by weight so that the main ingredients are at the top of the list.

For example, notice that the first two ingredients on the red box of cereal are rolled oats and sugar. Therefore, the box of cereal contains more oats, by weight, than sugar. What else, besides tunafish, is in the can of tuna shown on page 96?

Some labels also contain nutrition information. This information includes the amount of protein, vitamins, minerals, and other nutrients in each serving. The amount of fat, salt, and cholesterol might also be part of the nutrition information. Such information is especially important to consumers who are trying to limit the fat, salt, or cholesterol they eat. Notice the vitamins that are contained in the crackers shown on page 96. On several items you might notice the letters RDA. What do they mean?

The next time you go to the store, look for other information on food labels, such as the weight, date, name of manufacturer, and storage information. With a little practice, you can use food labels to become a better consumer.

*On Your Own*
Analyze one of the food labels on these two pages. Write the product name on a sheet of paper. Then answer the following questions. What is the ingredient in the largest amount? the lowest? What other information is given on the label? Which food group or groups does the food product belong to? What kinds of nutrients does it have?

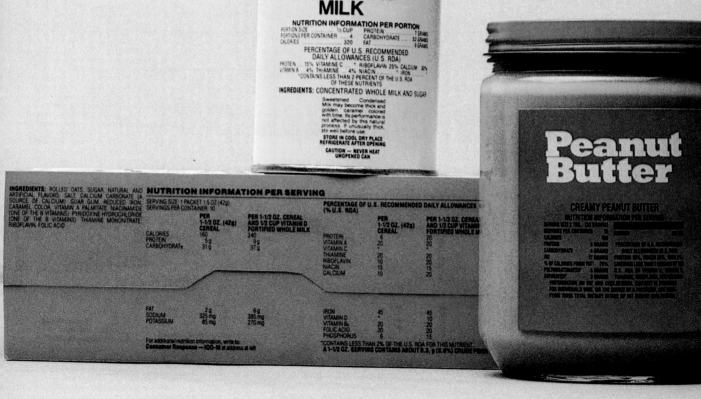

## How Can You Be a Wise Food Consumer in a Restaurant?

You have already learned in this chapter how to make healthy food choices in the supermarket and at home. Making healthy choices is important when eating in restaurants too. Some restaurant meals are high in fats, sugar, and salt. By choosing carefully, you can order a healthy meal.

Suppose you are at a restaurant, and a waiter gives you a menu like the one below. Which foods on the menu would you avoid if you want to limit fatty foods in your diet? Which foods would you avoid if you want to limit sweet foods in your diet?

When eating at a restaurant, you do not need to feel shy about ordering small portions or taking leftover food home. Some people tend to overeat at restaurants. Eating out can be a convenient and pleasant experience. You can use your knowledge about nutrition to make it a healthy experience too.

**Think Back** • *Study on your own with Study Guide page 321.*

1. What does a wise food consumer do to make the best possible food choices?
2. The first four ingredients on a certain box of cereal are sugar, oats, barley, and yeast. What does the box of cereal contain most, by weight? How do you know?
3. What kind of nutritional information might appear on a food label?
4. What healthy food choices can a wise food consumer make while eating at a restaurant?

Which foods would you choose for a healthy, good-tasting meal?

**Appetizers:** batter-fried onion rings; vegetable soup; raw vegetable platter with yogurt dip

**Dinners:** broiled fish; batter-fried fish; baked chicken; fried chicken; broiled steak; fried hamburger; beans, rice, and cheese casserole

**Beverages:** low-fat milk; whole milk; soda; orange juice; coffee; tea

**Desserts:** chocolate cake; fruit pie with ice cream; fresh fruit cup; yogurt with fresh blueberries

# Health Activities Workshop

## Investigating Food Labels

1. Bring to class a label from an empty food can, box, or jar from home. Then answer each of the following questions about the product:

• Which ingredient does this product contain the most of, by weight?
• What is the product's net weight—the weight of the product without the packaging?
• What vitamins does this product contain?
• Where would you write to send complaints or compliments about this product?

Using the information on the label, write at least five questions of your own. Exchange the list and labels with a classmate, and try to answer each other's questions.

2. Play an ingredients game. At home, write down the ingredients of several food products. At school, list the ingredients of each product on one side of the chalkboard. List the food products on the other side of the chalkboard in any order, as shown. See if your classmates can match each product with its list of ingredients.

3. Design your own food label. Use your imagination and what you have learned in this chapter to make the label both attractive and useful for consumers. If you wish, tape your label onto a can, jar, or box. You might design a label for a familiar brand name or make up your own brand name.

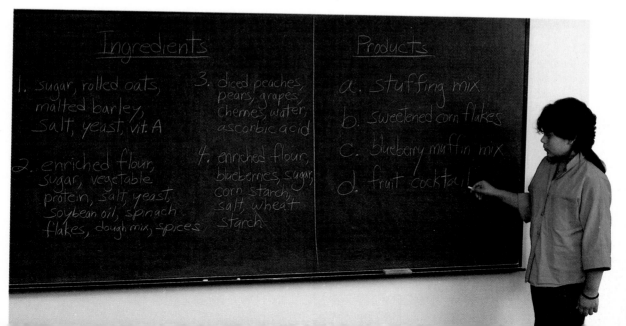

# Health Focus

## An Important Discovery About Disease and Diet

In the early 1700s, sailors in the British Navy led a very dangerous life. Fierce battles and raging storms at sea claimed many lives. Perhaps the greatest hazard of naval life, however, was a disease called *scurvy* (skėr/vē). On long voyages, scurvy often caused sore gums, a loss of teeth, bleeding within the body, and death. In fact, during wartime more British sailors died of scurvy than of battle wounds.

Then in the mid-1700s, a physician named James Lind studied this disease. He thought that scurvy might be related to the sailors' diets, which consisted only of salted beef and biscuits. Dr. Lind found that eating lemons prevented and cured scurvy. The painting shows Dr. Lind giving lemon juice to a sailor suffering from this disease. Lemon juice was included in the sailors' diets, and scurvy disappeared from the British Navy practically overnight.

Dr. Lind knew that something in the juice of lemons prevented scurvy. That "something" was later discovered to be vitamin C. Today scurvy is rare in the United States because most people include fruits and other sources of vitamin C in their diets.

The discovery of the cure for scurvy shows the importance of a varied diet. Eating a variety of foods helps provide the vitamins needed for good health.

### Talk About It

1. Why is Dr. James Lind an important person in medical history?
2. Besides getting scurvy, what other kinds of food-related problems might have developed by eating a diet consisting only of salted beef and biscuits?

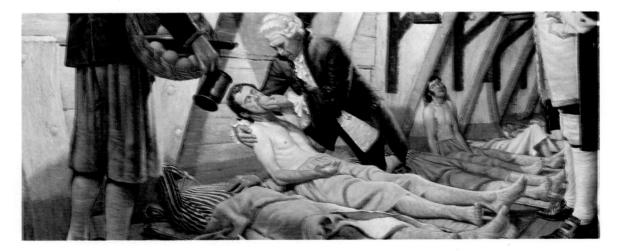

## Breaking the Salt Habit

Eating too much salt over a long period of time can lead to high blood pressure in some people. Your body does need some salt—about a tenth of a teaspoon each day. The average American, however, consumes two or four teaspoons every day!

Many food products you buy at the store contain added salt. You can become aware of which products contain salt by examining the labels of foods in your kitchen or pantry. Look also for the word *sodium,* the chemical symbol Na, and any term that includes *sodium.*

With so many products containing salt, you might think it is impossible to avoid too much salt. However, the tips below can help you and your family break the salt habit. You might want to share these tips with your family.

• Cut down on extremely salty foods. These foods include potato chips and other snack chips, pretzels, salted peanuts, olives, pickles, and lunch meats.
• Try to reduce the amount of salt added to food while cooking.
• Borrow a low-salt cookbook from the library. Many recipes use herbs and spices rather than salt to add flavor to food. Ask if you can plan a meal or help cook a meal from a low-salt cookbook.
• Taste before adding salt to anything you eat. Better yet, remove the saltshaker from the table altogether.

## Reading at Home

*Junk Food—What It is, What It Does* by Judith S. Seixas. Greenwillow, 1984. Find out what junk food is, how it affects you, and what you can do about it.

*Stuffin' Muffin: Muffin Pan Cooking for Kids* by Strom Scherie. Young People's Pr. Mar., 1982. Have fun cooking meals from this very special cookbook.

# Chapter 3 Review

## Reviewing Lesson Objectives

1. List the six kinds of nutrients and explain how getting the proper amount of each nutrient helps the body to function. (pages 76–81)
2. Describe what a healthy diet should include. List the basic four food groups and the suggested servings from each group. (pages 82–87)
3. List four ways of processing food. Explain how each method affects the quality of food and how a person can choose foods processed the healthiest ways. (pages 90–95)
4. Explain what important information is on food labels. Tell how to make wise food choices when away from home. (pages 96–98)

For further review, use Study Guide pages 320-321

Practice skills for life for Chapter 3 on pages 344-346

SKILLS FOR LIFE

## Checking Health Vocabulary

Number your paper from 1–11. Match each definition in Column I with the correct word or words in Column II.

### Column I

1. a substance found in food that the body needs to stay healthy
2. a group of nutrients needed in small amounts to keep the body working properly; examples include A and D
3. a carbohydrate that helps move food and wastes through the body
4. the changing of food before it is eaten
5. the group of nutrients that builds, repairs, and maintains body cells
6. the group of nutrients that includes sugar, starch, and fiber
7. any substance added to food for a particular purpose
8. a fatlike substance that is made naturally in the body and is present in foods from animal sources
9. a group of nutrients that provides energy and carries certain vitamins through the body
10. a group of nutrients needed to provide healthy teeth, bones, muscles, and blood cells
11. an additive that helps keep food from spoiling

### Column II

a. additive
b. carbohydrates
c. cholesterol
d. fats
e. fiber
f. food processing
g. minerals
h. nutrient
i. preservative
j. proteins
k. vitamins

## Reviewing Health Ideas

Number your paper from 1–15. Next to each number write the word or words that best complete the sentence.

1. The carbohydrate that helps move food and wastes through the body is _____ .
2. Potatoes, rice, macaroni, and bread are all good sources of _____ , a kind of carbohydrate.
3. Like carbohydrates, _____ are a group of nutrients that supply energy.
4. Nutrition experts recommend that people choose _____ sources as well as animal sources of protein.
5. Minerals that help build strong bones include _____ and phosphorus.
6. A healthy diet includes a _____ of foods every day.
7. A person should have two servings from the _____ group every day.
8. A person should eat _____ servings each day from the fruit-vegetable group.
9. Nutrition experts think people should limit foods that contain much sugar, fat, cholesterol, and _____ .
10. Drying and freeze-drying removes water from food so that _____ cannot grow in it.
11. Some _____ in canned foods leak out into the water packed in the can.
12. Food that has nutrients added to it would have the word fortified or _____ on its package.
13. Fresh vegetables lose much of their vitamins if they are cooked until _____ .
14. A wise food consumer reads and _____ food labels.
15. Ingredients are listed in order by _____ .

## Understanding Health Ideas

Number your paper from 16–25. Next to each number write the word or words that best answer the question.

16. What are the six major groups of nutrients?
17. What nutrients do experts think should make up half of your diet?
18. How can a person best be sure of getting all the vitamins and minerals he or she needs?
19. What are the basic four food groups and the recommended daily servings from each group?
20. What health problem can too much fat and cholesterol in the diet cause?
21. What health problem might too much salt in the diet cause?
22. What are four common methods of food processing?
23. Why are additives used in food?
24. Which government organization studies and tests additives?
25. How can you make wise choices in a restaurant?
26. What are some alternative cooking methods to frying?
27. What is a food consumer?
28. What information can be found on a food label?

## Thinking Critically

Write the answers on your paper. Use complete sentences.

1. Why are vitamin pills probably unnecessary if someone has a balanced diet?
2. Suppose you had a glass of milk, half a grapefruit, two slices of toast, and a soft-boiled egg for breakfast. List foods for the rest of the day that would provide a healthy daily diet.

# Chapter 4

# Becoming Physically Fit

"We did it!" The feelings of joy and accomplishment are obvious in those words and this picture. Whether participating in a sporting event or doing daily activities, being physically fit helps you perform your very best.

This chapter explains how exercise and physical fitness can help you have a healthy life. You will learn how you can become physically fit and have fun doing it. The chapter includes several exercises you might do. Through proper exercise, you will discover how to stay fit throughout your life.

## Health Watch Notebook

In your notebook, write three fitness goals that you would like to achieve. As you read the chapter, note ways in which you can meet your goals. Keep track of your progress as you develop a personal fitness plan.

1　How Does Exercise Improve Health?
2　How Does Exericse Help Control Body Fatness?
3　What Is Skills Fitness?
4　How Can You Set Good Fitness Goals?
5　How Can You Achieve Your Fitness Goals?

# 1 How Does Exercise Improve Health?

After a good night's sleep and a campfire breakfast, Allison was ready for a morning hike with the rest of her scout troop. In the afternoon the girls went canoeing around the lake. After dinner Allison helped organize a softball game. Exercise is important to Allison. It helps her enjoy an active, healthy life. Most people enjoy doing some kind of exercise. What kinds of exercise do you like to do?

## What Areas of Health Can Exercise Improve?

You probably know that exercise can improve physical health. You might be surprised to learn that exercise can also improve mental health. Relieving stress is one important way exercise can improve mental health. If you are worried or angry, physical activity can help you feel calmer and more relaxed.

Exercise can also improve your mental health by helping you feel good about yourself. Regular exercise can help you look your best. You feel good about yourself when you know you look the best you can. Physical activity also helps build strong, fit muscles that help you have good posture. Having good posture helps you look and feel your best.

Exercise can help you feel good about yourself by giving you a feeling of accomplishment. The girls in the picture have run the entire length of the beach for the first time. How does that help them feel good about themselves?

How does exercise help people enjoy life?

106

Exercise can also improve your social health. The students in the picture have found that taking part in exercise is a good way to meet people and make friends. Such team sports as volleyball and basketball help people learn to communicate and cooperate. These skills can help you get along well with other people all through your life.

The area of health most affected by exercise is physical health. Exercise improves your **physical fitness.** If you are physically fit, you do not get tired easily during exercise. Your body parts work at their best. You are also less likely to develop certain diseases. Exercise helps you look, feel, and be as healthy as you can be.

**physical fitness,** the ability to exercise, play, and work without tiring easily and without a high risk of injury.

What social skills are being developed here?

## How Can Exercise Affect Your Cardiovascular System?

Many parts of your body work together as body systems. Your heart, blood, and blood vessels make up your **cardiovascular system.** This system takes oxygen and nutrients to your cells and carries carbon dioxide and other wastes away from your cells. Exercise that involves all parts of your body can improve the way your cardiovascular system works.

For example, exercise can make your heart stronger. Notice in the drawings that a strong, fit heart pumps more blood with each beat. A strong heart beats less often and rests longer between beats. This extra rest helps the heart stay strong, just as the right amount of sleep helps you stay healthy.

Your blood takes oxygen to your muscles and carries carbon dioxide and other wastes away from them. When you exercise hard, your muscles use more oxygen and make more wastes. Muscles become tired and cannot work if they do not get enough oxygen and if the wastes are not removed. A fit heart is able to supply the extra blood your muscles need when they are exercising. What activities would you enjoy more and be better at if your muscles did not tire quickly?

The heart pumps blood through blood vessels called arteries. Sometimes fatty material builds up on the inside walls of an artery. If too much fatty material builds up over the years, the flow of blood through the artery might become slower or might even stop. Regular exercise helps keep your arteries clear of fatty material.

The heart of a more active person pumps more blood with each beat.

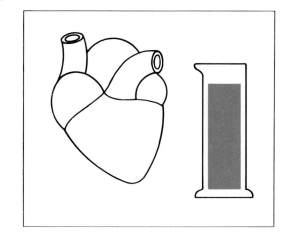

108

Look carefully at the two hearts below. The heart on the right has a richer network of blood vessels than the other heart. People who exercise regularly often develop more branching of the arteries in the heart. This richer network of arteries helps to carry more oxygen to the heart.

### How Can Exercise Affect Your Respiratory System?

Your **respiratory system** works with your cardiovascular system. Your nose, air passages, and lungs make up your respiratory system. Air flows into your lungs when you breathe in. In the lungs, oxygen from the air passes into your bloodstream, and carbon dioxide passes from your bloodstream into the air. The carbon dioxide leaves your body when you breathe out.

As the drawings to the right show, muscles move your chest up and out when you breathe in. This action makes your chest cavity larger. Air moves into your lungs, and they expand to fill up the extra space in your chest. When you breathe out, the muscles contract. Your chest cavity gets smaller and moves air out of your lungs.

The muscles that move your chest become stronger when you exercise regularly. Stronger muscles make the chest cavity larger when you breathe in. Therefore, you can take in more oxygen and get rid of more carbon dioxide with each breath. You breathe more deeply and less often, so you get the air you need with less effort. You can exercise longer and harder without getting out of breath.

**respiratory** (res′pər ə tôr′ē) **system,** the body system that includes the nose, air passages, and lungs. This system helps bring oxygen to the body and remove carbon dioxide from the body.

Ribs

Lung

Sheet of muscle

Breathing in

Ribs

Lung

Sheet of muscle

Breathing out

The heart of a more active person often has a richer network of arteries.

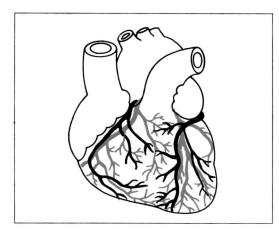

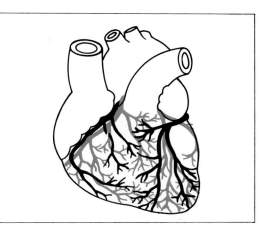

**flexibility** (flek′sə bil′ə tē),
the ability to move the joints
fully and to move body parts
easily.

**muscular endurance**
(en dyùr′əns), the ability of
muscles to work for long
periods of time without
getting tired.

### How Does Exercise Improve Your Muscles?

You have more than six hundred muscles in your body. Large muscles in your thighs help you stand and run. Tiny muscles in your skin raise hairs and cause goosebumps to form when you are cold. Exercise cannot make you grow more muscles, but regular exercise does improve your muscles in the three ways shown here.

Athletes do stretching
exercises like this one to
build **flexibility.** Flexible
muscles allow your body
parts to move fully and
easily without causing injury.

Exercises that cause your
muscles to lift more than
they normally do make your
muscles stronger. This
gymnast needs a lot of
muscular strength to lift his
body to this position.

110

Muscles that have strength, flexibility, and endurance are not easily injured and do not become sore easily. Muscles that have strength, flexibility, and endurance can help a person perform certain activities better. Which sports and jobs could you perform better if you had good strength? good flexibility? good muscular endurance?

Cardiovascular fitness, muscular strength, flexibility, and muscular endurance are parts of physical fitness. These parts of fitness are called health fitness because they help you have good health and resist certain diseases.

**Think Back** • *Study on your own with Study Guide page 322.*
1. How can regular exercise improve mental and social health?
2. How can regular exercise improve the cardiovascular system? the respiratory system?
3. In what three ways can exercise improve muscles?

Activities that make your muscles work for longer periods of time than normal build **muscular endurance.** Muscles with endurance can exercise for a long time without tiring. These bicyclists have trained their muscles to keep working through the entire race.

## 2 How Does Exercise Help Control Body Fatness?

Your body is made up of many different kinds of tissue. Two kinds of tissue are muscle and bone. Another is fat. The amount of a person's weight that is body fat is called **body fatness.** Body fatness is another part of health fitness.

Many people think body fat is something bad. However, a certain amount of fat is important to your health. Fat stores certain vitamins, such as A, D, E, and K. Fat helps keep your body warm during cold weather. Fat cushions and protects your organs from injury when your body is bumped. A certain amount of fat helps give your body its shape. Also, body fat stores energy. In fact, that is exactly what fat is— stored energy. The body uses stored fat to provide energy if it cannot get enough energy from foods.

About half of your body fat surrounds your organs and muscles. The other half is found under your skin. A doctor is doing a skinfold test on the boy in the picture. A tool called a caliper is used to measure the thickness of a fold of skin and fat on the boy's arm. The measurement tells the doctor how much body fat the boy has.

A skinfold test can measure body fatness.

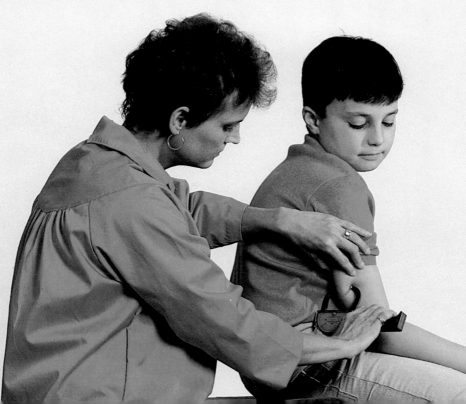

## How Much Body Fat Does a Person Need?

Having some fat is important to good health. However, too little or too much fat can cause problems. Without enough fat, the body does not have enough stored energy and cannot work properly. People who try to lose weight sometimes lose too much body fat. Losing too much fat can be harmful. Without enough stored energy, muscle tissue might begin to break down to give the body the energy it needs. A person who loses too much weight can become very weak and develop serious diseases.

Having too much fat can also be unhealthy. Too much fat can keep a person from being able to work and play actively. A person who has too much fat usually gets tired more quickly than someone who is lean. Adults who have too much fat are more likely to develop heart disease, high blood pressure, and diabetes than other adults.

The amount of body fat a person your age needs is about 10 to 15 percent of his or her total body weight. This amount will probably change as you grow older. Boys and girls both develop more muscle as they grow older, but a healthy girl usually needs to have more body fat than a healthy boy. This combination of muscle and fat helps people look their best. The picture shows the average amounts of fat and other tissues in a physically fit man and woman.

What percentage of a physically fit person's body is fat?

Male

Other 25%
Muscle 45%
Bone 15%
Fat 15%

Female

Other 25%
Muscle 36%
Bone 12%
Fat 27%

## How Can You Control Body Fatness?

The best way to control body fatness is to balance the amount of energy you take into your body with the amount of energy your body uses. Your body gets energy from the food you eat. The energy in food is measured in units called **Calories.** The number of Calories you need depends partly on how active you are. If you are a very active person, you need more energy and more food than someone who is less active. Most people your age need to take in between two thousand and three thousand Calories every day. However, individuals differ in the amount of Calories they need.

If you take in more Calories than you use, your body stores the energy in the form of body fat. You gain weight. If your body uses more Calories than you take in, your body begins to use up stored energy—body fat. You lose weight. When the number of Calories you use is the same as the number of Calories you eat, your weight stays the same.

Regular exercise can help prevent a person from gaining too much body fat. Regular exercise increases the amount of Calories that a person uses. Eating the right kinds and amounts of food is important too. Foods such as candy, cake, and potato chips are high in Calories but have very few nutrients. The sensible way to take in the right amount of Calories and nutrients you need is to choose foods from the basic four food groups in the daily food guide shown in Chapter 3.

The Calorie and activity chart on the next page shows how many Calories certain activities use in fifteen minutes. Notice that the number of Calories used depends partly on how long the activity is done without stopping. The number of Calories used also depends on a person's weight—the greater the body weight, the more Calories used.

The chart shows that jogging and bicycling are good activities to use up extra Calories. These activities can be done for a long time without stopping. Therefore, more Calories are used. What other activities on the chart can be done for a long time without stopping?

1. Why is a certain amount of body fat important for good health?
2. What is the best way to control the amount of body fat?
3. How does exercise help control the amount of body fat?

## Calories Used in Fifteen Minutes of Certain Activities

| Activity | Calories Used in 15 Minutes by Persons Weighing | | | |
|---|---|---|---|---|
| | *65 pounds* | *75 pounds* | *85 pounds* | *95 pounds* |
| badminton (recreation) | 38 | 42 | 48 | 56 |
| basketball (half-court) | 33 | 37 | 42 | 48 |
| basketball (full-court, moderate) | 47 | 53 | 59 | 69 |
| bicycling (level ground, 5½ miles per hour) | 34 | 38 | 42 | 49 |
| bicycling (level ground, 13 miles per hour) | 72 | 81 | 91 | 105 |
| dance, modern (moderate) | 28 | 32 | 35 | 41 |
| football (moderate) | 34 | 38 | 43 | 49 |
| hiking (with 40-pound pack, 3 miles per hour) | 46 | 52 | 58 | 67 |
| horseback riding (walk) | 23 | 25 | 28 | 32 |
| jogging (5½ miles per hour, 11 minutes to jog a mile) | 72 | 81 | 91 | 105 |
| jogging (7 miles per hour, 8½ minutes to jog a mile) | 94 | 106 | 118 | 137 |
| skating, ice (moderate) | 38 | 44 | 48 | 56 |
| skiing, cross-country (5 miles per hour) | 78 | 89 | 99 | 114 |
| soccer (moderate) | 60 | 68 | 76 | 87 |
| swimming (pleasure, 25 yards in 1 minute) | 41 | 46 | 51 | 59 |
| swimming (crawl, 50 yards in 1 minute) | 71 | 80 | 90 | 104 |
| walking (2 miles per hour) | 23 | 26 | 30 | 35 |

**agility** (ə jil′ə tē), the ability to change the position of the body quickly and to control body movements.

**coordination** (kō ôrd′n ā′shən), the ability to use the senses together with body parts or to use two or more body parts together.

# 3 What Is Skills Fitness?

Cardiovascular fitness, muscular strength, muscular endurance, flexibility, and body fatness make up the five parts of health fitness. All of these parts of fitness can be improved by regular exercise. Physical fitness also includes skills fitness, the ability to perform well in activities that require certain skills. Exercise can improve your skills fitness in ways that will help you all through your life.

**Agility** is the ability to change your body position quickly and to control the movement of your whole body. Agility is important in sports such as soccer and gymnastics and in jobs such as construction work.

Balance is the ability to stay upright while standing or moving. Balance is an important skill in skiing, skating, and most sports. What jobs do you think would be better performed with good balance?

**Coordination** is the ability to use your senses, such as sight, together with your body parts or to use two or more body parts together. People with good hand-eye or foot-eye coordination are good in hitting and kicking games such as soccer and ping pong. For what other sports would coordination be important? Why is coordination important for surgeons and typists?

116

## What Are the Parts of Skills Fitness?

Skills fitness has six parts. Each of these parts is useful in many different sports and jobs. Think about activities that involve each part of skills fitness as you read the descriptions of skills fitness on these two pages.

**Think Back** • *Study on your own with Study Guide page 322.*

1. How is skills fitness different from health fitness?
2. What are the six parts of skills fitness?

Power is the ability to quickly do activities that require strength. This part of skills fitness involves both strength and quickness. Power is important in sports such as swimming and football and in jobs such as household moving and ranching.

Reaction time is the amount of time it takes you to start moving once you observe the need to move. Good reaction time helps people who enjoy fencing or karate to avoid fast attacks. Good reaction time is important for many people who work on factory assembly lines.

Speed is the ability to perform a movement or cover a distance in a short period of time. Speed is important in running and skating and for many factory jobs.

## Examining Some Parts of Fitness

1. You can use a yardstick to test your reaction time. Ask a partner to hold the top of the stick with the thumb and first finger. Hold your thumb and fingers on either side of the stick, as shown, but do not touch it.

Your partner should drop the stick without warning you. Try to catch it between your thumb and fingers as quickly as possible. Do this test three times. Record how many inches slip through your hand before you catch the stick each time. Then switch places with your partner.

2. Choose a food high in Calories from those listed in the first chart. Write down the name of the food, the serving size, and the number of Calories in the food. Look at the second chart. Find the weight closest to your own. Use the column that gives your weight to complete this activity.

How long would you have to walk to use up the Calories in the food you chose? How long would you have to jog? Why might some people avoid this food as a snack? Try this activity with other foods from the first chart.

3. Make a poster that you think would effectively urge someone to exercise for fitness.

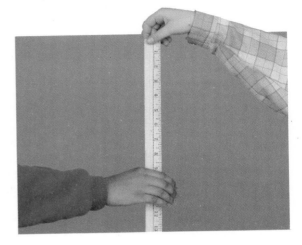

### Calories Provided by Certain Foods

| Food/Serving Size | Calories |
|---|---|
| apple, 1 medium | 80 |
| gelatin, flavored, 1 cup | 140 |
| orange, 1 medium | 70 |
| pretzels, 10 sticks | 230 |
| carrot, 1 medium | 30 |
| cookies, chocolate chip, 3 | 165 |
| chocolate candy, 1 ounce | 150 |
| ice cream, 1 cup | 260 |
| celery, 1 stalk | 7 |
| cola, carbonated, 12 ounces | 140 |
| French fries, 1 average serving | 300 |
| cupcake, chocolate cake with icing, 1 | 170 |

### Calories Used in 15 Minutes by

| Persons Weighing | 75 | 85 | 95 (pounds) |
|---|---|---|---|
| **Activity** | | | |
| walking | 26 | 30 | 35 |
| jogging | 81 | 91 | 105 |

## Looking at Careers

4. Some large companies provide exercise classes and other kinds of physical recreation for employees. These companies often hire **activity specialists.** The specialist tests employees for physical fitness and helps plan their fitness goals. Then the specialist can set up fitness programs that help people meet their goals.

A **recreational therapist** uses knowledge of physical fitness to help handicapped children. A recreational therapist works with a child's doctor. Together they plan activities that improve the fitness of the child. These activities might include sports, games or dance.

Activity specialists and recreational therapists might work in hospitals, schools, nursing homes, sports centers, and company buildings. To become an activity specialist or recreational therapist, you must finish high school and four years of college.

Many other kinds of jobs are available in the fields of fitness and recreation. Some positions, such as **camp counselor** and **playground leader,** can be filled by people still in high school or college. The camp counselors shown here are also guides and organizers.

You might visit your local park district or community center to find out more about these kinds of jobs. Talk to the people about any special skills and abilities needed. People often like to share information about their jobs.

For more information write to the National Recreation and Park Association, 1601 North Kent Street, Arlington, VA 22209.

# 4 How Can You Set Good Fitness Goals?

**On Your Own**
Choose two sports from the following list. Write the name of each sport at the top of a sheet of paper. Then list the parts of skills fitness a person interested in each sport would need to develop. Finally, explain how each part of skills fitness would help the person perform that sport.

| | |
|---|---|
| basketball | auto racing |
| football | bicycling |
| gymnastics | golf |
| ice skating | hiking |
| rodeo event | ping-pong |
| running | soccer |
| softball | swimming |
| tennis | volleyball |

Some people think only athletes need to be physically fit, but this idea is not true. Physical fitness is important for everybody. Being physically fit helps you look and feel your best. Being physically fit is one of the most important goals you can set for yourself. Setting fitness goals can help you build fitness, and you can have fun doing it.

You can help decide what your fitness goals should be by determining your needs, interests, and abilities. Deciding how fit you are right now can also help you set your fitness goals.

## What Are Your Needs, Interests, and Abilities?

People want to be physically fit for different reasons. Most people want to be fit in order to have good health and to feel good about themselves. They can reach these goals by working to improve each of the five parts of health fitness. Some people want to be fit because they are interested in certain sports. These people might need to develop all six parts of skills fitness.

Many people need extra ability in certain parts of health and skills fitness. Which parts of health and skills fitness does the construction worker especially need? Which parts does the gymnast especially need?

These people especially need certain parts of fitness.

Understanding your abilities can help you decide what your fitness goals should be. The kind of body you have helps determine some of your abilities. Everyone is born with a certain kind of body. Notice the three main adult body types in the pictures.

Some people are naturally more muscular than others. Such people might have greater strength. They can also build their muscles more easily than other people.

Some people have thin body types. Such people have a harder time building large muscles. However, they can develop good muscular endurance and cardiovascular fitness as easily as other people.

Some people have a body type that makes it easy for them to gain body fat. These people can stay lean, build muscle, and do well in many sports, but it might take extra effort.

Your body type and natural abilities make it easier to improve some parts of fitness, but harder to improve other parts. You can work to improve the parts of fitness that are more difficult for you. A little more effort often makes up for a lack of ability.

Different people have different body types.

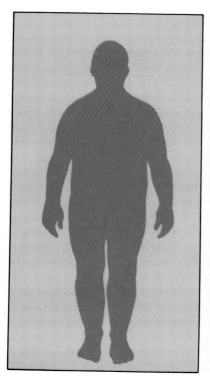
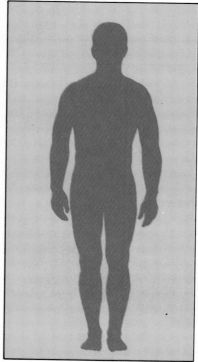
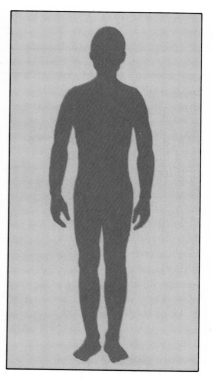

## What Kind of Health Fitness Do You Have?

Before you can set good fitness goals, you need to determine which parts of physical fitness you are strong in and which parts you need extra work in.

Try the activities on these two pages. As you perform each one, think about what part of health fitness it measures and how that part of health fitness is different from the others. These activities will help you understand more about each part of health fitness and show you what parts you might need to improve.

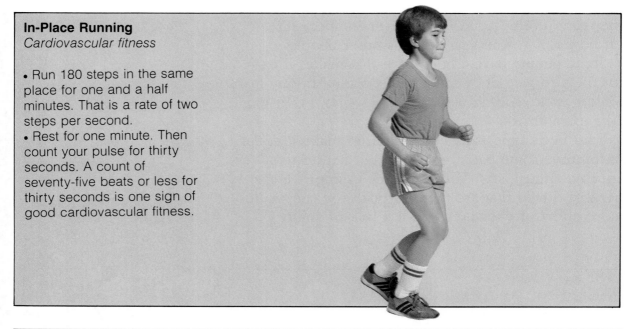

### In-Place Running
*Cardiovascular fitness*

• Run 180 steps in the same place for one and a half minutes. That is a rate of two steps per second.
• Rest for one minute. Then count your pulse for thirty seconds. A count of seventy-five beats or less for thirty seconds is one sign of good cardiovascular fitness.

### Push-Up
*Strength*

• Face the floor and support your body on your hands and feet.
• Keep your body straight as you lower yourself until your nose touches the floor.
• Push with your arms to return your body to the starting position. Keep your body straight as you push up.
• Try to do five push-ups.

### Bent Knee Push-Up

• Lie face down with your hands on the floor next to your shoulder and your knees and feet on the floor.
• Keep your body straight as you push the upper part of your body off the floor.
• Keeping your knees and feet on the floor, lower your body until your nose or chest touches the floor.
• Try to do five bent knee push-ups.

While getting an idea of your health fitness, you will find it helpful to measure your pulse. Your pulse is caused by the rush of blood into the arteries after each beat of your heart. To check your pulse, place your index and middle fingers of one hand on the wrist just below the thumb of the other hand. Notice this position in the picture. Press gently and you should feel your pulse.

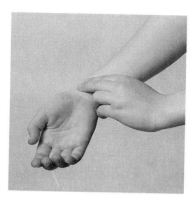

### Two-Minute Jump
*Muscular endurance*

• Put your hands behind your head. Bend your knees slightly.
• Place your right foot in front of a line on the floor. Place your left foot behind the line.
• Jump in place, switching your feet so that you land with your left foot in front of the line and your right foot behind it.
• Try to jump 240 times in two minutes. That is a rate of two jumps every second.

### Two-Hand Ankle Grab
*Flexibility*

• With your heels together, bend forward and reach with your hands between your legs and behind your ankles.
• Reach around your ankles and clasp your hands in front of your ankles. Interlock your hands for at least the full length of your fingers.
• Hold for a count of five while keeping your feet still.

## What Kind of Skills Fitness Do You Have?

You can do some simple activities to help you understand more about the parts of skills fitness and to find out what parts of skills fitness you might want to improve. Try each activity on these two pages. As you perform each one, think about how the part of skills fitness the activity measures is different from other parts of skills fitness.

### Line Jump
*Agility*

• Balance on your right foot on a line drawn on the floor or ground, or made with tape.
• Jump so that your left foot lands to the right of the line.
• Jump to the left side of the line, landing on your right foot.
• Jump again, landing on the line with your left foot.
• Practice once. Then see if you can do the activity two out of three times without losing your balance.

### Backward Hop
*Balance*

• Hop backward on one foot for five hops with your eyes closed. Do not allow your other foot to touch the ground.
• Stop after the last hop and hold your balance for three seconds.
• Try this activity twice. Then repeat it while hopping on the other foot.

### Double Ball Bounce
*Coordination*

• Hold a volleyball or basketball in each hand.
• Starting at the same time with each hand, bounce both balls at the same time. Bounce the balls at least knee high.
• Bounce both balls three times in a row without losing control of either ball.
• Try this activity three times.

1. How can your interests and needs help you set good fitness goals?
2. How can determining your abilities help you set good fitness goals?

### Standing Long Jump
*Power*

• Make a line on the floor with chalk or with masking tape. Lie down on the floor so that your feet are even with the line. Then ask a partner to make another line by your head so that the two lines represent the length of your body.
• Stand with your toes at the edge of one line.
• Swing your arms forward and try to jump beyond the second line. You should not run or hop before jumping.
• Try this activity twice.

### Tube Catch
*Reaction time*

• For this activity, roll a sheet of paper to make a paper tube. Keep the tube together with tape.
• Lay the tube on a table or desk so that slightly less than half of the tube extends over the edge.
• Tap the tube so that it flips off the table or desk. Try to catch the tube before it hits the floor.
• See how many times you can catch the tube out of five tries.

### Run In Place
*Speed*

• Stand with your feet about shoulder width apart.
• When a partner says "Go," run in place as fast as you can for ten seconds. As you run in place, count the number of times each foot touches the ground. Your partner should watch the clock or have a watch with a second hand.
• Try this activity twice.

# 5 How Can You Achieve Your Fitness Goals?

Remember that special feeling of accomplishment you had when you first learned to ride a bicycle? You had set a goal. You worked very hard. You probably took a few tumbles, but you finally achieved your goal—and you had fun doing it.

You can earn that same sense of accomplishment by achieving your physical fitness goals. Setting fitness goals can be fairly easy. Achieving those goals takes time, but it can be done—and it can be fun!

The charts on these two pages list many sports activities that can help you achieve your fitness goals. Notice which areas of fitness each activity improves. Once you have set goals to improve certain areas of fitness, try activities that will strengthen those areas.

## Skill-Related Benefits of Sports Activities

| Activity | Improves balance | Improves coordination | Improves reaction time | Improves agility | Improves power | Improves speed |
|---|---|---|---|---|---|---|
| Badminton | Fair | Excellent | Good | Good | Fair | Good |
| Baseball | Good | Excellent | Excellent | Good | Excellent | Good |
| Basketball | Good | Excellent | Excellent | Excellent | Excellent | Good |
| Bicycling | Excellent | Fair | Fair | ____ | ____ | Fair |
| Bowling | Good | Excellent | ____ | Fair | Fair | Fair |
| Canoeing | Good | Good | Fair | ____ | Good | ____ |
| Dance, Aerobic | Fair | Good | Fair | Good | ____ | ____ |
| Dance, Ballet | Excellent | Excellent | Fair | Excellent | Good | ____ |
| Football | Good | Good | Excellent | Excellent | Excellent | Excellent |
| Gymnastics | Excellent | Excellent | Good | Excellent | Excellent | Fair |
| Jogging | Fair | Fair | ____ | ____ | ____ | ____ |
| Racquetball; Handball | Fair | Excellent | Good | Excellent | Fair | Good |
| Skating, Ice | Excellent | Good | Fair | Good | Fair | Good |
| Skating, Roller | Excellent | Good | ____ | Good | Fair | Good |
| Skiing, Cross-Country | Fair | Excellent | ____ | Good | Excellent | Fair |
| Soccer | Fair | Excellent | Good | Excellent | Good | Good |
| Softball | Fair | Excellent | Excellent | Good | Good | Good |
| Swimming | Fair | Good | ____ | Good | Fair | ____ |
| Tennis | Fair | Excellent | Good | Good | Good | Good |
| Volleyball | Fair | Excellent | Good | Good | Fair | Fair |
| Walking | Fair | Fair | ____ | ____ | ____ | ____ |

Notice that some activities are not very helpful for improving certain parts of fitness. For example, swimming does not do much to improve reaction time, as shown by the dash in the *reaction time* column for swimming. However, swimming is a good or excellent activity for improving other parts of skills and health fitness. You should not stop doing an enjoyable activity just because it does not improve a certain part of fitness. Instead, try to include additional activities that can help you achieve your fitness goals.

## Health-Related Benefits of Sports Activities

| Activity | Develops cardiovascular fitness | Develops muscular strength | Develops muscular endurance | Develops flexibility | Helps control fatness |
|---|---|---|---|---|---|
| Badminton | Fair | ____ | Fair | Fair | Fair |
| Baseball | ____ | ____ | ____ | ____ | ____ |
| Basketball (half court) | Fair | ____ | Fair | ____ | Fair |
| Bicycling | Excellent | Fair | Good | ____ | Excellent |
| Bowling | ____ | ____ | ____ | ____ | ____ |
| Canoeing | Fair | Fair | Good | ____ | Fair |
| Dance, Aerobic | Excellent | Fair | Good | Good | Excellent |
| Dance, Ballet | Good | Good | Good | Excellent | Good |
| Football | Fair | Good | Good | ____ | Fair |
| Gymnastics | Fair | Excellent | Excellent | Excellent | Fair |
| Jogging | Excellent | ____ | Good | ____ | Excellent |
| Racquetball; Handball | Good-Excellent | ____ | Good | ____ | Good-Excellent |
| Skating, Ice | Fair-Good | ____ | Good | ____ | Fair-Good |
| Skating, Roller | Fair-Good | ____ | Fair | ____ | Fair-Good |
| Skiing, Cross-Country | Excellent | Fair | Good | ____ | Excellent |
| Soccer | Excellent | Fair | Good | Fair | Excellent |
| Softball | ____ | ____ | ____ | ____ | ____ |
| Swimming | Excellent | Fair | Good | Fair | Excellent |
| Tennis | Fair-Good | ____ | Fair | ____ | Fair-Good |
| Volleyball | Fair | Fair | ____ | ____ | Fair |
| Walking | Good | ____ | Fair | ____ | Good |

## How Much Physical Activity Do You Need?

Fitness experts suggest that you exercise at least three times a week to build and maintain fitness. You should exercise hard enough to make your heart beat at a rate of 135 to 155 beats per minute. You need to keep your heart beating at this rate for at least fifteen minutes at a time. Your heart is a muscle. Making your muscles work harder than usual makes them stronger. Making your heart work harder for at least fifteen minutes will build cardiovascular fitness. You can check your pulse to keep track of how hard your heart is working while you exercise.

## How Can You Exercise Safely?

You need to follow a few safety guidelines as you exercise to meet your fitness goals. These guidelines will help you avoid injuries and soreness.

• **Warm up before you exercise.** You should warm up your muscles with gentle exercises before you do more active exercises. The side stretch, toe reach, and jumping jack described on page 130 are good warm-up exercises. They stretch muscles and help prevent muscle injuries. Slow walking or slow jogging are other good warm-up exercises that stretch muscles and get your heart ready for more active exercises.

Comfortable clothing allows free movement during exercise.

• **Dress properly for exercise.** How is the boy in the picture dressed correctly for active exercise? He is wearing comfortable exercise shoes that support and protect his feet. His clothes are loose enough to allow free movement.

• **Use safe equipment and exercise in a safe place.** Make sure any exercise equipment you use is in good condition. Unsafe equipment, such as a cracked baseball bat or a bicycle that is too large for its driver, can cause serious injuries. Also make sure that the area you plan to exercise in is safe. Joggers should run in a smooth area free of holes. Bicycle drivers should use safe bicycle paths. If your community has no bicycle paths, ride in an area that is known to be safe.

• **Make sure you are fit for a sport before you take part in it.** Sports can build good fitness, but you need to have a certain amount of fitness to attempt certain sports. A few weeks of exercising can help you build fitness for a sport.

• **Cool down after you exercise.** A complete exercise routine always includes cooling down with gentle exercises after you finish more active exercise. Cooling down helps prevent soreness and helps you slowly lower your heart rate back to normal. The same exercises used for warming up are good for cooling down.

• **Gradually increase the amount of exercise you do.** If you have not exercised for a long time, you need to start slowly. As you continue, you can gradually build up the amount of exercise you do. For example, you might exercise two times during the first week. Then you can gradually build up to exercising five times every week. Starting slowly and increasing gradually helps prevent injuries.

**Think Back** • *Study on your own with Study Guide page 323.*

1. What kind of activities should a person choose when achieving fitness goals?
2. How often should a person exercise to build and maintain fitness?
3. What are six guidelines for exercising safely?

# project keep fit

Project Keep-Fit is an exercise program that can help you improve your physical health and your physical abilities. Be sure to have your teacher help you learn how to do these exercises correctly. Also, it is a good idea to check with your doctor before beginning any exercise program.

The program begins with warm-up exercises to stretch muscles and prepare your body for more vigorous activity. The warm-up exercises can also be used for the cool-down, preparing your body to return to its normal amount of activity. The main part of the program, called the *Workout,* includes exercises that build all parts of fitness.

## Warm-Up

**Side Stretcher**
• Stand with your feet about twelve inches apart. Hold your right hand up over your head.
• Bend as far as you can to the left. Reach as low as you can with your left arm and as far over your head as you can. Hold for six seconds. Then stand up straight.
• Switch hands and bend to your right.
• Do five stretches to each side.

**Toe Reach**
• Sit on the floor with your legs straight. Spread them about three feet apart.
• Bend your body forward over your right leg and reach toward your toes. Reach as far as you can. Try to touch your head to your knee. Keep your leg straight. Hold for six seconds.
• Return to the starting position and repeat over your left leg.
• Return to the starting position and repeat reaching midway between your legs.
• Do five stretches to each side and to the middle.

**Jumping Jacks**
Do jumping jacks for one minute.

# Workout

To help you experience the fun of becoming fit, the exercises for the workout of Project Keep-Fit have been developed into an exercise circuit, as the map shows. A circuit adds variety to your exercise. You might think of other ways to arrange the activities into a circuit, depending on the kind of space you have.

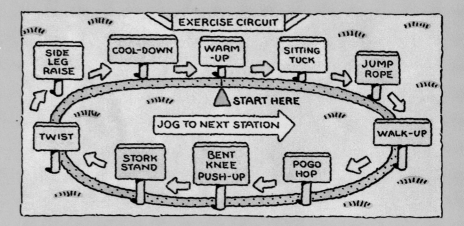

EXERCISE CIRCUIT

SIDE LEG RAISE → COOL-DOWN → WARM-UP → SITTING TUCK → JUMP ROPE

START HERE

JOG TO NEXT STATION

TWIST — STORK STAND ← BENT KNEE PUSH-UP ← POGO HOP — WALK-UP

## 1. Sitting Tuck
• Sit on the floor with your knees bent and arms stretched to your sides.
• Lean back and balance on your hips with the knees bent near your chest and feet off the floor.
• Straighten your knees so the body forms a V.
• Bend your knees to the chest again.
• Do as many sitting tucks as you can up to ten.

131

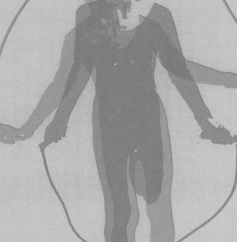

### 4. Pogo Hop
• Lock your hands behind your head and place your right leg forward and your left leg back.
• Jump in the air, changing positions of your legs so that when you land your left leg is forward and your right leg is back.
• Do as many pogo hops as you can for up to two minutes.

### 2. Jump Rope
• Jump rope in place.
• Do as many jumps as you can for up to two minutes.

### 3. Walk-Up
• Support your body with your arms and feet in a push-up position.
• Slowly bring your feet forward as if walking toward your hands, but do not move your hands. Walk forward as far as you can.
• Walk your feet slowly back to where you started.
• Do as many walk-ups as you can up to fifteen.

## 5. Bent-Knee Push-Up

• Lie on your stomach with the palms of your hands on the floor next to your shoulders.
• Keep your knees touching the floor while you push the upper part of your body off the floor.
• Lower your body to the starting position.
• Do as many push-ups as you can up to fifteen.

## 6. Stork Stand

• Stand with your arms out to the sides.
• Lean forward on one foot, lifting your other leg up behind you. Hold the position for a count of ten.
• Repeat standing on the other foot.
• Do this activity three times for each foot.

## 7. Twist

• Stand with your arms out to the sides.
• Twist your body to the right as far as you can. Hold the position for a count of ten.
• Repeat to the left.
• Do as many twists to each side as you can up to three.

## 8. Side Leg-Raise

• Lie on your left side. Use your arms to help keep you balanced there.
• Keep your body stiff while you lift your left leg in the air.
• Lower your leg.
• Switch to your right side and repeat the exercise.
• Do as many leg raises as you can up to fifteen with each leg.

## Cool-Down

Use the warm-up exercises on page 130 as your cool-down exercises.

134

# Keep Fit While You Sit

## Book Curl
- Hold a book, such as a textbook, in one hand.
- Lift the book from your lap to your shoulder. Keep your elbow in near your waist.
- Repeat the exercise with the other arm.
- Do as many curls as you can up to fifteen with each arm.

## Back Zipper
- Reach behind your head and down your back with one hand. Reach up and behind your back with your other hand.
- Try to reach far enough so that the fingers of your two hands touch.
- Hold for ten seconds.
- Repeat this exercise reversing the positions of the hands.
- Do three reaches for each position.

## Fitness Counts on Everglades Adventure

You can probably think of many ways that being physically fit contributes to health. You might not realize that fitness can also contribute to enjoyment of a vacation. The students from East Haddam, Connecticut, can tell you fitness was an extremely important part of their vacation.

One winter, twelve students from Connecticut took a guided cruise through the Florida Everglades. Why would they need to be physically fit for such a trip? This cruise was made in canoes that the students paddled themselves for two weeks!

During the two weeks the students had many adventures. They paddled through the quiet marshes and peaceful woodlands of the Florida coast. Here they saw many animals they had never seen before. Large storks perched on the tops of trees. Alligators peered at them from fallen logs. Porpoises swam playfully beside them.

However, not everything about the trip was peaceful. On the first day of canoeing the students battled fierce winds and waves. With the rough weather, progress was slowed to a snail's pace. Then it took the students several hours to put up their tents. The winds were so strong the tents kept blowing over.

Because the students were physically fit, they were able to enjoy the canoe trip despite the weather. Before they left Connecticut, each person passed a fitness test. Each one had to run several miles and show that he or she could swim and canoe well. Being physically fit allowed the students to paddle through the Everglades with ease on peaceful days and handle the hardships during the more difficult days.

### Talk About It

1. How did being physically fit help the students on their trip through the Everglades?
2. On what other types of vacations would it be helpful to be in good physical shape?

## Participating in Lifetime Activities

Many games and sports can be enjoyed by people of all ages. These games are called lifetime activities. Unlike many sports, these activities can be done all through your life. Badminton, golf, jump rope, cross-country skiing, bicycling, skin diving, running, tennis, skating, dancing, swimming, and walking are just a few of the lifetime activities you can enjoy.

These activities can be a good way for a family to spend time together because people of all ages can participate. Also, many of the activities do not need costly equipment or large groups of players. A person does not have to be highly skilled to enjoy these activities.

Help your family plan a fitness break. You might play indoors with a sponge ball or have a jump rope contest. Ask members of your family to go bicycling or play badminton on a Saturday afternoon. Your family could take a walk together after dinner. What activities might your family enjoy doing together?

Lifetime activities can help your family become interested in physical fitness and maintain fitness all through life.

## Reading at Home

*The New Physical Fitness* by Richard Lyttle. Watts, 1981. Learn to take care of your body through exercise and diet.

*Your Muscles and Ways to Exercise Them* by Margaret Cosgrove. Dodd, Mead, 1980. Read about the effects of exercise on muscles.

# Chapter 4 Review

## Reviewing Lesson Objectives

1. Recognize the role that regular, vigorous activity plays in promoting a positive self-concept and healthy body. (pages 106–111)
2. Explain how the right amount of body fat is important to health. Explain how regular, vigorous activity can help control body fatness. (pages 112–115)
3. Explain what skills fitness is. List the six parts of skills fitness. (pages 116–117)
4. Explain how interests, needs, and abilities help a person set fitness goals. (pages 120–125)
5. Explain how a person can achieve fitness goals. (pages 126–129)

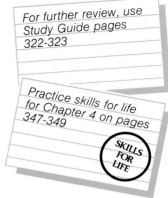

For further review, use Study Guide pages 322-323

Practice skills for life for Chapter 4 on pages 347-349

SKILLS FOR LIFE

## Checking Health Vocabulary

Number your paper from 1–8. Match each definition in Column I with the correct word or words in Column II.

### Column I

1. the ability to exercise without tiring easily and without a high risk of injury
2. the ability of muscles to exercise for a long time without tiring
3. the body system that includes the air passages and lungs
4. a unit used to measure the energy in food and the energy used in activity
5. the ability to change body position quickly and to control the movement of the whole body
6. the body system made of the heart, blood, and blood vessels
7. the ability to move the body parts fully and easily
8. the ability to use the senses with the body parts or to use two or more body parts together

### Column II

a. agility
b. Calorie
c. cardiovascular system
d. coordination
e. flexibility
f. muscular endurance
g. physical fitness
h. respiratory system

Number your paper from 9–20. Next to each number write a sentence using that part of fitness.

9. cardiovascular fitness
10. muscular strength
11. flexibility
12. muscular endurance
13. body fatness
14. agility
15. balance
16. coordination
17. power
18. reaction time
19. speed
20. skills fitness

## Reviewing Health Ideas

Number your paper from 1–14. Next to each number write the word that best completes the sentence.

1. _____ can improve mental health by relieving stress.
2. A stronger heart pumps _____ blood with each beat than a weaker heart.
3. People who exercise regularly often develop more branching of the _____ in the heart.
4. Stronger chest muscles let a person take in more oxygen and get rid of more carbon _____ with each breath.
5. Stretching exercises make the muscles more _____.
6. Fat is stored _____.
7. About half of a person's fat is under the _____.
8. A person who uses up more Calories than he or she takes in will likely _____ weight.
9. Cardiovascular fitness, muscular strength, flexibility, muscular endurance, and body fatness are parts of _____ fitness.
10. Being able to meet a ping-pong ball with a paddle is a result of good hand-eye _____.
11. The tube catch can be used to test the part of skills fitness called _____.
12. People need to exercise at least _____ times a week to build and maintain fitness.
13. Before beginning highly active exercise, a person should do _____ exercises.
14. Cooling down after active exercise helps to slowly lower the heart _____ back to normal.

## Understanding Health Ideas

Number your paper from 15–22. Next to each number write the word or words that best answer the question.

15. What skills important to social health can people learn while playing team sports?
16. What happens to muscles if they do not get enough oxygen and do not have wastes taken away?
17. What kind of tissue can break down if a person does not have enough body fat?
18. If a person eats food that contains 2,500 Calories and uses up 2,000 Calories, what happens to the other 500 Calories?
19. What part of skills fitness involves covering a certain distance in a short period of time?
20. What three things should a person determine before setting fitness goals?
21. What should people do if they enjoy an activity that does not improve a part of fitness that they want to improve?
22. How fast should the heart beat during exercise to build and maintain fitness?

## Thinking Critically

Write the answers on your paper. Use complete sentences.

1. For each part of skills fitness write the name of a sport, job, or daily activity that requires that part. Explain why the part of skills fitness is important to the activity.
2. What advice would you give to someone who wanted to become physically fit?

# Chapter 5

# Safety and First Aid

What do all the hats in the picture have in common? They are all worn by people who are concerned with safety or first aid—for themselves and for others. Where might you see each kind of hat being worn?

This chapter shows how you can make safety a part of your everyday life. You will learn how to prevent accidents. The chapter also discusses ways that you can help someone, and perhaps save someone's life, during an emergency. Practicing safety and developing first-aid skills is an important part of your future health.

## Health Watch Notebook

Look through newspapers or magazines for an article about an accident. Paste the article in your notebook. Write a paragraph describing what caused the accident, what its consequences were, and how the accident could have been prevented.

1   How Can You Prevent Accidents?
2   How Can You Act Safely at Home?
3   How Can You Be Prepared for Emergencies?
4   How Can You Help in a Medical Emergency?

**POOL RULES**

- SHOWER BEFORE ENTERING POOL.
- CAPS MUST BE WORN BY ALL SWIMMERS.
- ONLY QUALIFIED SWIMMERS MAY SWIM IN THE DEEP END.
- NO ROUGH PLAY.
- ONLY ONE PERSON ON THE DIVING BOARD.
- NO RUNNING.

# 1 How Can You Prevent Accidents?

"Accidents do not just happen; they are caused." This statement means that people usually cause accidents by taking unnecessary risks. Swimming in an off-limits area and playing around railroad cars are two unnecessary risks that could lead to accidents. You can prevent many accidents by avoiding unnecessary risks.

How is the girl in the picture avoiding unnecessary risks? She is picking up some clothes and other items that are on the stairs. Think about the accidents that could occur if those items were left on the stairs.

Following safety rules can also prevent accidents. Safety rules, such as those shown here, often appear at a swimming pool. Sometimes you might feel that such rules prevent you from having fun. Remember that the purpose of safety rules is to protect you and others from harm. Imagine what would happen if students were allowed to run in school halls. Think about how dangerous swimming would be without a lifeguard.

How is this person avoiding unnecessary risks?

## What Are Some Traffic Safety Rules?

The people in these pictures are avoiding unnecessary risks and accidents by following traffic rules. Notice that the girl is going to cross the street at a crosswalk. She is also watching for traffic. Being careful around traffic is one way to avoid accidents.

The teenager in the picture is avoiding unnecessary risks by taking a training class for his all terrain vehicle. He knows that his new vehicle can be fun, but very dangerous. Taking a training class can help him become a safe driver.

The girl in the car is avoiding unnecessary risks by wearing a safety belt. How is the bicycle rider avoiding unnecessary risks and helping prevent injuries?

**Think Back** • *Study on your own with Study Guide page 324.*

1. In general, how can accidents be prevented?
2. How could someone avoid unnecessary risks while climbing stairs?
3. What are three ways people can prevent traffic accidents?

How are the people in these pictures avoiding unnecessary risks?

## 2 How Can You Act Safely at Home?

What comes to mind when you hear the word *accident*? Many people think of automobile crashes and accidents that happen away from home. A large number of accidents, however, occur inside the home. Falls, fires, and other accidents often occur because of unnecessary risks at home.

### How Can You Prevent Falls?

You have probably fallen at one time or another. You might have slipped on a wet floor or tripped on a stair. Falls are the most common type of accident in the home. Most falls result in minor bumps and bruises, but some falls can be very serious.

By knowing the most common causes of falls, you can take actions to prevent them. For example, a rug on a slippery floor can lead to dangerous falls. The people in the picture are helping to prevent this kind of accident. They are putting rubber backing on the rug to keep it in place when people walk on it. The chart lists several other safety rules to prevent falls. Try to practice these rules at home.

Rubber backing keeps the rug in place.

144

## How Can You Prevent Poisonings?

A **poison** is a substance that is harmful if it gets inside the body. When you think of poisons, you might imagine bubbly potions in a laboratory, or a rattlesnake's venom. Actually, such common items as cleaning fluids, bleaches, detergents, and paint thinner are poisons. They can cause severe illness or death if they get into the body. Even the fumes of these substances can be poisonous. Medicines also can poison you if they are not used properly.

The labels of some poisons carry the familiar skull and crossbones or other warning signs. The labels also explain how to use the products safely.

Many poisonings happen to young children. They cannot read the warning signs on labels and will put almost any substance into their mouths. Therefore, all poisons and medicines should be kept out of reach of small children. Many people store their household cleaners on high shelves so that young children cannot reach them. Some people lock these materials in a cabinet. The picture shows a kind of lock that helps prevent small children from opening the cabinet doors. The lock can be released only by pushing down on the white bar. The chart lists other ways to prevent poisonings.

**poison,** a substance that is harmful if it gets inside the body.

### Safety Rules to Prevent Poisonings

- Label poisons clearly, and keep them out of the reach of young children.
- Store poison in its original container so it will not be mistaken for something else.
- Read labels carefully before taking medicines or using household products.
- Store medicines and household products out of reach of young children.
- Check medicines from time to time and properly dispose of all old medicines.
- Properly dispose of all empty containers that have held poisons or medicines.

145

## Safety Rules to Prevent Electric Shock

- Do not touch the metal prongs of a plug when putting it into an outlet.
- Do not plug too many appliances into the same outlet.
- Use safety plugs to cover unused outlets.
- Do not allow electrical appliances to get near water or use them when you are wet.
- Do not use an appliance if its cord is damaged.
- Tell an adult if you see a damaged cord, wire, or electrical appliance.

## How Can You Prevent Electric Shocks?

When you walk across a carpet and then touch a metal object, you often get a slight electric shock. This shock is not harmful. Other electric shocks, however, can be strong enough to kill a person. You can prevent electric shocks by practicing the rules shown to the left.

Many electric shocks occur when someone uses plugs and outlets improperly. When you put a plug into an outlet, be careful not to touch the metal prongs on the plug. Also, do not plug too many appliances into the same outlet. Such an overload can cause a fire. Unused outlets should be covered so that young children cannot stick tiny objects into them.

Electricity flows through water easily. Therefore, you should never touch a radio, hair dryer, or other electrical appliance when any part of your body is wet. Also, never allow these appliances near water.

Plastic or rubber coatings on wires protect a person from electric shocks. Sometimes these coatings can become cracked and worn. If you see any damaged wires, tell an adult immediately.

How are these people helping to prevent a fire?

## How Can You Prevent Fires?

The picture shows several ways of preventing another common type of home accident—fires. Notice the people putting a screen around the fireplace. The screen prevents sparks and small pieces of burning wood from falling into the living room. The boy is moving the magazines away from the fireplace in case some sparks get through the screen. The woman is disconnecting a plug so that the outlet is not overloaded.

Now look at the people in the kitchen. The man is putting the matches in an upper cabinet out of reach of the young child. Meanwhile, the girl is dampening the burnt-out match to make sure it cannot start a fire when she throws it away. The chart lists other ways to avoid risks that could lead to a fire.

Unlike a fall or poisoning, a fire often harms more than one person. If you live in an apartment building, a fire in your apartment can spread throughout the entire building. You protect your family and your neighbors, as well as yourself, whenever you do something to prevent a fire.

### Safety Rules to Prevent Fires

- Install smoke detectors.
- Handle matches carefully.
- Dispose of used matches properly.
- Keep matches and other fire sources away from young children.
- Keep flammable materials away from the stove and other heat sources.
- Throw out flammable materials, such as newspapers, cardboard boxes, and old rags.
- Keep electrical wiring in good working order by replacing damaged cords, cracked plugs, and loose connections.
- Never overload an outlet.
- Turn off space heaters before leaving a room or going to bed.

## How Can You Act Safely When You Are Home Alone?

Sometimes you might be home alone. Perhaps you get home from school before the rest of your family comes home. You might stay home on a Saturday morning while your family goes shopping. Preventing accidents at home is especially important when you are alone because help might not be available right away if an accident occurs.

Knowing how to act safely toward strangers is also important while you are alone. Suppose you were home alone and heard a knock at the door. Would you open the door right away? To be safe, you should first find out who is on the other side of the door. You could look out a window or look through a peephole, as shown. If the caller is a stranger, do not open the door. Instead, ask "Who is it?" through the closed door.

You should never let a stranger know you are home alone. If the stranger asks to see your father, for example, you might say that he cannot come to the door right now and ask the caller to come back later. This safety rule also applies to strangers who call on the telephone.

When someone calls at the door, find out who is there.

Sometimes you might meet a stranger while outside. For example, someone in a car might ask you for directions. You do not have to give the directions. You can tell the stranger to ask an adult or go to a nearby service station. If you choose to give directions, stay several feet away from the car, as these girls are doing. The chart lists other safety rules you should follow when dealing with strangers.

You probably think of your home as a place of safety and protection. You have seen, however, that many daily activities, such as climbing the stairs or using a household cleaner, can involve a certain amount of risk. By avoiding the unnecessary risks, you can help keep your home safe for yourself and your family.

**Think Back** • *Study on your own with Study Guide page 324.*

1. What are three ways to help prevent a fall?
2. What are three ways to help prevent poisonings?
3. What are three ways to prevent electric shock?
4. What is the safe way to dispose of used matches?
5. What should someone do if he or she is home alone and a stranger knocks at the door?

**On Your Own**

Some people have small chains on the doors to their homes. These chains allow someone to open the door a few inches to see the person outside. On a sheet of paper, explain why it would not be safe to open a door to a stranger even if the door was chained.

**Safety Rules of Acting Toward Strangers**

- When someone knocks at the door or rings the doorbell, look through a window or peep hole to see who it is.
- Never open the door to a stranger.
- Do not let a stranger know that you are home alone.
- If a motorist asks you directions, stay several feet from the car. Remember, you can tell the motorist to ask an adult.
- Never enter a stranger's car.

How are these people acting safely toward a stranger?

# Health Activities Workshop

## Exploring Ways to Practice Safety

1. The boy in the picture is picking up a shovel from the sidewalk. Write the different kinds of accidents that could result if the shovel were left on the sidewalk or if a rake were left on the lawn.

2. The skull and crossbones and the Mr. Yuk symbol are two warning signs of poisons. Design your own warning sign for poisons. Give the sign a name.

3. Think of ways you can avoid unnecessary risks and prevent accidents in your daily activities. For example, first write down a common activity, such as washing before school. Then write what kinds of accidents could occur during that activity. Finally, list several ways to avoid the unnecessary risks that could cause those accidents. In this example, you could list using nonskid mats on the bathroom floor and wiping up any water on the floor to avoid falls.

4. Draw a picture or find one in a newspaper or magazine that shows a person with a high-risk job. You might look for a firefighter, test pilot, race car driver, police officer, tree trimmer, or football player. Glue or tape the picture onto a sheet of paper. Then, write a paragraph describing the risks of the job and how that person avoids unnecessary risks while on the job. You might need to use an encyclopedia or other book to get your information.

 ## Looking at Careers

5. When your house or apartment was built, one or more construction inspectors probably looked at it. These people check buildings, bridges, roads, dams, and other structures to make sure they are safe for people to use. Different kinds of inspectors check for different things.

**Building inspectors** check the plans of a building before construction begins. During construction, the inspectors check the foundation, materials, and building methods. **Electrical inspectors** examine the wiring, lighting, and other electrical parts. A building with unsafe or incorrect wiring can be a fire hazard. **Mechanical inspectors** inspect the plumbing, including septic tanks, sewer systems, and heating systems.

Construction inspectors must be at least high school graduates. Many inspectors also have studied

architecture or engineering in college.

You can discover a career you might like by making a list of your interests and the things you care about. For example, if you enjoy building models and working outside and you care about people's safety, you might like to be a construction inspector. Make up a list of your interests. Keep the list in a folder and add to it as your interests change.

To find out more about construction inspectors, write to the International Conference of Building Officials, 5360 South Workman Mill Rd., Whittier, CA 90601.

**emergency,** a sudden need for quick action.

## 3 How Can You Be Prepared for Emergencies?

Notice the picture of the fire station. A firefighter checks face masks, gas tanks, fire extinguishers, and other special gear on the vehicle. He makes sure everything is ready for use. The proper knowledge, skills, and equipment make this firefighter well prepared for an emergency.

An **emergency** is a sudden need for quick action. No one can predict exactly how he or she will react in an emergency. However, by being prepared, you have the best chance of reacting correctly and safely. For example, your school's fire drill procedure can prepare you for a fire emergency.

### How Can You Get Help Quickly?

One way to be prepared for all kinds of emergencies is to know how to get help. For most emergencies, help is only a telephone call away. Knowing who to call and what to say might save someone's life.

Firefighters are well prepared for an emergency.

The police department, fire department, doctor's office, hospital, and poison control center are some places you can call in an emergency. The telephone numbers of these places should be listed near the telephone, as shown. This list should also include numbers of several nearby friends and numbers where family members can be reached at work.

If you need emergency help and you do not have the right telephone number nearby, you can dial 0 for operator. He or she will get you help. Many communities use 911 as a special emergency number. Find out if your community has such a number.

When you call for help, you need to give certain information. For most emergencies, the person you call will need to know *what* the emergency is and *where* it is. Also, the person will likely need your name and address. He or she might ask you questions about the emergency. Try to stay calm so you can answer the questions clearly. Be sure you do not hang up the telephone until you have given all the needed information.

**On Your Own**
Make a list of emergency numbers for your own home. You might want to make a smaller list to tape to the telephone receiver. This list could include the police and fire department numbers.

What telephone numbers should be listed in case of an emergency?

| DOCTOR | 262-( |
| POLICE | 911 |
| FIRE | 911 |
| POISON CONTROL CENTER | 795-2 |
| HOSPITAL | 262-1 |
| DAD | 795-2 |
| JIM | 262-3 |
| DEBBY | 262-( |

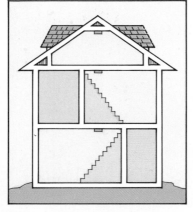

Why should a building have several smoke alarms?

## How Can You Be Prepared for Fire Emergencies?

Fire drills help prepare you for fire emergencies at school. You can prepare for fire emergencies at home too. The woman shown to the left is increasing her family's chances of surviving a major fire. She is installing a smoke alarm. A smoke alarm makes a loud, shrill noise when smoke reaches it. The drawing shows that a smoke alarm should be installed in several places throughout a home or other building. With the proper equipment, people are alerted to a fire no matter where it starts.

What would you do if you saw a small fire in a trash can at home? This kind of emergency might require the use of a fire extinguisher. Every household should have at least one fire extinguisher to put out small fires. You need to know where the extinguisher is located and how to use it before an emergency occurs. By being prepared, you would not have to waste precious seconds looking for the extinguisher and learning how to use it.

How would these items be helpful during an emergency?

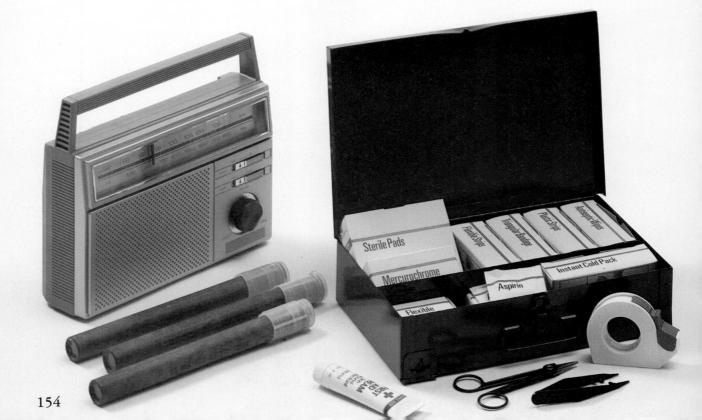

Some home fires are too large to be put out with a small fire extinguisher. If a large fire occurs, leave the building immediately. Have two or three escape routes already planned. You can practice these escape routes by having fire drills, just as you do at school. Once you are safely out of the building, call for help from a neighbor's house.

### What Items Should a Home Have for Any Emergency?

A fire extinguisher is one item your family should have in case of an emergency. The picture shows other items you might need. A battery-operated radio, a flashlight, and candles and matches will be useful if the electricity goes out. An emergency escape ladder, as shown here, can help you safely leave a building. The first-aid kit can help you and your family treat minor medical emergencies. The kit shown here includes bandages, gauze, cotton, scissors, tweezers, and an antiseptic to treat small wounds. Be sure to read the directions on the items in the first-aid kit. If you know how to use emergency supplies, you will be prepared if you need to use them.

**Think Back** • *Study on your own with Study Guide page 325.*

1. Whose telephone numbers should be posted near the telephone in case of an emergency?
2. What information might you need to give when calling for emergency help?
3. How can you prepare for fire emergencies at home?
4. What are some emergency items every home should try to have?

## 4 How Can You Help in a Medical Emergency?

Some emergencies involve people who are injured or ill. A person might be choking on a piece of food. A hot iron might fall on someone's arm. Such emergencies require immediate medical attention—**first aid.** Different emergencies require different kinds of first aid. However, certain rules apply for all kinds of emergencies and first aid.

Giving first aid requires clear thinking and correct, quick actions. Therefore, the first thing you need to do is stay calm. Second, send for help as quickly as possible. If no one else is near, go for help only after the person is out of immediate danger. For example, a person who has stopped breathing will need your immediate attention. Tell someone else to call for help while you start first aid. Third, do not move an injured person unless you must, such as moving someone away from a burning building. Moving the person often makes the injury worse.

Finally, do not do more than you know how to do. The information in this lesson shows only some basic ways to perform first aid. In order to be trained properly, people in the picture are attending a first-aid class. First-aid classes teach people how to develop the knowledge and skills that might one day save a person's life.

First-aid classes teach first aid thoroughly.

## How Can You Help Someone Who Is Choking?

Choking occurs when a piece of food or other object blocks air from moving through the windpipe. A person who is choking usually tries to cough up the object. Do not interfere as long as the person can cough or speak. However, you must start first aid if the person cannot cough, speak, or breathe. If someone else is nearby, ask them to call for help. The following pictures show the first aid you can give to someone who is choking.

1. Stand behind the person. Put your arms around the person just above the navel.

2. Make a fist with one hand. The thumb of the fist should be toward the person. Wrap your other hand around the fist.

3. Quickly thrust your fist against the person's abdomen. Use an inward and upward motion.

4. Repeat these three steps until the object comes out.

157

**artificial respiration**
(är′tə fish′əl
res′pə rā′shən), a method
of first aid that forces air into
the lungs.

## How Can You Help Someone Who Has Stopped Breathing?

Choking, poisoning, or a near drowning can all cause a person to stop breathing. First aid for stopped breathing includes **artificial respiration**—a method of forcing air into the lungs. Starting artificial respiration right away is very important. Most people suffer brain damage or die after only four to six minutes without oxygen. The pictures and captions on these two pages show how to perform artificial respiration.

1. Find out if the person is conscious. Gently shake the shoulder and ask loudly, "Are you OK?" If you do not get an answer, send someone for medical help if you can. Then begin artificial respiration.

2. Place the person on his or her back. Put one hand on the person's forehead. Open the air passage by gently lifting the chin up with your fingers. Remove any food or other material in the person's mouth.

3. Place your cheek and ear close to the person's mouth and nose. Look at the chest to see if it rises and falls. Listen and feel for air to be exhaled for three to five seconds.

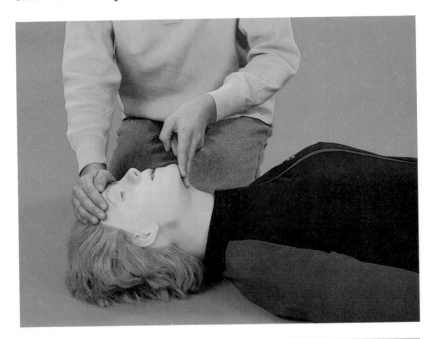

Some situations, such as a heart attack, can cause a person's heartbeat as well as breathing to stop. First aid for such cases includes cardiopulmonary resuscitation (CPR). In giving CPR, a person applies rhythmic pressure on the chest to force the blood to circulate. A person should use CPR only if he or she has been trained to do so.

4. If the person is still not breathing, keep the airway open and pinch the nostrils closed. Keep one hand under the chin for support. Then, seal your mouth tightly over the person's mouth and give two full breaths. As you give the breaths, you should be able to see the person's chest rise.

5. Look, listen, and feel again for breathing. If the person is still not breathing, give one breath every five seconds for anyone over eight years old. Continue giving the breaths until the person breathes without assistance or until help arrives. For children under eight years old, give one breath every four seconds. For infants, give one puff of air every three seconds.

6. If the person is still unconscious but breathing on his or her own, continue to maintain the open airway.

## How Can You Help Someone Who Has a Burn?

You have probably experienced a minor burn at some time in your life. Perhaps you touched a dish that just came out of a hot oven. You might have relieved the pain by running cool water over your fingers. Applying cool water is one of the correct ways to give first aid for a minor, first-degree burn.

The chart shows the correct ways to give first aid for all kinds of burns. Notice that for first-degree and second-degree burns, the general treatment is to apply cool water and to cover the burn with a sterile cloth or bandage. Third-degree burns are more serious and require the immediate attention of medical professionals. A third-degree burn should be covered with a sterile dressing until help arrives.

## First Aid for Burns

| Signs | Type of burn | Treatment |
|---|---|---|
| Redness<br>Mild pain and swelling<br>Unbroken skin | First-degree:<br>Injures only the outside layer of skin. Possible causes are sunburn, brief contact with hot objects, and hot water or steam. | Immediately run cool water over the injured area or put the injured area in cool water until the pain stops. Do not use ice directly on a burn. Gently pat the skin dry. Cover the skin with a bandage called a sterile dressing. Do not apply ointments, sprays, or home remedies. |
| Redness<br>More skin damage<br>Blisters<br>Swelling (lasts several days) | Second-degree:<br>Injures layers of skin beneath the surface. Possible causes are deep sunburn, hot liquids, and flash burn from gasoline. | Follow the treatment for a first-degree burn. Do not break the blisters. Do not apply an ointment, spray, or home remedy. Take off the dressing if the pain returns. Put a clean cloth wrung out in cool water over the area. When the pain stops, carefully dry the area and cover with a new dressing. Get medical help quickly. |
| Charred or white appearance.<br>Complete loss of all skin layers.<br>Little pain because nerve endings have all been destroyed | Third-degree:<br>Destroys all layers of skin. Possible causes are fire, electricity, and prolonged contact with hot substances. | Cover the burn with a sterile dressing or clean cloth. Get medical help quickly. Be ready to begin artificial respiration if breathing stops. Do not remove any clothes stuck to the injured area. Do not apply any treatment to the burn itself. |

*Note:* A victim's burns might include a combination of degrees. Be sure to look at all injured areas.

## How Can You Help Someone Who Is in Shock?

Shock occurs when the heart, lungs, brain, and other organs do not get enough blood. The body functions slow down. Any kind of accident or severe illness can cause a person to go into shock. This condition is often more serious than the injury or illness that caused the shock. Common signs of shock include cold, damp skin; nausea; faintness; trembling; rapid breathing; rapid, weak pulse; and unusual thirst.

First aid for shock includes laying the person down and keeping the person warm, as shown. Unless the person has a leg, chest, or head injury, you should raise the legs to improve circulation of the blood. First aid also includes sending someone for help. If no one is nearby, you should get help yourself after the person is lying down and covered.

People in a serious accident should be treated for shock even if the signs of shock do not appear. Early treatment can help prevent the person from going into shock later.

**shock,** a condition that occurs when the body fails to circulate blood adequately, causing body functions to slow down.

**Think Back** • *Study on your own with Study Guide page 325.*

1. What should a person remember when giving any kind of first aid?
2. What is the first-aid procedure for choking?
3. What are the steps of artificial respiration?
4. How does first aid for a first-degree burn differ from first aid for a third-degree burn?
5. How should someone treat a person for shock?

What is the proper first aid for shock?

## Leslie's First Aid Saves Her Mother's Life

When Leslie Maack was learning about first aid in her sixth-grade health class, she never thought she would use it so soon. Just two weeks later, however, Leslie performed first aid that saved her mother's life.

Leslie awoke one night to find her mother lying on the bedroom floor. A blood vessel in her brain had ruptured. She was not breathing, and her heart had stopped beating. Leslie's older sister and grandmother were stunned, but Leslie knew exactly what to do. She immediately started giving her mother artificial respiration and CPR—a kind of first aid that circulates the blood artificially.

For five minutes, Leslie performed this first aid and kept her mother alive. An ambulance arrived shortly and took her mother to the hospital.

Leslie's successful experience at CPR made her the star of her health class. The class had studied first aid for victims of stopped breathing, choking, drowning, and other kinds of accidents. The students had been able to practice artificial respiration and CPR on a Red Cross manikin.

Besides learning the correct procedures for first aid, the class had also learned how to react to an emergency. Leslie's knowledge of first aid would not have done much good if she had panicked when she saw her mother lying on the floor. Fortunately, she remained calm and started first aid immediately. Leslie's ability to manage a life-threatening situation shows the importance of learning first aid.

### Talk About It

1. What are two ways in which Leslie's training helped her save her mother?
2. How do you think you would react to an emergency like the one described here? What might help you react correctly?

123

NING POST

Leslie Maack's 45 minutes of CPR training enabled her to save her mother's life.

Leslie Maack, 11, awoke at 2 a.m. to see her mother on the bedroom floor, blue, breathless and Before she gave herself a chance ulmonary rescue

## Planning and Practicing Fire Drills

You probably have three or four fire drills a year at school. Do you have any fire drills at home? People often panic during a fire and get confused about how they should act and where they should go. Home fire drills, like the one shown here, will help you and your family react correctly if a real emergency occurs.

Decide on two escape routes, if possible, from the building. Decide where your family should meet outside. By meeting outside, you can find out if everyone is safe.

Practice your escape routes several times a year. Be sure to practice during the day and at night. Follow the escape routes as quickly as possible, but remember these safety rules.
- Walk quickly down the stairs.
- Keep a flashlight next to each bed for night fire drills.
- Keep all doorways and hallways clear of objects so that you do not fall during the fire drill.
- Practice crawling close to the floor to avoid dangerous smoke and vapors.

## Reading at Home

*By Yourself* by Sara Gilbert. Lothrop, 1983. Learn about how to deal with being home alone and how to handle various emergency situations.

*Fractures, Dis-Lo-Ca-Tions, and Sprains* by Alan E. Nourse. Watts, 1978. Find out what each of these injuries is and how to take care of them.

*In Charge—A Complete Handbook for Kids with Working Parents* by Kathy S. Kyte. Knopf, 1983. Discover how it is possible to take care of yourself and deal with a possible crisis while your parents are at work.

# Chapter 5 Review

### Reviewing Lesson Objectives

1. Describe several ways to avoid unnecessary risks and accidents, including traffic accidents. (pages 142–143)
2. Describe several safety precautions that can prevent falls, poisonings, electric shocks, fires, and other possible dangerous situations at home. (pages 144–149)
3. List the kinds of telephone numbers and other items that help in preparing for an emergency. (pages 152–155)
4. Explain the guidelines for giving first aid for choking, stopped breathing, burns, and shock. (pages 156–161)

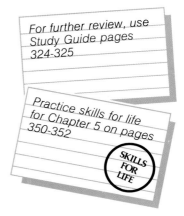

For further review, use Study Guide pages 324-325

Practice skills for life for Chapter 5 on pages 350-352

SKILLS FOR LIFE

### Checking Health Vocabulary

Number your paper from 1–5. Match each definition in Column I with the correct word or words in Column II.

*Column I*

1. a condition that occurs when the body fails to circulate blood adequately
2. a method of first aid that forces air into the lungs
3. a substance that is harmful if it gets inside the body
4. immediate medical care given to someone who is injured or suddenly ill
5. a sudden need for quick action

*Column II*

a. artificial respiration
b. emergency
c. first aid
d. poison
e. shock

Number your paper from 6–8. Next to each number write a sentence describing the kind of burn listed below.

6. first-degree burn
7. second-degree burn
8. third-degree burn

Number your paper from 9–16. Next to each number write a sentence using each word or words.

9. unnecessary risk
10. safety belt
11. accident
12. crosswalk
13. electric shock
14. stranger
15. smoke alarm
16. first-aid kit

## Reviewing Health Ideas

Number your paper from 1–15. Next to each number write the word or words that best completes the sentence.

1. You can avoid unnecessary risks while riding in a car by wearing a _____ _____.
2. Picking up objects left on a stairway is one way of avoiding _____.
3. Falls are the most common type of accident at _____.
4. Cleaning fluids and medicines can be _____, and should be kept out of the reach of young children.
5. Unused outlets should be _____ in some way if children are around.
6. You should never let a stranger know you are home _____.
7. A list of emergency telephone numbers is most useful if it is near the _____.
8. Every household should have at least one fire _____.
9. During any emergency, it is important to stay _____.
10. During an emergency, you should send for _____ as soon as possible.
11. Start first aid immediately if a choking person cannot cough, _____, or breathe.
12. First aid for choking includes thrusting a fist against the _____.
13. During artificial respiration, you open the air passage by pulling the _____ up and tilting the head back.
14. While breathing into a person's mouth during artificial respiration, you should keep the person's _____ closed.
15. A _____-degree burn can be treated by running cool water over the burn.

## Understanding Health Ideas

Number your paper from 16–25. Next to each number write the word or words that best answer the question.

16. What is one way a person can avoid unnecessary risks on a bicycle?
17. What should a person do before throwing away a burnt-out match?
18. If you are home alone and someone knocks at the door, what should you do first?
19. What should you do if you are giving directions to a motorist?
20. Who should you call if you need the police, but do not have the telephone number?
21. What information will a person need if you call for emergency help?
22. What items should a home have for any emergency?
23. After opening the air passage, what should you check before continuing artificial respiration?
24. What kind of burn should be covered and treated further only by a medical professional?
25. What should people in serious accidents always be treated for?

## Thinking Critically

Write the answers on your paper. Use complete sentences.

1. Write a paragraph in response to the following statement: "Safety rules only stop me from having fun."
2. For each situation, explain the correct way to respond.
   a. A motorist asks you to come near the car to give directions.
   b. The child you are babysitting for has just swallowed cleaning fluid.

# Chapter 6

## Drugs: What They Are and What They Do

The old-fashioned medicine containers in the picture might be interesting to look at, but the medicines they once contained often were not safe. This chapter describes the safe use of medicines and the harmful effects of using illegal drugs. You will also learn the dangers of other substances, such as alcohol and tobacco. In addition, the chapter suggests ways to resist trying drugs—an important choice for a healthy life.

### Health Watch Notebook

Look through magazines or newspapers for an article describing how drug use has affected society. Place the article in your notebook. Write a paragraph describing how the drug user, as well as others, was harmed.

**drug,** any chemical substance that changes the way the body works. The physical changes might cause changes in emotions and behavior.

# 1 What Are Drugs?

Suppose that you, like the student shown in the picture, were asked to write a definition of *drug*. What would you write? Suppose, too, that you were asked to name some common products that have drugs in them. What would you name? Compare your ideas with the information on these two pages.

A **drug** is a chemical that changes the way the body works. The changes might be physical, such as the heart beating faster. The changes might also affect a person's emotions and behavior. Different drugs cause different changes. Medicines, for example, are drugs that produce changes in the body to prevent, treat, or cure an illness.

A mild drug called caffeine is in some teas, coffees, and soft drinks. The small amounts of caffeine in these drinks increase the activity of the brain and other parts of the nervous system. Too much caffeine can make a person sleepless and nervous. Most doctors recommend that young people limit drinks with caffeine. Many caffeine-free teas, coffees, and soft drinks are now available.

Alcohol is a drug that slows down the work of the nervous system. Alcohol can cause changes in the way a person thinks, feels, and acts. The kind of changes depend on how much alcohol is in the body.

Tobacco and tobacco smoke contain a drug called nicotine. This drug causes the blood vessels to narrow and the heart to beat faster. Other substances in tobacco and tobacco smoke irritate the nose, throat, and lungs.

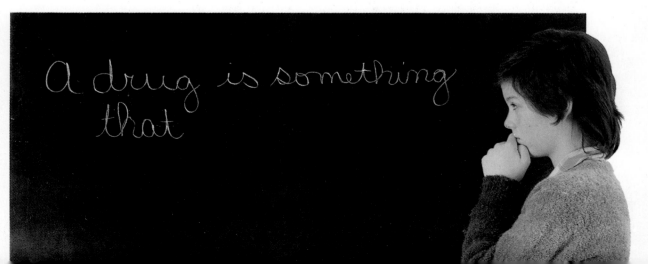

You might be surprised to learn that the glue shown in the picture can have harmful, druglike effects on the body. The fumes from such products as glue, paint thinner, paints, and gasoline are poisonous. Inhaling these fumes can make a person feel dizzy and sick. The products are not intended to be used in ways that are harmful to health.

The items mentioned on these two pages are common products that you have probably seen in a store, at home, or in an advertisement. They are legal to use, although age restrictions might apply. Some drugs, however, are illegal to sell, buy, or use because of their extremely dangerous effects. Some illegal drugs can easily cause death, even in small amounts. You will learn more about the effects of these drugs later in the chapter.

All drugs, including medicines, can be harmful. People need to know the facts about drugs to make the wisest decisions about health.

**Think Back** • *Study on your own with Study Guide page 326.*
1. What is a drug?
2. What are some products that contain drugs?
3. What are some products that have druglike effects on the body if used in ways that are not intended?

Glues, paints, and thinners can be harmful if misused.

## 2 What Are Medicines and How Do People Use Them Safely?

Almost everyone has taken some kind of medicine at one time or another. During an illness, a doctor might have given you certain medicine to relieve pain or to help cure a disease. Medicines are drugs intended to be used for health reasons. Hundreds of medicines have been developed to prevent, treat, or cure many diseases.

### How Do Medicines Get into the Body?

As the pictures show, medicines get into the body in different ways. Medicine for an eye infection might be a liquid dropped directly into the eyes. Medicine for a skin problem might be a lotion rubbed on the skin. Medicine for a nasal problem might be sprayed into the nose.

Sometimes a doctor or nurse injects medicine into the body through a hollow needle. Such shots are often given deep in the muscles of the upper arm. The muscle cells absorb the medicine, which then passes into the bloodstream. The blood carries the medicine to all parts of the body, including the part that is ailing. Sometimes medicine is injected directly into a vein.

Medicines get into the body in different ways.

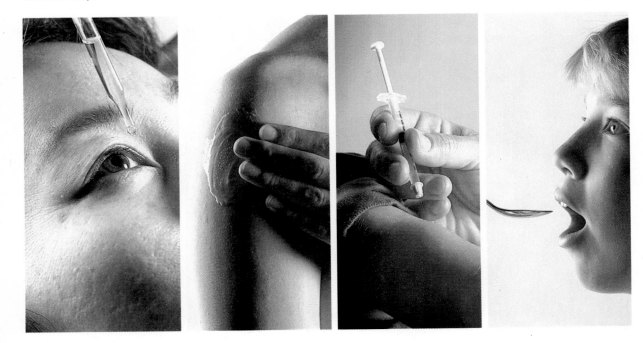

More often than not, people take medicine orally—through the mouth. Such medicine might be in the form of a pill, capsule, or liquid. Once the medicine is swallowed, it travels to the stomach within a few seconds. Stomach juices might dissolve the medicine. Then it can pass through the walls of the stomach and small intestine into the bloodstream. The blood carries the medicine to all parts of the body, including the part that needs it.

### What Are Prescription and OTC Medicines?

Some medicines can be bought only with a prescription—a doctor's order for a specific medicine. These medicines are **prescription medicines**—Rx medicines. Notice the prescription shown here. It includes the kind and amount of medicine and directions for safe use. A pharmacist follows the doctor's order in preparing the medicine.

Buying **over-the-counter medicines**—OTC medicines—does not require a prescription. Aspirin, some cough syrup, and cold tablets are some OTC medicines usually found on store shelves. OTC medicines are intended only for occasional, short-term use. Although OTC medicines are generally not as powerful as prescription medicines, they can be dangerous if not used correctly.

**prescription** (pri skrip′ shən) **medicine,** a drug that can be purchased only with an order from a doctor.

**over-the-counter medicine,** a drug that can be purchased without a doctor's order.

What information is on this prescription?

## How Can People Use Medicines Safely?

Like all drugs, medicines cause changes in your body. Therefore, medicines must be used with caution. The labels on medicine containers help you to use medicine safely.

Notice the label of the prescription medicine below. It lists the name of the doctor, pharmacy, and patient. The patient listed is the only person who should take that medicine. The label also includes directions about how much medicine to take and how often to take it. Special warnings and directions for safe storage might be included. All these directions should be followed exactly. What other information can you find on the prescription label?

Directions for safe use are on OTC medicines too, as the label to the right shows. These labels tell the purpose of the medicine, how much medicine to take, and any special warnings. Always read a warning carefully. Some people might not be able to use some OTC drugs if they have certain health problems or are currently taking other medicines.

What important information is on Rx and OTC medicine labels?

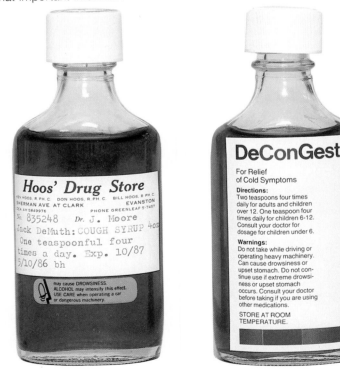

Notice that the label on the OTC medicine also describes possible side effects—unwanted effects of the medicine. Headache, stomach upset, and drowsiness are common side effects of OTC and prescription medicines. Prescription medicine labels do not always list possible side effects. This information must come from your doctor or pharmacist. Be sure you are aware of the possible side effects before taking any medicine.

**drug misuse,** incorrect use of a medicine in a way that can harm health.

The chart lists safety guidelines to follow when using medicine. Taking medicine without following these guidelines is **drug misuse**—incorrectly using a medicine in a way that could harm health. Examples of drug misuse include taking more medicine than directed, taking two or more medicines at the same time without a doctor's permission, or taking medicine prescribed for someone else. You can prevent most drug misuse by reading and following the information on medicine labels.

**Think Back** • *Study on your own with Study Guide page 326.*
1. What is a medicine?
2. What happens to medicine after it is swallowed?
3. How do prescription and over-the-counter medicines differ?
4. What guidelines should people follow for using medicines safely?

## Safety Guidelines for Using Medicine

- Do not take medicine without the permission of a doctor, parent, or other responsible adult.
- Read and follow all directions and warnings on the label.
- When the doctor prescribes a medicine, ask him or her what side effects you might expect.
- If an OTC medicine has a harmful or unexpected side effect, stop taking it immediately. Tell an adult member of your family about the side effect. If a prescription medicine has an unexpected side effect, call the doctor immediately.
- Do not use a medicine for every minor ailment. Occasional sleeplessness, headache, and slight cold can often be relieved with rest and relaxation.
- Keep medicine in its original container.
- Never take a medicine prescribed for someone else.
- Keep all medicines in places where young children cannot reach them.
- Take a prescription medicine for as long as the doctor directed, even if you feel well before then.

## 3 What Are the Dangers of Drug Abuse?

The proper use of medicine helps millions of people around the world every day. Some people, however, use medicines and other drugs in harmful, dangerous ways. The intentional use of drugs for reasons other than health is **drug abuse.**

The abuse of drugs can produce many harmful effects. Some of these effects are immediate. They occur within a few minutes or hours after taking the drug. A sick feeling in the stomach is one common immediate effect of drug abuse. Others include headache, sleeplessness, high blood pressure, vomiting, and even death if a person takes too much of the drug.

Some dangerous effects of drug abuse occur after a period of continued abuse. These long-term effects include tolerance and dependence.

**Tolerance** occurs when a person's body gets used to a drug. The abuser must use more and more of the drug to get the same effect. For example, suppose a person starts the bad habit of taking a sleeping pill every night to fall asleep. That person's body will soon build tolerance to the sleeping pill. Then two pills might be needed to make the person sleepy. As tolerance continues to build, the person might need three or four pills each night to fall asleep.

This person needed emergency medical help to recover from an overdose.

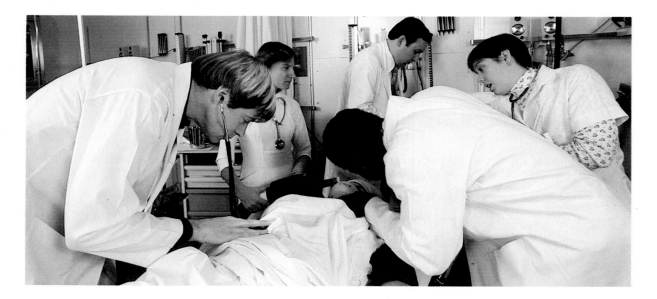

These larger amounts of sleeping pills might lead to an **overdose**—an amount of a drug too large for the body to use. An overdose can cause serious health problems. The patient shown on page 174 suffered from a drug overdose. The emergency team was able to save this person's life, but many other people die from overdoses.

**Dependence** is the need for a drug. The need might be mental or physical. A mentally dependent person *thinks* he or she needs the drug to function or make it through the day. With physical dependence, a person's body needs the drug to avoid feeling sick. A person can be both mentally and physically dependent on a drug.

Sometimes a person who is physically dependent on a drug stops taking it. The person might then suffer from a sickness called **withdrawal.** The symptoms of withdrawal can vary, depending on the drug that had been used. Withdrawal symptoms can be unpleasant and dangerous. Usually the person becomes nervous, depressed, or panicky. Other symptoms include chills, fever, vomiting, and severe aches and pains. People withdrawing from certain drugs often need to be hospitalized for a short time.

Usually, after a short withdrawal period, the body learns to function without the drug. Physical dependence stops. Mental dependence, on the other hand, is often more difficult to stop. A person can overcome dependence, but he or she must be willing to get proper help and find healthier, more constructive ways to deal with problems.

The picture shows one way of dealing with drug-related problems. A person who wants help is talking with someone who has special training and experience in helping others with their problems. Some organizations in your community probably provide such counseling.

## What Are the Most Commonly Abused Drugs?

The most commonly abused drugs can be placed into five groups. They are depressants, stimulants, narcotics, hallucinogens, and inhalants. The charts on the next few pages describe these groups of drugs.

**overdose,** an amount of a drug that is too large for the body and can cause a dangerous reaction.

**dependence** (di pen′ dəns), the need for a drug. This need might be mental, physical, or both.

**withdrawal** (with drô′ əl), the symptoms that occur when a person who is physically dependent on a drug stops taking it.

Talking about drug-related problems helps.

**stimulant** (stim′ yə lənt), a drug that speeds up the work of the nervous system.

**depressant** (di pres′ nt), a drug that slows down the work of the nervous system.

## Stimulants

*What They Are:* **Stimulants** are drugs that speed up the work of the nervous system. Stimulants can cause a feeling of being more awake or having more energy than usual. Strong stimulants include amphetamines, crank, "ice," cocaine, and crack. Amphetamines are illegal without a prescription. Crank, "ice," cocaine, and crack are illegal.

*Harmful Effects:* Misuse of amphetamines can cause a person to feel anxious or confused. The person might have trouble sleeping, become irritable, and lose his or her appetite. Also, heavy doses can dangerously increase the heart rate. Crank and "ice" cause extreme fear, anger, and violence and can damage the brain, heart, lungs, and kidneys. Cocaine is a strong stimulant that increases the heart rate and blood pressure. Crack is an especially potent form of cocaine. Cocaine and crack act upon the nervous system and cause a feeling of excitement that soon wears off. Then the user is likely to feel depressed. Other effects of cocaine and crack use include sleeplessness and hallucinations—seeing or hearing things that are not really there. Tolerance and dependence can develop from the use of amphetamines and cocaine. Crack, crank, and "ice" users develop tolerance and dependence very rapidly. An overdose of stimulants can cause death.

## Depressants

*What They Are:* **Depressants** are drugs that slow down the work of the nervous system. The brain and nerves work more slowly, muscles relax, and the body takes longer to react. Alcohol, tranquilizers, and barbiturates are depressants. Doctors sometimes prescribe mild depressants, such as minor tranquilizers, to calm people or to help them sleep. Such prescriptions are for short-term use. Doctors might prescribe barbiturates to relax patients before surgery. Alcohol is illegal for sale to minors. Tranquilizers and barbiturates are illegal without a prescription.

*Harmful Effects:* Because doctors prescribe tranquilizers and barbiturates at times, some people think such drugs are safe to use as they choose. This idea is a mistake. Depressants often cause such symptoms as confusion, slurred speech, and staggering. A person who takes heavy doses of barbiturates usually has difficulty thinking and working effectively. As a result, that person might not remember how many doses he or she has taken and might accidentally take an overdose. Then the person's breathing and heart rate will slow down so much that the person might pass out, go into a coma, or die. People can develop tolerance and mental and physical dependence for depressants.

## Narcotics

*What They Are:* **Narcotics** is a term for a group of depressant drugs that are made from opium or from a substance like opium. Narcotics include morphine, codeine, and heroin. Narcotics, like other depressants, slow down the work of the nervous system. Narcotics also stop the brain from feeling pain. Doctors use codeine and morphine to produce sleep and to relieve pain in operations and serious illnesses. However, doctors use these drugs with great care. As soon as they can, doctors stop giving these drugs. Morphine and codeine are illegal without a prescription. Heroin is not used medically in the United States and is illegal.

*Harmful Effects:* Narcotics are especially dangerous because they can produce physical and mental dependence quickly. Even people who want to give up taking a narcotic might find that they cannot. Withdrawal symptoms can be severe and usually include chills, fever, and stomach pains. Other health problems occur when people abuse a narcotic. They often spend so much time using or thinking about the drug that they neglect other body needs. Many narcotic abusers become malnourished. Infections, such as hepatitis and AIDS, can result from unsterile needles that abusers use to inject heroin.

## Hallucinogens

*What They Are:* **Hallucinogens** are drugs that cause changes in the senses. A person who uses a hallucinogen might see, hear, smell, or feel things that are not really there. Hallucinogens change the messages carried by the nerves to the brain. Therefore, a whisper might sound like a shout. Time might appear to pass very slowly. Hallucinogens include LSD and PCP. All hallucinogens are illegal.

*Harmful Effects:* Hallucinogens increase the heart rate and blood pressure. Feet and hands might feel numb, and the stomach might become upset. Some hallucinogens affect people's moods. Hallucinogens are very unpredictable. Even in the same person, the effects of a hallucinogen can change each time the drug is used. Some users become violent or frightened. Some people injure themselves because they are not aware of danger. In some cases, users have gone into a coma and died. Continual use of hallucinogens can lead to mental problems and permanent brain damage.

**narcotic** (när kot′ ik), a legal term for a drug made from opium or from a substance like opium that is produced artificially.

**hallucinogen** (hə lü′ sn ə jen), a drug that causes changes in the senses, often making a person see, hear, smell, or feel things that are not really there.

### Did You Know?
Some young people use anabolic steroids, a group of drugs similar to a male hormone. Some young people use steroids to build muscle quickly. They mistakenly believe that these drugs have no harmful effects. However, anabolic steroids are known to cause dangerous side effects, including severe liver damage, mental problems, skin problems, and the appearance of male characteristics in female users. Because they are so dangerous, the use of anabolic steroids is illegal in most athletic competitions.

**inhalant** (in hā′ lənt), a substance that gives off fumes, which could produce druglike effects when breathed deeply into the body.

## Inhalants

*What They Are:* **Inhalants** are substances that give off fumes, which could produce druglike effects when breathed deeply into the body. Dangerous inhalants include the fumes from lighter fluid, cleaning fluid, gasoline, paint thinner, airplane glue, nail polish remover, pesticides, and oven cleaners. The picture shows a safe way to use some of these household products. People who abuse these substances breathe the fumes deeply into the body. Then changes occur in the body similar to changes caused when drugs are taken.

*Harmful Effects:* At first a person who inhales fumes might think that he or she has more energy. However, this feeling does not last long. Soon other effects take place. A person might feel irritable or dizzy. He or she might have trouble speaking clearly. Vomiting might occur. Headaches, nosebleeds, and loss of memory are common. A person might become drowsy or pass out. Constant or deep sniffing of fumes can permanently damage the nose, throat, lungs, brain, liver, and kidneys. Inhalants can cause death by stopping the heartbeat or breathing.

How is this person using the paints and thinner safely?

## How Does Drug Abuse Affect Society?

Drug abuse affects society as well as the person taking the drug. As the picture suggests, one effect of drug abuse on society is increased crime. Many people who abuse drugs obtain them illegally. Because the price of illegal drugs is often high, abusers often steal to pay for them. Abusers obviously cause harm to theft victims and sometimes police officers. Also, the arresting, trying, and imprisoning of abusers costs society millions of dollars.

People who abuse drugs affect society in another way. Drug abusers cause many accidents resulting in injuries or death to themselves or others. More than half of all motor vehicle accidents involve someone who has abused a drug.

**Think Back** • *Study on your own with Study Guide page 326.*

1. What is one possible long-term effect of drug abuse?
2. How can stimulants damage the body?
3. What are some harmful effects of depressants?
4. Why are the changes caused by hallucinogens dangerous?
5. What are some products that give off fumes that could be harmful unless the products are used properly?
6. How does drug abuse affect society?

*Did You Know?*
Society is affected by drug use in ways other than crime and accidents. Society loses when students do not learn or drop out of school because of drug use. Society also loses when workers miss work, work slowly, or make mistakes at work because of drug use. Society also loses when the babies born to alcoholic or drug-addicted mothers are born sick and brain damaged. These babies may never be able to develop into persons who can care for themselves. Therefore, they may have to be supported by society throughout their lives.

How does drug abuse lead to an increase in crime?

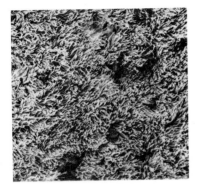

Cilia in healthy lungs

Cilia are destroyed by marijuana smoke.

# 4 How Does Marijuana Affect Health?

Marijuana is a drug that comes from the hemp plant. Marijuana cigarettes contain the dried leaves and stems of the plant. Scientists have been studying marijuana for over twenty years. Their findings show that using this drug harms health in many ways.

Marijuana contains more than four hundred chemicals—some of which can be harmful to the body. Like all drugs, marijuana can cause changes in the way the body works. It can also change the user's moods and actions.

The main mind-altering chemical in marijuana is called THC. When marijuana is smoked, the THC is absorbed by many body tissues and organs. The greater the amount of THC in the marijuana, the greater the effects will be on the user. Tests show that the THC from just one cigarette can stay in the body for about a month. Therefore, THC easily builds up in the body of a marijuana user.

When marijuana is smoked, the heartbeat speeds up. Blood vessels behind the eyes might become irritated. However, scientists think the most damaging physical effects of marijuana occur in the lungs. Marijuana smoke inflames the lining of the lungs and prevents them from working properly. The first picture above shows that air passages in healthy lungs are lined with hairlike cilia that sweep particles away from the lungs. Notice in the second picture that the cilia in a marijuana smoker have been completely destroyed. Chemicals in marijuana smoke can help cause lung cancer and other serious diseases of the lungs. In addition, evidence indicates that long-term marijuana use reduces the body's ability to resist diseases in general.

Use of marijuana can affect a person's timing and coordination. As a result, driving a bicycle or a car can be dangerous. Many traffic accidents are caused by people who use marijuana. Notice in the chart on the next page other driving skills affected by the use of marijuana. Think about how each skill is important to traffic safety. How does driving become dangerous if that skill is weakened?

Marijuana use can also affect a person's mood. Some users find that marijuana makes them feel nervous. Others say it makes them irritable. Some users become loud and talkative. Marijuana affects the moods of different people differently. It can also affect the same person differently at different times.

The use of marijuana is especially damaging to young people. It interferes with physical, emotional, and mental growth. For example, studies show that marijuana use might decrease the levels of certain hormones during puberty. This action slows the rate at which a young person matures. Also, young people who use marijuana to escape their problems might not learn the skills necessary to deal with everyday problems of growing up.

Many young people who use marijuana notice that their school grades drop, partially because marijuana can interfere with a person's ability to learn. The drug affects memory and thinking skills. Also, as a marijuana user becomes more interested in the drug, he or she often becomes less interested in school, activities, and friends.

Because of its danger to health, there are laws against growing, selling, and possessing marijuana.

**Think Back** • *Study on your own with Study Guide page 327.*
1. How can marijuana use affect the body?
2. How might the use of marijuana lead to driving accidents?
3. How can marijuana affect a user's mood?
4. Why can the use of marijuana be especially harmful to young people?

> **Did You Know?**
> Marijuana can harm the reproductive system. As young people go through puberty, proper amounts of the male and female hormones are essential for normal growth. Marijuana has been shown to change the amount of these hormones. These changes can result in abnormal sexual development.

**Driving Skills that Marijuana Weakens**
- Coordination
- Reaction time
- Ability to follow a moving object
- Perception of flashing lights
- Ability to adjust quickly to a sudden bright light

# 5  How Does Alcohol Affect Health?

**On Your Own**
Use the chart on this page to answer the following questions on a sheet of paper.
• At what percentage level of blood alcohol content does risk of accidents increase? Why?
• How does the risk of accidents change as the percentage increases? Why?

Alcohol is a depressant drug. It is probably the most abused drug in the United States today. Alcohol is illegal for people under a certain age. This drug is found in such beverages as whiskey, beer, and wine.

Alcohol does not break down in the body the same way other foods do. It is absorbed right into the bloodstream from the stomach and the small intestine. Within two minutes after a person drinks alcohol, that alcohol starts to enter the bloodstream. The blood carries the alcohol to every part of the body.

### What Are the Immediate Effects of Alcohol?

Because alcohol is a depressant, it slows down the activity of the brain, which slows other parts of the body. Like many drugs, alcohol can change a person's mood, emotions, or actions.

The degree to which alcohol affects a person depends on the blood alcohol level—the percentage of alcohol in the person's blood. The chart shows the effects of different blood alcohol levels on a person's bodily functions and behavior. Note that the higher the blood alcohol level, the more severe the effects of alcohol on the person. However, even a low level of alcohol can interfere with a person's ability to perform.

Effects of Blood Alcohol Level

| Blood Alcohol Level (percent) | Examples of Effects |
|---|---|
| 0.01-0.04 | Blood circulates more rapidly; inhibitions lessened; user feels dizzy; ability to think clearly decreases; coordination lessens; judgment and memory are weakened; risk of accidents increases. |
| 0.05-0.09 | Unable to think clearly; behavior changes; judgment and reasoning become unreliable; coordination impaired; risk of accidents much higher. |
| 0.10 | Vision, hearing, speech, and balance are impaired; coordination poor; considered intoxicated by law in most states; risk of accidents very high. |
| 0.20 | Most behaviors are affected; standing and walking are difficult; user might lose bladder control; risk of accidents extremely high. |
| 0.30 and up | Vomiting might alternate with unconsciousness; deep coma; death. |
| 0.40-0.50 | Usually causes death. |

A person's weight affects the blood alcohol level. A smaller person has a higher blood alcohol level than a larger person if both drink the same amount of alcohol. A smaller person has less body fluids, which dilute the alcohol. Why do you think young people would feel the effects of alcohol faster and more strongly than adults? Other things affect the blood alcohol level. The level rises quickly if a person drinks many drinks in a short period of time or if the stomach is empty. Also, each person's body chemistry is different and reacts to alcohol differently.

As the blood alcohol level increases, people lose their coordination. They lose their ability to walk, talk, and see properly. They lose memory and alertness, and they can lose self-control. They might do things that would be embarrassing to them if they were sober. Some people might argue, fight, or act in a silly way. The higher the alcohol level, the greater its effects. As the chart shows, a person with high levels might vomit or lose consciousness and could even die. The dangers are especially great among young people because alcohol affects them very quickly and severely.

Notice the facts in the chart below. Some of these figures might surprise you. They highlight one of the most disastrous effects of alcohol—accidents caused by drunk drivers.

**Some Facts About Drunk Driving in the United States**

- About 26,000 people are killed in drunk driving accidents every year.
- Nearly 70 people are killed in drunk driving accidents every day.
- About 750,000 people suffer crippling and other serious injuries every year in drunk driving accidents.
- On an average weekend night, one out of ten drivers on the road is drunk.

**cirrhosis** (sə rō′sis), a disease of the liver that is often caused by heavy, long-term use of alcohol.

**alcoholism** (al′kə hô liz′əm), a disease in which a person cannot control his or her use of alcohol.

## What Are the Long-Term Effects of Alcohol?

People who drink alcohol heavily over long periods of time suffer certain long-term effects. A common long-term effect of drinking alcohol is **cirrhosis,** a disease of the liver that can result in death. Notice in the picture how the diseased liver differs from the healthy liver. Alcohol can also cause brain damage, nerve damage, and ulcers—sores in the lining of the stomach. Many people who drink alcohol over a long period of time suffer from malnutrition. Although it provides Calories, alcohol contains none of the vitamins, minerals, or proteins that are needed for growth and health. In addition, many people who are long-time, heavy users of alcohol lose their appetites and do not eat nourishing meals.

Another long-term effect of drinking alcohol is physical and mental dependence. A person who develops such dependence on alcohol suffers from a progressive disease called **alcoholism.** An alcoholic cannot control his or her heavy drinking.

An alcoholic often drinks so heavily and so often that drinking interferes with everyday life. The alcoholic might be unable to do school work or hold a job. Family relationships are often ruined as alcohol becomes the most important thing in the person's life.

Healthy liver                                   Liver with cirrhosis

An alcoholic needs treatment. The disease can be controlled with proper help. However, the alcoholic must want help before he or she can be helped. A physician or a psychologist might provide counseling and treatment for the alcoholic.

One organization that helps many alcoholics stop drinking is Alcoholics Anonymous, or AA. Special branches of AA help family members of alcoholics. The branch for husbands, wives, other relatives, and friends is called Al-Anon. The branch for sons and daughters from age twelve to eighteen is Alateen, and the branch for sons and daughters who are under twelve is Alatots. The picture shows an Al-Anon meeting in session. Here, family and friends of alcoholics help each other by sharing their experiences and discussing ways to help solve their problems.

**Think Back** • *Study on your own with Study Guide page 327.*
1. Why does alcohol affect the body so quickly?
2. What are some immediate effects of alcohol?
3. What diseases can long-term alcohol abuse cause?
4. What can be done to help alcoholics?

Help is available for friends and families of alcoholics.

# 6 How Does Tobacco Affect Health?

Every pack of cigarettes and all cigarette advertisements must carry one of the statements shown to the left. In addition, cigarettes cannot be advertised on radio or TV, and it is illegal for young people to buy cigarettes. The government has made these laws because of the dangers of tobacco.

## What Happens When Cigarettes Are Smoked?

When a cigarette is puffed, smoke passes into the lungs. In this smoke is a mixture of particles, gases, and other chemicals. Almost all the harmful substances that are inhaled stay in the body. The three most damaging substances are nicotine, carbon monoxide, and tars.

Nicotine is a stimulant drug. It speeds up the heartbeat and can cause dependency.

Carbon monoxide is a poisonous gas. It replaces some of the oxygen in the blood. Then the smoker has to breathe faster to take in enough oxygen.

Tar is a yellow or brown substance with hundreds of chemicals in it. As the tars cool in the smoker's lungs, they form a brown, sticky mass. The picture demonstrates how tar accumulates in the lungs. The tar irritates the lungs and the lining of air passages. Tar in the lungs can cause lung cancer.

**Did You Know?**
Scientists estimate that a two-pack-a-day smoker shortens his or her life by about eight years.

What does this smoking demonstration show?

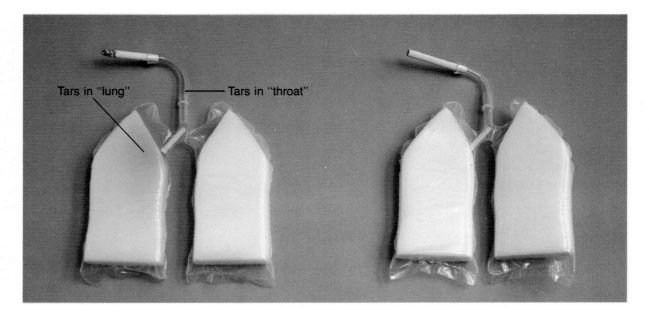

Tars in "lung" — Tars in "throat"

## What Are the Long-Term Effects of Cigarette Smoking?

When a person first starts smoking cigarettes, he or she might feel sick. Sometimes the person might cough a lot or feel dizzy. If a person continues to smoke, the body develops tolerance. The person no longer feels uncomfortable. However, the person becomes dependent on the nicotine in tobacco. Dependent people feel nervous or jittery if they cannot smoke a cigarette.

Other clues that show a person has been smoking for a long time are shown in the chart. Perhaps you know someone who has been affected in one or more of these ways.

Besides causing unattractive traits and dependence on nicotine, smoking for several years can cause certain diseases. For example, long-term smoking can increase the risk of developing high blood pressure. The chances of having a heart attack or a stroke are greater in a smoker. Smoking can also cause lung cancer.

Emphysema is another disease that can be caused by cigarette smoking. In emphysema, tiny air sacs in the lungs are weakened and destroyed. People with this disease have trouble breathing. Sometimes they have to carry a supply of oxygen with them wherever they go. Emphysema cannot be cured.

Chronic bronchitis is still another disease caused by cigarette smoking. People with chronic bronchitis develop irritating coughs and have difficulty breathing.

**On Your Own**
Write a paragraph discussing why the following advice on smoking is a healthy idea: "The best tip is not to start."

### Clues that a Person Is a Smoker

- The tars in cigarette smoke can stain a smoker's teeth.

- The odor of stale smoke clings to a smoker's clothes.

- A smoker's fingertips can be stained yellow or brown from holding cigarettes.

- A smoker might have bad breath.

- A smoker might develop a brown or black fur-like coating on the tongue.

### How Does Second-Hand Smoke Affect Health?

Today, more and more people say, "Yes, I *do* mind if you smoke." Being in the same room with a smoker exposes nonsmokers to second-hand smoke. Second-hand smoke comes from someone else's cigarette.

Second-hand smoke is of two kinds and has two sources. Sidestream smoke comes from the end of a burning cigarette. Mainstream smoke is exhaled by the smoker. Sidestream smoke is more dangerous than mainstream smoke. Sidestream smoke contains twice as much tar and nicotine and five times as much carbon monoxide as mainstream smoke does. Second-hand smoke can be especially dangerous for people who have allergies, asthma, other lung diseases, or heart disease.

More and more restaurants and public places have sections for nonsmokers. Some communities have passed laws requiring this. Also, an increasing number of signs are appearing in stores and other places suggesting that people not smoke there. Where have you seen signs like the one shown below?

Why are non-smoking areas important to public health?

188

## How Does Smokeless Tobacco Affect Health?

In addition to being smoked, tobacco is sometimes used in the form of chewing tobacco and snuff. Chewing tobacco is coarsely ground tobacco leaves. Snuff is a powder made from grinding tobacco leaves and stems. It is usually sniffed through the nose.

Many young people mistakenly believe that smokeless tobacco is safe to use. Using chewing tobacco or snuff, like cigarette smoking, is very harmful to a person's health. Cancers of the mouth and throat, gum diseases, high blood pressure, and stomach trouble can quickly develop among people who use smokeless tobacco. Users also have bad breath and discolored teeth. What message does the poster give about smokeless tobacco?

**Think Back** • *Study on your own with Study Guide page 327.*
1. What are the three main harmful substances in cigarette smoke?
2. How do these substances affect the body?
3. What health hazards do smokers risk?
4. How is smoking dangerous to nonsmokers?

What is the message here?

Sometimes the worst things come in the best packages.

## Learning More About the Harmful Effects of Drugs

1. Investigate the cost of smoking cigarettes. Find out what one pack of a certain brand costs. Suppose a person smokes a pack a day. How much money will he or she spend in a week? in a year?

2. Investigate and make a report on the topic "How Did Smoking Start?" A helpful book that might be in the library is *Smoking and You* by Arnold Madison.

3. Bring in clippings from the newspaper about accidents during a one-week period. Make a special note of articles that mention accidents as a result of the use of alcohol by car drivers or pedestrians.

4. Look at the information on the bottle of aspirin shown here. Then answer these questions.

- What is the adult dose?
- What cautions must be taken in the use of this medicine?

5. Design and make a poster that might prevent someone your age from using drugs. Be sure to include both a statement and a picture to get your message across.

Use Only If Printed Seal Under Cap is Intact

**Adult Dose:** 1 or 2 tablets with water every 4 hours, up to 12 a day.
**WARNINGS: Consult a physician** before giving this medicine to children, including teenagers, with chicken pox or flu. Keep this and all drugs out of the reach of children. In case of accidental overdose, seek professional assistance or contact a poison control center immediately. As with any drug, if you are pregnant or nursing a baby, seek the advice of a health professional before using this product. See important directions in leaflet, including use in arthritis and rheumatism.

## Looking at Careers

6. Many people who have a health-related job work in factories where medicines are made. **Pharmaceutical plant workers** help make and package most of the medicines found in stores. These workers perform many different jobs. Some people mix substances following careful procedures and directions to produce tablets, capsules, or solutions. Others might weigh pills to make sure they include the right amount of medicine. Some workers operate machines that fill bottles of liquid medicine.

Other pharmaceutical plant workers work in the maintenance department. They repair equipment and keep the plant clean. Workers in the shipping department are responsible for delivering the medicines to hospitals and stores on time.

**Chemists** also work at a pharmaceutical plant. Some chemists are involved with research. They try to find ways to improve medicines or develop new ones. Other chemists, called quality control chemists, make sure the medicine made in the plant is being produced properly.

Use an encyclopedia or science book to find out what other kinds of chemists do. Describe your findings in a paragraph or two.

For more information write to the Pharmaceutical Manufacturing Association, 1155 Fifteenth St. N.W., Washington, DC 20005.

People who enjoy hobbies or other activities usually have no desire to try drugs.

## 7 How Can People Make Healthy Decisions About Drugs?

Many people make decisions not to abuse drugs. Such people know the harmful effects certain drugs have on those who misuse or abuse them. These people also realize that certain drugs are illegal.

Even though people know the dangers of drug abuse, sometimes they are tempted to try a drug because of the influence of a friend. These people might be afraid they will lose the friend if they say no. If this should ever happen to you, ask yourself if this person really is a friend. Would a true friend want you to do something that could harm you?

The best way to refuse drugs is to learn to say no. You could just say "No, thanks," or say you have something else to do. If the person continues to pressure you, you could just walk away. You do not have to let people tease or push you into something you do not want to do.

Another way to resist pressure to abuse drugs is to keep busy with activities you enjoy doing. You might want to develop a skill, such as writing or painting. You could try participating in team sports, or activities such as swimming and bicycling. You could develop a hobby such as collecting stamps or coins. The pictures suggest some activities you might enjoy.

If you are in a situation where you need to make a decision about drugs, follow the five steps to making healthy decisions. The following example shows how a healthy decision about drugs might be made. Barbara had a week to finish a report comparing two books. She was telling her friend Kathy that she had only read one book and might have to stay up late each night to finish the report. Kathy offered her some amphetamine pills to help her stay awake. Barbara used a decision chart like the one on the next page and made a wise decision not to use the drug. Read the chart to find out how she arrived at her decision.

Barbara was able to make the right decision because she knew the dangers of drug abuse. She also knew how to make decisions through a five-step process. Barbara found out she could resist pressure from a friend and that drugs are not a solution to a problem.

**Think Back** • *Study on your own with Study Guide page 327.*
1. What might influence a person to abuse drugs?
2. What information about drugs helps people decide not to abuse them?
3. What are some ways to resist pressure from friends to abuse drugs?

### Barbara's Decision-Making Chart

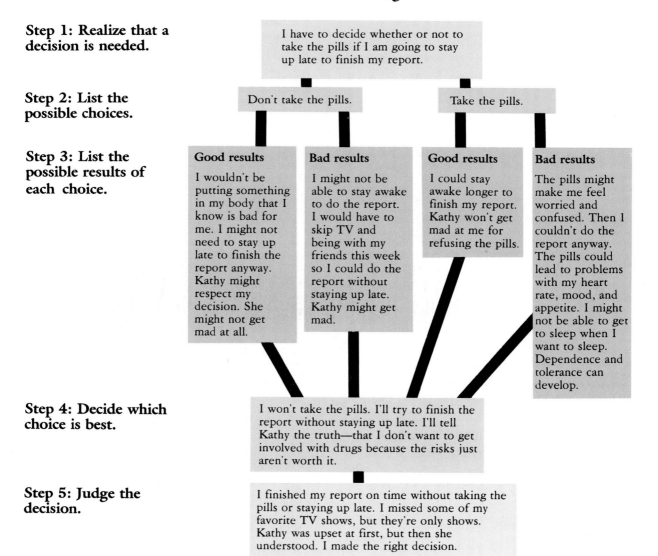

**Step 1: Realize that a decision is needed.**

I have to decide whether or not to take the pills if I am going to stay up late to finish my report.

**Step 2: List the possible choices.**

Don't take the pills.

Take the pills.

**Step 3: List the possible results of each choice.**

**Good results**

I wouldn't be putting something in my body that I know is bad for me. I might not need to stay up late to finish the report anyway. Kathy might respect my decision. She might not get mad at all.

**Bad results**

I might not be able to stay awake to do the report. I would have to skip TV and being with my friends this week so I could do the report without staying up late. Kathy might get mad.

**Good results**

I could stay awake longer to finish my report. Kathy won't get mad at me for refusing the pills.

**Bad results**

The pills might make me feel worried and confused. Then I couldn't do the report anyway. The pills could lead to problems with my heart rate, mood, and appetite. I might not be able to get to sleep when I want to sleep. Dependence and tolerance can develop.

**Step 4: Decide which choice is best.**

I won't take the pills. I'll try to finish the report without staying up late. I'll tell Kathy the truth—that I don't want to get involved with drugs because the risks just aren't worth it.

**Step 5: Judge the decision.**

I finished my report on time without taking the pills or staying up late. I missed some of my favorite TV shows, but they're only shows. Kathy was upset at first, but then she understood. I made the right decision.

## Kids Saving Kids

"We think we can help young people live drug-free lives," says sixteen-year-old Peter True about the Kids Saving Kids program. Peter is actively involved in this program, in which high-school students talk to fifth- and sixth-graders about the dangers of drug and alcohol abuse. Peter is one of about thirty teens in the Hempfield School District in Pennsylvania who serve as positive role models.

The first requirement to join Kids Saving Kids is to be able to stand up and say, "I am drug and alcohol free." Then the teens go through a two-day training session and correctly answer 138 questions about drugs and how they affect the body. Once accepted, the teens are further trained by someone from the National Federation of Parents for Drug Free Youth.

Although becoming part of Kids Saving Kids involves work, the teens use fun to reach their audience. The teens perform skits to get their point across. One skit is called "Keggers." In this skit some teens want to have a beer party. Others want to be alert for skiing the next day. The "keggers" get so sick they cannot enjoy the skiing. Other skits are about tobacco, marijuana, and other drugs.

Throughout the skits, the teens include facts about the harm caused by drugs. "The point at the end is that 'Drugs are stupid, drugs are bad,'" says Peter. Then each teen leads a small group in a discussion.

"The most important thing is to reach young people before they get the wrong idea that drugs are OK," says Peter. "The biggest problem is pressure from friends and others in school," he adds. "The teens in Kids Saving Kids provide an alternative group for the young people to turn to."

### Talk About It

1. What do the teens in Kids Saving Kids do to help prevent drug abuse?
2. Besides the one mentioned above, what other situation would make a good skit for the Kids Saving Kids program?

## Checking the Home for Drug Safety

Your parents and other family members are likely to be very interested in what you have learned about drugs at school. Think over some of the ideas you might share with them. What can you tell them about drugs?

You might also join some family members at home in a medicine safety check. Here are some things to look for in your home.

• Is old medicine thrown away? If not, it should be. Old medicine can lose strength or get stronger. Check the expiration date on the label. If the date has expired, flush the medicine down the toilet. Throw empty containers in the garbage. If you are not sure if a medicine is still fresh, you could ask a pharmacist.

• Is medicine kept where small children cannot get it? Is it in child-proof containers? Is it in a locked cabinet?
• Do members of the family avoid calling any medicine "candy"? Young children might look for the "candy" and take dangerous doses of medicine.

## Reading at Home

*Drug Use and Drug Abuse* by Geraldine Woods. Watts, 1979. Find out the medical uses of various drugs and the effects of drug abuse.

*Over-the-Counter Drugs* by Ann E. Weiss. Watts, 1984. Learn about how over-the-counter drugs can be helpful and harmful.

# Chapter 6 Review

## Reviewing Lesson Objectives

1. Explain what drugs are, and list some common products that contain drugs. (pages 168–169)
2. List the guidelines for using medicines safely. (pages 170–173)
3. State the harmful effects of abusing each major kind of drug. (pages 174–179)
4. State the harmful effects of marijuana. (pages 180–181)
5. Describe the short- and long-term effects of alcohol abuse. Tell where alcohol abusers can get help. (pages 182–185)
6. Explain how tobacco can harm the health of users and nonusers. (pages 186–189)
7. Identify factors that contribute to alcohol, tobacco, marijuana, and other drug use. Describe some ways to resist pressure to abuse drugs. (pages 192–193)

For further review, use Study Guide pages 326-327

Practice skills for life for Chapter 6 on pages 353-355

SKILLS FOR LIFE

## Checking Health Vocabulary

Number your paper from 1–16. Match each definition in Column I with the correct word or words in Column II.

### Column I

1. an amount of a drug that is too large for the body to use
2. a drug that can be used only with a doctor's order
3. a condition in which the body gets used to a drug
4. the symptoms that occur when a person who is physically dependent on a drug stops taking it
5. the incorrect use of medicine in a way that could harm health
6. a drug that can be purchased without a doctor's order
7. the intentional use of drugs for reasons other than health
8. a drug that speeds up the work of the nervous system
9. a drug that causes changes in the senses, often making a person see, hear, or feel things that are not really there
10. a drug that slows down the work of the nervous system
11. a drug made from opium or opiumlike substances
12. a substance that gives off fumes, which could produce druglike effects when breathed deeply into the body
13. the physical or mental need for a drug
14. any chemical substance that causes changes in a person's emotions, behavior, or the way the body works
15. a disease in which a person cannot control his or her use of alcohol
16. a disease of the liver that is often caused by heavy, long-term use of alcohol

### Column II

a. alcoholism
b. cirrhosis
c. dependence
d. depressant
e. drug
f. drug abuse
g. drug misuse
h. hallucinogen
i. inhalant
j. narcotic
k. over-the-counter medicine
l. overdose
m. prescription medicine
n. stimulant
o. tolerance
p. withdrawal

## Reviewing Health Ideas

Number your paper from 1–15. Next to each number write the word or words that best complete the sentence.

1. Some teas, coffees, and soft drinks contain a mild drug called _____.
2. Medicine that enters the body is carried by _____ to all parts of the body.
3. The name of a doctor, pharmacy, and patient would be found on a _____ medicine label.
4. Taking medicine prescribed for someone else is an example of drug _____.
5. Tolerance for a drug can lead a person to take an _____ of the drug.
6. A person who is _____ dependent on a drug *thinks* he or she needs it.
7. Two strong stimulants are amphetamines and _____.
8. Tranquilizers and barbiturates belong to the group of drugs called _____.
9. Inhalants can cause death by stopping the _____ or breathing.
10. The use of marijuana can lead to _____ cancer.
11. Studies show that the use of marijuana might decrease the levels of certain _____ during puberty.
12. Cirrhosis and ulcers are some long-term effects of abusing _____.
13. Carbon monoxide from tobacco smoke replaces _____ in the blood.
14. Gum diseases and cancers of the mouth and throat can develop from using _____ tobacco.
15. The best way to refuse drugs is to learn to say _____.

## Understanding Health Ideas

Number your paper from 16–25. Next to each number write the word or words that best answer the question.

16. What are three kinds of information found on OTC medicine labels?
17. How do stimulants generally affect the body?
18. What depressant drugs are especially dangerous because they produce quick dependence and severe withdrawal symptoms?
19. What is the main mind-altering chemical in marijuana?
20. How long can the THC from one marijuana cigarette stay in the body?
21. What factors might influence a person to abuse drugs?
22. What is a blood alcohol level?
23. What is Alcoholics Anonymous?
24. What are the three most damaging substances in cigarette smoke?
25. What diseases can long-term smoking help cause?

## Thinking Critically

Write the answers on your paper. Use complete sentences.

1. Suppose you have an earache. You remember that your father had an earache a month ago, and the doctor gave him a prescription medicine. Since you know where this medicine is, should you take it? Explain your answer.
2. Suppose you see a friend smoking marijuana. You advise your friend not to use the substance but he or she replies, "Why not? What's wrong with it?" What would you tell your friend?

197

# Fighting Against Disease

What is unusual about this human heart? Look at the two large arteries that supply blood to the heart. The yellow spots show material that has built up inside the arteries. Material that builds up in arteries can lead to several diseases.

This chapter discusses these diseases and a wide range of others—from the common cold to cancer. You will discover how your body fights disease every day of your life and how your health practices can help prevent disease now and in the future.

## Health Watch Notebook

Each day, write in your notebook activities you do to prevent disease. For each activity, explain how it helps keep you healthy.

1   What Causes Communicable Diseases?
2   How Does Your Body Fight Communicable Diseases?
3   What Are Some Diseases of the Respiratory System?
4   What Causes Noncommunicable Diseases?
5   What Is an Allergy?
6   How Can a Healthy Lifestyle Help Prevent Disease?

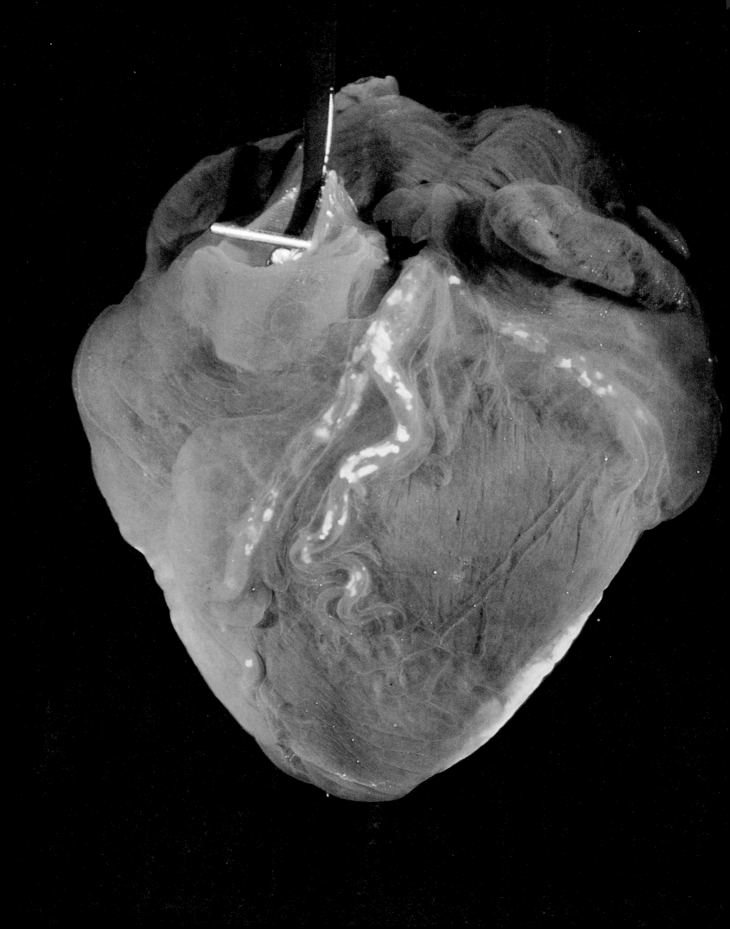

**communicable**
(kə myü′nə kə bəl) **disease,**
a disease that can spread,
usually from one person to
another.

# 1  What Causes Communicable Diseases?

Try to think of the last time you had a cold or the flu. Was anybody else in your family sick at about the same time? Perhaps you had a cold just as your mother was getting over hers. A few days later your brother or sister might have started coughing and sneezing. Sometimes a disease seems to pass from one family member to the next.

Diseases that can spread from one person to another are called **communicable diseases.** Tiny organisms or substances called disease germs cause these diseases. Bacteria and viruses are two of the most common kinds of disease germs.

### How Do Certain Kinds of Bacteria Harm Your Body?

Bacteria are the most numerous kinds of organisms. They exist in the air, ground, water, and your body. Bacteria are so tiny that millions of them could fit on a pinhead. The pictures show the various shapes of different kinds of bacteria seen through a microscope.

Bacteria have a variety of shapes.

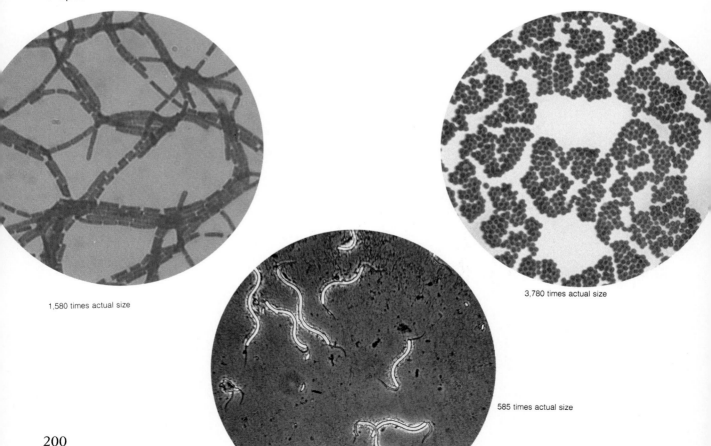

1,580 times actual size

3,780 times actual size

585 times actual size

Some kinds of bacteria are harmless, and many are helpful. A few kinds of bacteria, however, are harmful to humans and cause diseases. Such bacteria grow in your body and harm you by giving off wastes that are harmful to your cells.

A small number of harmful bacteria are not enough to make you sick. Bacteria, however, grow and reproduce very quickly. They grow best in warm, dark, moist places. The human body offers many such growing places for bacteria. The pictures show how quickly bacteria can reproduce and increase their numbers. Bacteria give off some wastes that act like poisons. A large number of harmful bacteria can produce enough poisonous wastes to make you sick.

Some diseases can be caused by different bacteria, and the same bacteria can sometimes cause different diseases. For example, several different kinds of bacteria can cause pneumonia. The bacteria that cause pneumonia can also cause sore throats, ear infections, and sinus infections. Bacteria that usually cause strep throat can also cause skin or sinus infections.

Bacteria reproduce quickly.

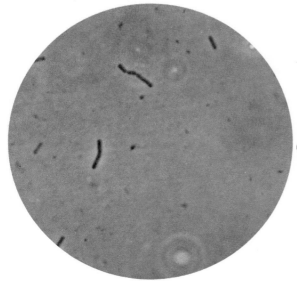

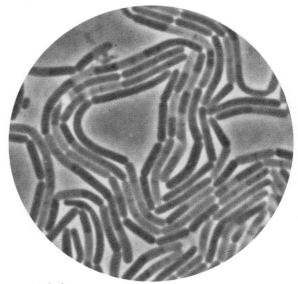
600 times actual size

## How Do Viruses Harm Your Body?

Viruses are even smaller than bacteria. They cause more illness than any other kind of disease germ. Viruses harm your body by entering and damaging body cells. The picture shows a virus invading a cell. Inside the cell the outer coat of the virus breaks down, and the virus reproduces rapidly. The new viruses use the cell's energy and crowd the inside of the cell, keeping it from working properly. The cell dies when the viruses break out of it. Then the viruses invade other cells. As with other kinds of disease germs, small numbers of viruses are not harmful. If the viruses reproduce, however, they can damage so many cells that you become sick.

In the last fifty years, scientists have identified hundreds of different kinds of viruses. Each kind of virus causes only one disease. For example, the virus that causes measles does not cause any other disease. A virus that causes a cold cannot cause any other disease. Flu, mumps, and chicken pox are also each caused by a certain kind of virus.

Viruses invade cells, use the cells' energy to reproduce, and break out to invade other cells.

1. Virus enters cell

3. DNA of virus reproduces itself

2. Outer coat of virus breaks down

4. Outer coat forms around new DNA and viruses leave cell

Viruses can be seen only by using an electron microscope, like the one in the picture. This important tool helps scientists compare, identify, and study the activities of viruses. This microscope can magnify a virus up to two million times its actual size. An electron microscope enlarged the viruses shown here. Notice the variety of shapes and sizes.

**Think Back** • *Study on your own with Study Guide page 328.*

1. What is a communicable disease?
2. What are the two most common kinds of disease germs and how does each cause disease?
3. Can a virus that causes flu also cause mumps? Explain your answer.

What instrument enables scientists to see these viruses so clearly?

685,880 times actual size

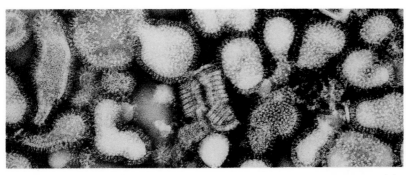

164,480 times actual size

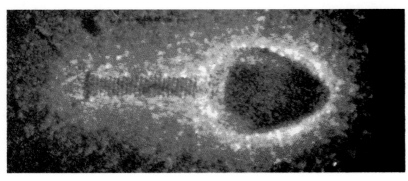

357,150 times actual size

## 2  How Does Your Body Fight Communicable Diseases?

Disease germs exist everywhere. In fact, the air you are breathing right now contains disease germs. You might wonder, then, why you do not get sick more often than you do.

### What Are Your First-Line Defenses?

Your body has three major ways to defend itself against disease germs. Your first-line defenses work to keep disease germs out of your body's tissues and bloodstream.

The most noticeable defense is your skin. Most disease germs cannot enter the body through unbroken skin. However, disease germs can enter your body easily through such openings as your mouth and nose. There the germs are likely to be trapped in mucus—a sticky liquid that lines your nose, mouth, throat, windpipe, and lungs. Thousands of tiny hairlike structures, or cilia, are in the nose and sweep mucus and disease germs to the throat. Then the material can be coughed up or swallowed. Stomach acids usually kill the germs swallowed with mucus.

Some white blood cells destroy disease germs.

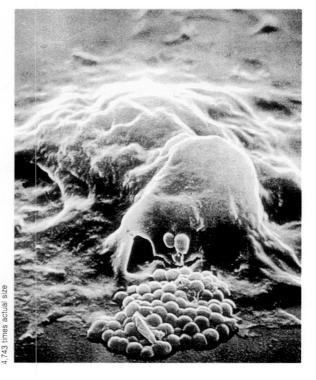

3,291 times actual size

4,743 times actual size

Dust particles and disease germs can enter your body through the openings around your eyes. Your body responds by producing tears. The tears clean your eyes and contain a substance that kills some disease germs.

Some germs might enter your body with your food. The saliva in your mouth might kill or weaken many of these germs. Others die when they mix with the strong acids in your stomach.

### What Is Your Second Line of Defense?

Sometimes your first-line defenses cannot prevent all disease germs from entering your body. Some might enter your bloodstream and other body tissues. Then your second line of defense goes to work.

Certain parts of your body produce white blood cells. Some of these cells circulate throughout your body. They surround and destroy disease germs, as shown in the pictures on these two pages. The first picture shows a white blood cell approaching a colony of bacteria, shown in green. In the second picture, the white blood cell has surrounded most of the colony. The colony has become a harmless jellylike mass inside the blood cell in the third picture.

**Did You Know?**
Instead of circulating in your bloodstream, some white blood cells stay in one place, such as your liver, spleen, or tonsils. White blood cells filter out disease germs as the blood passes through these organs.

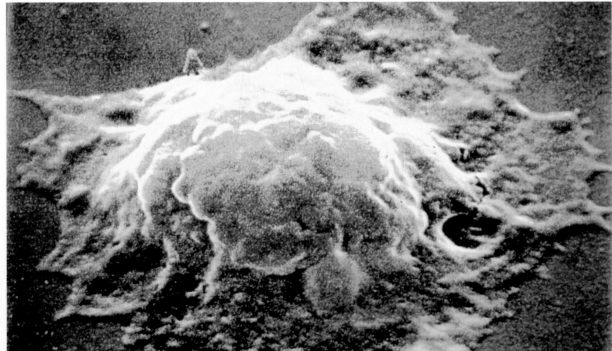

6,080 times actual size

**antibody** (an′ti bod′ē), a tiny substance made by white blood cells that attaches to a disease germ, making it harmless.

**immunity** (i myü′nə tē), the body's resistance to a disease through the presence of antibodies.

## What Is Your Third Line of Defense?

Sometimes disease germs reproduce so quickly that white blood cells cannot destroy them fast enough. Then your third line of defense—**antibodies**—helps your body fight off disease germs.

Antibodies are tiny substances produced by some white blood cells. The antibodies attach themselves to disease germs. The drawing shows that antibodies attach themselves to the germs and make them harmless. Later, other white blood cells can destroy the germs.

Each kind of antibody can attack only a specific kind of disease germ. For example, antibodies that attack the flu germ cannot harm the germ that causes any other disease. If a different kind of disease germ invades your body, your white blood cells must make a different kind of antibody.

Antibodies can do more than help fight off disease germs. Antibodies can also prevent you from getting a disease. For example, suppose you get chicken pox. Some of your white blood cells will form antibodies that can fight off the chicken pox germs. Some other white blood cells do not make antibodies right away. These white blood cells act as memory cells that "remember" to make the correct antibodies in the future. Long after you are cured, the memory cells will stay in your blood. If chicken pox germs enter your body again, these memory cells can quickly make the antibodies that can attack the germs. The antibodies will be made so quickly that the disease germs will not have a chance to make you sick. Therefore, if you have had chicken pox once, you will probably never get it again. You have an **immunity** to this disease. Measles, mumps, and polio each provide lifelong immunity once you have had the disease.

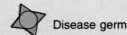
Disease germ

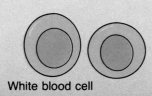
White blood cell

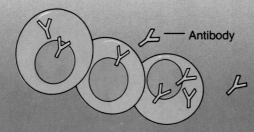
Antibody

Antibodies attach to germ

White blood cell

### How Do Vaccines Give You Immunity?

Having a disease can be a dangerous and painful way of building immunity. Today you can build immunity to certain diseases without having to get sick. Your body can be made to produce its own protection against certain disease germs. Preparations such as vaccines can be injected into the body. Or, in the case of polio vaccine, it can be taken into the body in syrup or on a sugar cube.

The girl shown here is receiving a vaccine that will give her immunity against mumps. A vaccine is a small dose of killed or weakened disease germs. These germs are not strong enough to make the girl feel sick. However, the germs do cause some of her white blood cells to make antibodies against mumps. Some other white blood cells become memory cells for mumps. If she is exposed to the germs that cause mumps, the memory cells will produce the correct antibodies quickly. These antibodies will attack only germs that cause mumps. She must have other vaccines to get immunity against other diseases.

The chart shows the vaccines you should receive. Notice that some vaccinations must be repeated in order to give you complete immunity to that disease.

Vaccines give immunity against certain diseases.

**Recommended Vaccines**

| Disease | First doses | Later doses |
|---|---|---|
| Diphtheria Whooping cough (pertussis) tetanus | 2 months, 4 months, 6 months, 18 months | DPT vaccine at 4 to 6 years then only tetanus-diptheria vaccine once every ten years |
| German measles (rubella) | 1 year to early teens | None |
| Measles | 15 months to adult | None, unless first dose was given before 12 months |
| Mumps | 1 year to adult | None |
| Polio | 2 months, 4 months, 18 months | 4 to 6 years |

**antibiotic** (an'ti bī ot'ik), a medicine that destroys or weakens bacteria.

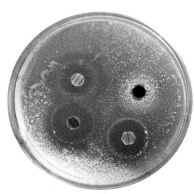

Antibiotics can kill some kinds of bacteria.

*Penicillium* forming on orange.

## What Else Helps Fight Communicable Diseases?

Vaccinations do not exist for every communicable disease. Also, your body's own defenses are not always enough to prevent or cure a disease. You might need medicines to help your body destroy certain disease germs.

**Antibiotics** are medicines that can kill many kinds of bacteria. Antibiotics are only helpful in treating diseases caused by bacteria. This type of medicine cannot kill viruses and, therefore, cannot help cure a cold or flu.

The picture to the left shows the effectiveness of some antibiotics. Bacteria are growing in the liquid in the disk. The four colored disks contain different antibiotics. The clear areas around three of the disks show that the antibiotic has killed the bacteria near the disks. The one disk with bacteria growing around it shows that some antibiotics cannot destroy certain kinds of bacteria.

The most familiar antibiotic is penicillin. It is used to help cure strep throat, some types of pneumonia, and other diseases. The discovery of penicillin was made accidentally. In 1928, a Scottish scientist, Sir Alexander Fleming, was searching for a substance that would kill harmful bacteria. To perform his experiments, he grew bacteria in special dishes. One day Fleming noticed spots of green, fuzzy mold in the dishes of bacteria. On further study, he noticed that the bacteria around the mold had died. The mold, *Penicillium,* made a substance that could kill bacteria. Fleming named this substance penicillin. The picture shows the kind of mold that produces penicillin.

## What is AIDS?

You probably have heard of a disease called acquired immune deficiency syndrome, or AIDS. AIDS is a preventable disease caused by a virus. The AIDS virus destroys the body's defense system against disease germs. This virus enters and destroys special white blood cells that signal the release of antibodies. Without these white blood cells, antibodies are not made to fight off disease germs.

The AIDS virus does not spread easily. It cannot spread by casual contact, such as sharing a room or touching. It does not spread through air, water, food, or by mosquitos. People can become infected with the AIDS virus if they get body fluids from an infected person into their bloodstream. One way people can become infected is by sharing needles used to inject illegal drugs. Another way the AIDS virus can spread is by sexual contact with an infected person. Also, mothers with the virus can transmit it to their babies during or after birth. Before 1985, some people became infected after receiving blood transfusions. Now, blood banks and hospitals test blood for the presence of the virus.

Most people who have become infected with the AIDS virus are not aware that they have been exposed to the disease. A person might look and feel well for many years after being infected. During this period, however, he or she can transmit the virus to others. In time, people with the virus might develop infections or diseases that they would not normally get if their defense system worked properly. They can get a rare form of pneumonia, a cancer called Kaposi's sarcoma, or other diseases that their bodies cannot fight off. Eventually, people with AIDS die of these diseases.

AIDS is a serious health problem. There is no cure for AIDS; however, scientists all over the world are working to find a cure and a vaccine. Although AIDS is mainly an adult disease, people of all ages should know how to protect themselves from the AIDS virus.

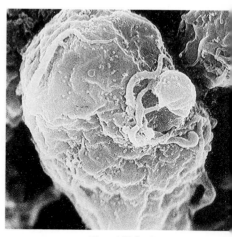

The AIDS virus

**Think Back** • *Study on your own with Study Guide page 328.*

1. How do skin, mucus, and tears each protect against communicable diseases?
2. How do white blood cells help fight against disease?
3. How do antibodies help provide immunity against some diseases?
4. Would antibodies help cure a disease caused by viruses? Why or why not?
5. What is AIDS? How does it cause illness in infected people?

## 3 What Are Some Diseases of the Respiratory System?

Almost everyone is familiar with the cough, sore throat, watery eyes, and runny nose of a cold.

Disease germs affect parts of the respiratory system and cause a cold. Your respiratory system includes your nasal passages, throat, windpipe, and lungs. The box shows some of the microscopic air passages and other structures in the lungs. All these organs work together to help you get oxygen from the air you breathe and to get rid of the carbon dioxide your body produces. Check the drawing as you read how colds and other communicable diseases affect the respiratory system.

**Respiratory System**

Nasal passage

Throat

Windpipe

Lungs

Air passages in lungs

## What Causes a Cold?

The most common disease in the United States is the cold. Most people catch at least one cold a year. Many people your age catch four or five colds a year.

Many different kinds of viruses cause colds. Two kinds of cold viruses are shown in the pictures. Cold viruses in the air can enter your nasal passages and throat easily when you inhale. Cold viruses on your skin can enter your body if you touch your hand to your mouth, nose, or eyes. The viruses reproduce quickly inside the respiratory system. One or two days later the growing viruses cause the familiar symptoms of the common cold.

The early stage of a cold usually lasts three or four days. During this time viruses continue to multiply in your nasal passages and throat. The tissue that lines your nasal passages produces extra mucus, and you get a runny nose. The tissue might also swell, making your nose stuffy. Other symptoms might include coughing, sore throat, sneezing, watery eyes, mild fever, and a loss of appetite. You might experience all of these symptoms or only a few of them during the early stage of a cold. The cold viruses can be passed on to others during this stage. Therefore, doctors suggest you stay at home during this time.

About a week later your body's defenses destroy the viruses. During this stage a person can no longer pass the viruses to others. The cold symptoms, however, continue for a few days.

You have probably heard that no cure exists for the common cold. More than 150 kinds of viruses cause colds, and scientists have not yet developed a vaccine that is effective against all of them. Antibiotics kill only bacteria, not viruses. Products such as cough syrup and cold tablets might make you feel better when you have a cold. However, these products treat only the symptoms, not the disease itself.

Your body's defenses can fight off the invading viruses. To help your body's own defenses, doctors recommend that you get plenty of rest and drink more fluids than usual. You should also avoid other people as much as possible so you do not spread the cold viruses.

49,000 times actual size

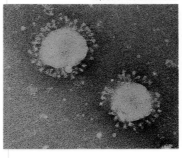

47,840 times actual size

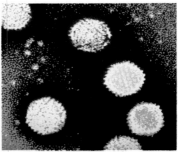

Two of the more than one hundred kinds of viruses that cause colds.

**sinusitis** (sī′nə sī′tis), a disease in which the sinus openings become blocked.

## When Does Sinusitis Occur?

The bones of your head and face have spaces within them called sinuses. The white arrows in the first picture show how these sinuses connect with the nasal passages. Mucus usually drains through the sinus openings into the nose and throat. If these openings become blocked, you can get **sinusitis.**

Sinusitis often occurs immediately after a cold. The same kind of tissue that lines the nose also lines the sinuses. The lining of the sinuses swells and produces more mucus than usual. Tissue around the sinus openings might swell and close off the openings. The mucus might thicken so that it blocks the openings. Then mucus accumulates in the sinuses, as shown in the second picture. The thick mucus might back up into your throat, making you cough.

Most cases of sinusitis are mild. However, certain bacteria can grow in the thickening mucus and make the sinusitis worse, especially if the openings of the sinuses are blocked. This blockage might result in headaches or a feeling of pressure behind your eyes. Antibiotics can help reduce the number of bacteria.

You can usually avoid a severe case of sinusitis by taking care of yourself when you have a cold. This care includes getting rest, drinking fluids, and taking medicines if they are suggested by your doctor.

Clear and blocked sinuses

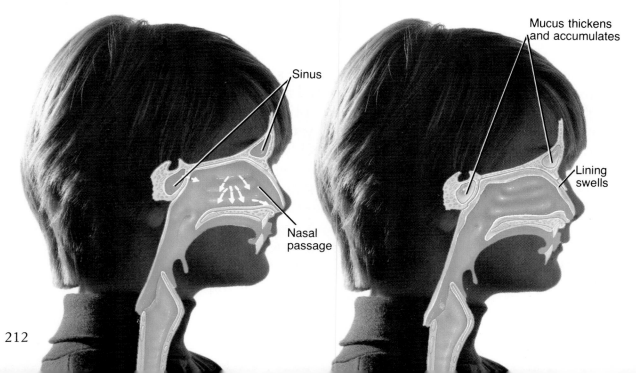

Sinus

Nasal passage

Mucus thickens and accumulates

Lining swells

## How Do You Get Influenza?

The flu—influenza—is similar to a cold in many ways. Like a cold, different kinds of viruses cause the flu. Flu viruses, like the one shown, invade the same parts of the body as cold viruses—the nose, throat, and air passages. Flu symptoms are similar to those of a cold, but much more severe. A person with the flu usually has fever, chills, aching muscles, and a general feeling of weakness. Other symptoms include headache, dizziness, sore throat, and coughing.

You can treat the flu as you do a cold. You should stay home for a few days to rest and to avoid spreading the disease germs to others. Flu is very easily spread. In fact, sometimes flu epidemics occur. The disease spreads so quickly that many people have it at the same time. With proper care, the flu usually lasts about four or five days.

As with a cold, no medicine can cure the flu or prevent you from getting the flu. No single vaccine can guard you against every kind of flu virus. Sometimes, however, scientists can predict what kinds of viruses will affect a population in a certain year. Then they can make a vaccine for those viruses.

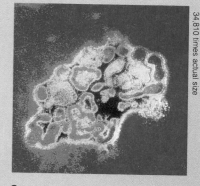

34,810 times actual size

Computer image of one kind of flu virus.

## What Is Pneumonia?

Pneumonia is an inflammation of the lungs. Most kinds are infectious and are caused by bacteria and viruses which begin growing in the nose and throat and then move to the lungs. The disease germs cause the tissue in the lungs to swell. Thick mucus collects in the lungs and interferes with breathing. Notice the X-ray picture of healthy lungs and a lung with pneumonia. The arrow points to the swollen tissue.

Symptoms of pneumonia include coughing, fever, chest pain, and noisy breathing. The treatment for this disease depends on what caused it. If bacteria caused the disease, antibiotics can help. If a virus caused the disease, the doctor might simply recommend bed rest and plenty of fluids.

## What Can Cause a Sore Throat?

Disease germs that grow in your respiratory system usually affect your throat. Therefore, a sore throat is a common symptom of many mild respiratory diseases, such as a cold or flu.

The X ray to the right clearly shows pneumonia in the lung.

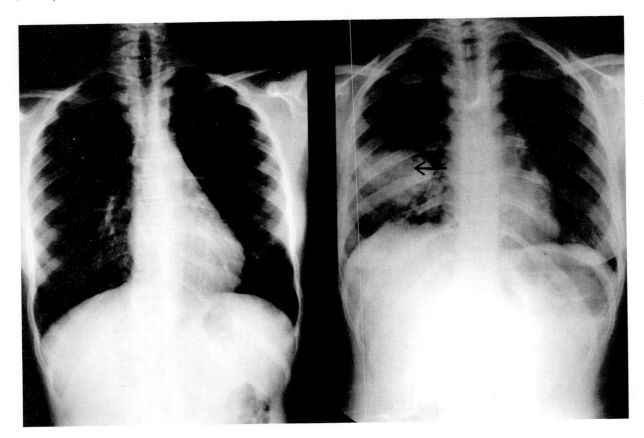

When you have a sore throat, you might notice a change in your tonsils. Notice in the first picture that tonsils are small, oval-shaped clumps of tissue on either side of the tongue. Disease germs can make the tonsils red and swollen, as shown in the second picture. The swollen tonsils make the throat sore.

If you get a severe sore throat, you might have strep throat. This disease can be serious if it is not identified and treated by a doctor. A certain kind of bacteria causes strep throat. An antibiotic, such as penicillin, is usually effective in treating strep throat.

By taking care of your respiratory system, you might be able to prevent some diseases. The box to the right lists some ways to care for your respiratory system. Even with proper care, you might get a few respiratory infections each year. The symptoms do cause discomfort, but you can recover quickly if you take care of yourself properly.

---

### Care of the Respiratory System

- Avoid exposure to people with respiratory infections.
- Help your body resist infection by eating a balanced diet and getting proper rest.
- Exercise regularly to keep your chest muscles strong.
- Do not smoke.
- Avoid breathing indoor pollutants such as sidestream smoke and aerosol sprays.

---

**Think Back** • *Study on your own with Study Guide page 328.*

1. What causes a cold and flu? What do doctors recommend for treating these diseases?
2. How can the sinuses become blocked?
3. What are some symptoms of pneumonia?
4. What respiratory diseases can be treated successfully with antibiotics?
5. How can you care for your respiratory system?

Healthy and swollen tonsils

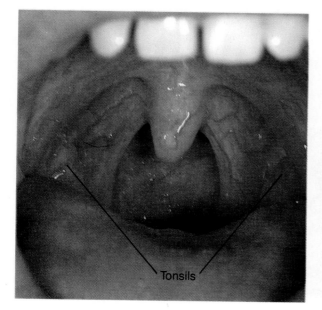

Tonsils

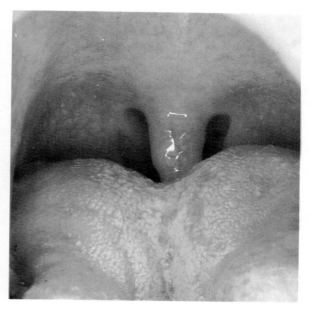

## Learning More About Communicable Disease

1. You might have noticed that many names of diseases end with *-itis*. Use a dictionary to find out what this suffix means.

2. Collect articles from current magazines and newspapers about new developments in fighting disease. Put the articles in a scrapbook. Along with each article, include one or two paragraphs that summarize the article. Share the information you have gathered with your class.

3. Look at the cartoon. Then write a paragraph describing what idea the cartoon shows.

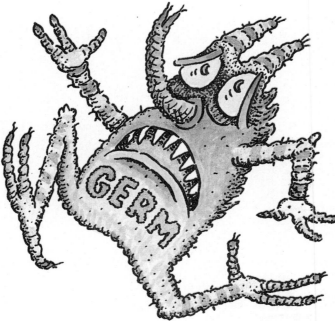

## Looking at Careers

4. "Get this to the lab right away." "We'll know more when we get the lab results." "Well, according to the lab report, . . ."

If you have ever spent time in a hospital or watched a medical program on television, you might have heard such statements. Before deciding upon the proper treatment for a patient, a doctor often needs to order laboratory tests. A sample of a patient's blood, urine, saliva, or body tissue is sent to the lab. Then a medical laboratory worker analyzes the sample. The doctor interprets the analysis and decides upon the best treatment for the patient. A laboratory employs several kinds of medical workers.

**Medical technologists** perform complicated tests and analyses. The technologist shown here is analyzing bacteria from a patient to determine the type of bacteria that is causing the patient's disease. By knowing the type of bacteria, the patient's doctor can decide how to treat the disease.

**Medical laboratory technicians** perform some of the same tests, usually under the guidance of a technologist.

**Medical laboratory assistants** assist technologists and technicians. Assistants perform some of the simpler tasks in the laboratory. For example, they might clean and sterilize equipment, store supplies, and prepare chemical solutions.

Each kind of laboratory worker needs a different amount of education. Technologists must have at least four years of college education. Technicians must have two years of college. Assistants must have taken a one-year course that includes laboratory training.

What school subjects do you think would be helpful in preparing someone for a career as a medical laboratory worker? Why would these subjects be helpful for this career?

For more information write to the American Society for Medical Technology, 330 Meadowfern Drive, Houston, TX 77067.

**noncommunicable**
(non/kə myü/nə kə bəl)
**disease,** a disease that is
not caused by germs and
that does not spread.

## 4 What Causes Noncommunicable Diseases?

At the beginning of this century in the United States, communicable diseases were the most deadly ones. Today, antibiotics, better health care, and better sanitary conditions make these diseases much less dangerous. The diseases that now account for the most deaths in the United States are **noncommunicable diseases.**

Disease germs do not cause noncommunicable diseases, such as heart disease and cancer. These diseases cannot spread from one person to another. Also, noncommunicable diseases often take years to develop in the body and might last a lifetime.

The known causes of noncommunicable disease can be placed into two main groups: heredity and environment. Heredity involves the passing of genes from parents to children. A person might inherit genes that cause a certain disease. For example, muscular dystrophy is an inherited disease of the muscles.

The environment includes your surroundings. You cannot control heredity, but you usually have some control over environmental causes of disease. Cigarette smoking, for example, is a cause of cancer that people have some control over.

How does plaque buildup in arteries affect health?

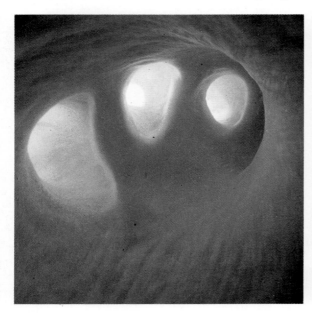

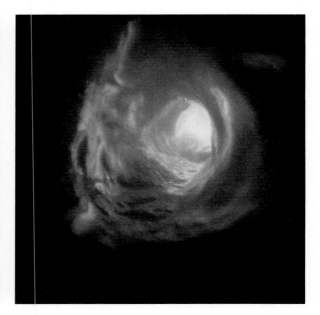

Heredity and environment usually act together to cause a noncommunicable disease. For example, heredity might make a person more likely than other people to have a heart attack. If the person smokes, however, his or her chances of having a heart attack become even greater.

### What Are Cardiovascular Diseases?

**Cardiovascular diseases** are diseases of the heart and blood vessels. The first three pictures show the insides of blood vessels called arteries. **Plaque**—a fatty substance—has built up on the inside walls of some of the arteries. This buildup of plaque is called **atherosclerosis.** As plaque continues to build up, the hollow part of the blood vessel becomes narrow.

The first picture shows the clear passageway through a healthy artery. Notice the smooth walls. The second picture shows a buildup of plaque on the artery walls. The heart has to pump harder to keep the blood flowing because the passageway through the artery is narrower. In the third picture, the passageway is even more blocked. The yellow spots in the fourth picture show another view of plaque buildup in arteries.

Atherosclerosis is serious because the buildup of plaque can prevent the body cells from getting oxygen and other materials that the blood usually brings. This buildup of plaque can cause other problems too.

**cardiovascular**
(kär′dē ō vas′kyə lər)
**disease,** a disease of the heart or blood vessels.

**plaque** (plak), a fatty substance that builds up along the inside walls of an artery.

**atherosclerosis**
(ath′ər ō sklə rō′sis), a cardiovascular disease in which material builds up inside the arteries.

Yellow spots show plaque in arteries.

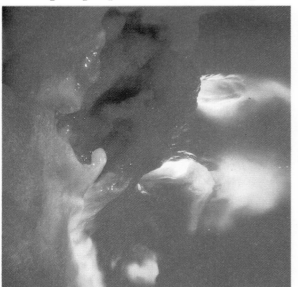
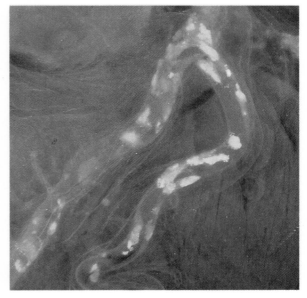

**hypertension**
(hī′pər ten′shən), high
blood pressure.

## What Other Diseases Can Atherosclerosis Lead To?

Atherosclerosis is often associated with **hypertension**—high blood pressure. Hypertension can cause artery walls to weaken, balloon out, and break, especially when the walls are already weakened by the buildup of plaque.

Atherosclerosis can also lead to a heart attack or a stroke. If an artery that supplies blood to the heart becomes blocked, part of the heart is damaged. The damage of part of the heart is a heart attack.

If an artery leading to the brain becomes blocked, part of the brain is damaged, and a stroke occurs. Part of the brain becomes damaged because it cannot get oxygen and other nutrients it needs. The inch-long (2.5 cm) piece of plaque in the picture caused a stroke. The drawing shows where the plaque built up in the neck. A stroke can also be caused by hypertension. The high blood pressure can cause an artery in the brain to weaken and burst.

## How Can You Help Prevent Cardiovascular Diseases?

Cardiovascular diseases are more common in adults than in people your age. However, good health practices begun at an early age can help prevent these diseases from occurring later in life. You can care for your cardiovascular system by eating properly, exercising, not smoking, and handling stress in healthy ways.

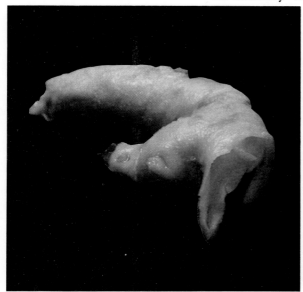

This plaque built up in an artery in the neck and caused a stroke.

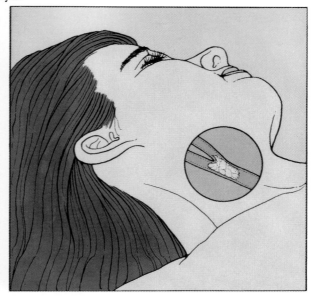

By reducing the amount of fat and cholesterol you eat, you can reduce the chance of building up plaque in your blood vessels. Cholesterol is a fatlike substance that makes up part of plaque. Food such as hot dogs, hamburgers, egg yolks, and butter are high in fat or cholesterol. These foods do not have to be eliminated, but they should be only a small part of your diet.

Exercise is an effective way to reduce the risks of heart disease. Exercise makes the heart larger and stronger. A stronger heart does not have to work as hard to pump blood. Also, a stronger heart can pump more blood with each beat. Exercise also reduces the amount of fat in the blood. Then the chances of building up plaque are less. Cycling, running, walking, and swimming are particularly helpful kinds of exercise.

Not smoking is one of the most effective ways to reduce the risk of heart attack and stroke. The nicotine in smoke narrows the blood vessels. Then the openings of the vessels become smaller, and blood pressure increases. Not smoking keeps the openings of the blood vessels as large as possible to keep blood flowing properly. Notice in the chart how smoking increases the risk of having a heart attack. What other factors, shown in the chart, increase the risk of having a heart attack?

Blood vessels also narrow when you are under stress. By learning to handle stress calmly, you can help keep your blood vessels healthy.

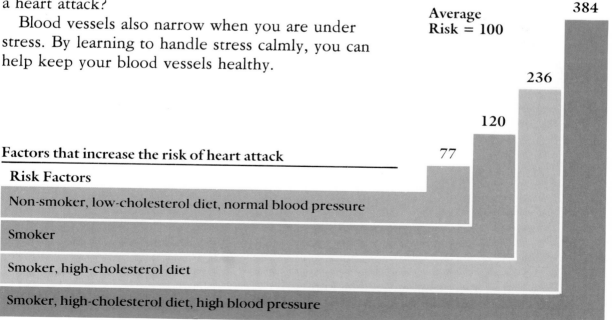

Average Risk = 100

384

236

120

77

Factors that increase the risk of heart attack

**Risk Factors**

Non-smoker, low-cholesterol diet, normal blood pressure

Smoker

Smoker, high-cholesterol diet

Smoker, high-cholesterol diet, high blood pressure

**cancer** (kan′sər), the uncontrolled growth of abnormal body cells.

**tumor** (tü′mər), a clump of useless tissue caused by the buildup of abnormal cells.

*On Your Own*
People often recognize possible signs of cancer in their bodies long before they see a doctor. Write a paragraph explaining why you think some people might put off seeing a doctor about such a serious illness.

## What Is Cancer?

People can get many different kinds of cancer. However, all cancers are alike in some ways. In all cancers certain body cells begin to grow and spread abnormally. The uncontrolled growth of abnormal body cells is called **cancer.** In some types of cancer, abnormal cells continue to grow and reproduce until they form a clump of tissue called a **tumor.** The drawing shows how a tumor forms. Tumors can form in the brain, lung, stomach, or other organs.

Not all tumors are cancerous. Sometimes cells clump and form fairly harmless tumors. They grow slowly, stay in one part of the body, and can usually be completely removed by surgery.

Cancer tumors are more dangerous. They grow rapidly and invade the surrounding tissue. Some cancer cells might break away from the tumor, travel through the bloodstream, and begin to grow in other parts of the body. Cancer cells damage healthy cells and interfere with the normal functions of the body.

Heredity plays a role in causing some cancers. However, many factors in the environment increase the chances of someone getting cancer. Cigarette smoking can lead to lung cancer in some people. Overexposure to the sun and to other kinds of radiation can cause skin cancer. A diet high in fat might contribute to other types of cancer.

Abnormal cells grow in an unorganized way to form a tumor.

## How Can Cancer Be Treated and Prevented?

Several treatments can help cancer patients live longer lives. The three major treatments include using surgery to remove tumors, using radiation to kill cancer cells, and using drugs to kill cancer cells. The kind of treatment used depends on the type of cancer. Often, a combination of treatments gives the best results. Some kinds of cancer can be cured if they are found in early stages. At early stages cancer cells are less likely to have spread in the body. Because of this, it is important to be aware of the warning signs of cancer, shown below in No. 7. If you notice any of these signs, notify your doctor.

Scientists have recently made much progress in treating cancer. However, the best way to fight this disease is to try to prevent it from occurring. The chart shows how you can help reduce the risks of developing cancer. You might notice that many of these health practices also help prevent other diseases.

**Think Back** • *Study on your own with Study Guide page 329.*
1. What are the two main causes of noncommunicable diseases?
2. How can atherosclerosis cause a heart attack?
3. What is the difference between cancerous tumors and noncancerous tumors?
4. How can a person reduce the risks of getting cancer or cardiovascular diseases?

**How to decrease the risk of developing cancer**

| | | | |
|---|---|---|---|
| 1 Do not smoke. | 2 Limit the amount of fat and cholesterol in your diet. | 3 Eat more poultry and fish and less red meat, such as beef. | 4 Eat more fruits and vegetables. |
| 5 Do not sunbathe, especially between 11:00 A.M. and 2:00 P.M. when the sun's rays can do the most harm. When in the sun, wear a protective sunscreen. | 6 Avoid unnecessary drugs. | 7 Be aware of the warning signs of cancer. These signs include a lump in the breast or elsewhere, a sore that does not heal, unusual bleeding, and changes in size or color of a wart or mole. | 8 Seek medical help if you feel you might have cancer. Many cancers can be treated successfully if discovered early enough. |

allergen (al′ər jən), a substance in the environment that causes an allergy.

## 5  What Is an Allergy?

Rain had fallen earlier in the day, but by afternoon the countryside was bathed in the warmth of the sun. Signs of spring were everywhere. Light-green leaves dotted the trees, and wildflowers lent a splash of color to the meadows. Gentle breezes carried nature's fragrances to the nearby farms.

For many people the spring day described above might be one of the most pleasant days of the year. For others, however, this day might be one of the most miserable. The flowers and breezes of spring often lead to sneezing, watery eyes, and other symptoms of allergies.

An allergy is a harmful reaction in some people's bodies to certain substances. An allergic reaction often resembles the symptoms of a cold. Something that causes an allergy is an **allergen.** Flowering plants, like those shown below, produce one of the most common allergens—pollen. Winds easily blow tiny pollen grains into the air. Then the pollen gets into the eyes, nose, and throat and causes a variety of reactions in millions of allergy sufferers.

Wind blows pollen from plants.

## What Are the Symptoms of Hay Fever and Asthma?

Hay fever and asthma are two of the most common allergies. When a person has hay fever, the tissue that lines the nasal passage becomes swollen. The swollen tissue makes breathing through the nose difficult. Other symptoms include sneezing, a runny or itchy nose, and red, itchy eyes.

Asthma often involves more serious symptoms. The lining of the air passages in the lungs becomes swollen. Mucus builds up in these passages, as shown. Tiny air passages in the lungs tighten. Breathing becomes very difficult. The person's breathing can cause whistling or wheezing sounds as air forces its way out through the narrowed passages.

The most common allergens of hay fever and asthma are materials that people inhale, such as pollen, dust, fur, and smoke.

Air passages become swollen during asthma.

Lining swells

Tiny air passages in lungs tighten

## What Are Some Other Kinds of Allergies?

About 35 million people in the United States have some sort of allergy. In fact, you could name any substance and chances are good that someone is allergic to it.

Some people are allergic to certain medicines, such as penicillin. This allergy might cause itchy skin, fever, or more serious effects. Other people are allergic to certain clothing material, such as wool. This allergy usually causes red, itchy rashes. Substances that cause an allergic reaction are called allergens. Nuts, milk, grains, chocolate, and shellfish are some common food allergens that can cause itchy skin rashes or the symptoms of hay fever and asthma.

The picture shows another common allergen. The stings of bees, wasps, and other insects cause discomfort for almost everyone. Some people, however, have allergic reactions to these stings. A rash might occur. The person might have a feeling of heat all over the skin. Later, he or she might feel weak and dizzy and have difficulty breathing. A person who has such allergic responses should get medical help immediately.

Insect stings are common allergens.

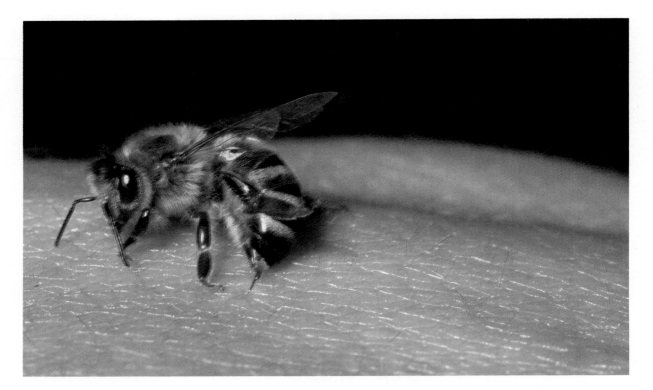

## What Can You Do About Allergies?

The first step in treating an allergy is to discover the allergens—the substances that cause the allergy. Quite often you can be the detective who figures out that you have an allergic reaction whenever you are in contact with a certain substance. Sometimes, however, a person has no idea what might be causing his or her allergy. The nurse in the picture is testing several substances on a patient to find out which ones cause an allergy.

If you have an allergy, the best way to treat it is to avoid the allergens. For example, a person might have to avoid certain foods or not keep a pet. Such allergens as pollen and dust are difficult to avoid. People who are allergic to these substances can take medicines to relieve the symptoms. Many people who have allergies take a series of shots. The shots gradually make the patient less sensitive to the allergen.

**Think Back** • *Study on your own with Study Guide page 329.*

1. What are some common allergens?
2. How does hay fever differ from asthma?
3. In addition to trouble with breathing, what other symptoms do people with allergies experience?
4. How can allergies be treated?

Searching for the allergens

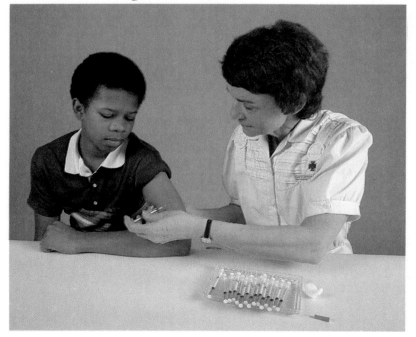

## 6 How Can a Healthy Lifestyle Help Prevent Disease?

The scene below is a common sight in any park. If you were to sit on a park bench for an hour, you would probably see dozens of people walking, running, skating, or bicycling past you. Today more and more people are adopting healthier lifestyles. They are taking better care of themselves by exercising, eating healthy foods, and giving up unhealthy habits.

Having a healthy lifestyle means doing things that will help you stay well. Staying physically fit is one part of a healthy lifestyle. Your body's defenses against disease work best if your body is in good physical condition. Regular exercise helps you keep fit, helps maintain proper body weight, and reduces the chances of getting cardiovascular diseases.

A healthy lifestyle also includes eating foods that are low in fat, sugar, salt, and cholesterol. Making wise decisions about tobacco, alcohol, and other harmful drugs is another part of a healthy lifestyle.

A healthy lifestyle includes exercise.

The picture on this page gives you a clue about another important part of a healthy lifestyle—keeping clean. Regular showering or bathing keeps harmful bacteria off your body. Brushing and flossing prevent the growth of bacteria on your teeth. Many people catch colds by spreading viruses from their hands to their eyes, nose, or mouth. Therefore, you should wash your hands frequently, especially when someone in the house has a cold.

A healthy lifestyle includes dealing with stress in healthy ways, such as facing your problems and trying to solve or accept them. Research studies show that your body's defenses work better if you deal with stress in calm ways.

A healthy lifestyle will not prevent you from ever getting sick. It will, however, greatly improve your body's ability to fight against harmful germs and to resist all kinds of disease.

**Think Back** • *Study on your own with Study Guide page 329.*

1. What practices does a healthy lifestyle include?
2. How does keeping clean help you stay healthy?

A healthy lifestyle includes keeping clean.

## Edward Jenner's Great Discovery

In 1796 George Washington was President of the United States. In that same year Edward Jenner, an English scientist, made a discovery that was a first step toward wiping out one of the most dreaded diseases in history—smallpox.

This disease got its name because of the little scars, called pockmarks, that formed on the face and body. Smallpox was very contagious. Sometimes whole families or villages died from it.

Dr. Jenner noticed that people did not get smallpox if they already had gotten cowpox. This disease was like smallpox, but much milder. Dr. Jenner thought that if people got cowpox on purpose, they would never get smallpox.

Dr. Jenner tested this idea in 1796 after many years of studying both diseases. He took material from a cowpox sore on a woman's hand. Then he rubbed this material into a scratch that he made on the arm of James Phipps, a healthy eight-year-old boy. The painting shows this historic vaccination.

The boy got cowpox, as Dr. Jenner expected. This disease gave James Phipps only a sore arm and a headache for a couple of days. Then, several weeks later, Dr. Jenner scratched the boy's arm again. This time he rubbed material from a smallpox sore into the scratch. James Phipps did not get smallpox. Dr. Jenner had discovered how people could be protected from this disease for the rest of their lives!

Edward Jenner discovered and developed the first successful vaccine. As a result of Dr. Jenner's discovery and a worldwide vaccination effort, in recent years smallpox has been eliminated throughout the world.

### Talk About It

1. What was Edward Jenner's great discovery?

2. How was material from a cowpox sore able to provide immunity from smallpox?

## Controlling the Spread of Disease Germs

Disease germs spread easily from one person to another, especially among people living in the same place. You can help control the spread of disease germs at home in many ways.

You can stop some germs from spreading by covering your nose or mouth when you sneeze or cough. A sneeze or cough releases many dust particles and droplets of moisture into the air. These particles and droplets contain millions of disease germs. Other people inhale the germs.

You can stop the spread of many disease germs by washing your hands after you sneeze, cough, or blow your nose. Germs on your hands can spread to every doorknob, light switch, and other object you touch. Washing is especially important before eating, setting the table, or preparing meals.

Disposing of garbage properly is another way you and your family can control the spread of disease germs. Hungry animals easily overturn garbage cans with loose-fitting lids. Disease germs, which grow quickly in garbage, spread to racoons, dogs, rats, and other animals that eat the garbage. These animals can spread the germs by biting or just being near other animals and people. How is the girl in the picture disposing of garbage properly?

Share the information on this page with your family. Try to make these practices part of your everyday life. They will help keep you, your family, and your community healthy.

## Reading at Home

*Germs* by Dorothy Hinshaw Patent. Holiday House, 1983. Learn how germs were discovered, how they affect you, and what exciting research is taking place concerning the control of germs.

*Medicine: The Body and Healing* by Gordon Jackson. Watts, 1984. Explore the function of the major body systems, some of the main causes of illness, and how the body deals with infection.

# Chapter 7 Review

## Reviewing Lesson Objectives

1. Describe some major kinds of disease germs that cause communicable diseases. (pages 200–203)
2. Describe the first-, second-, and third-line defenses against communicable diseases. Explain what occurs when a person becomes infected with AIDS. (pages 204–209)
3. Describe the major causes, symptoms, and treatment of some common respiratory diseases. (pages 210–215)
4. Explain some causes of and some ways to help prevent cardiovascular diseases and cancer. (pages 218–223)
5. Describe the symptoms and the causes of several kinds of allergies. (pages 224–227)
6. List health practices that help prevent and control diseases. (pages 228–229)

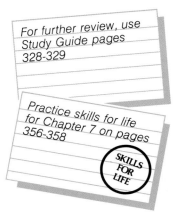

For further review, use Study Guide pages 328-329

Practice skills for life for Chapter 7 on pages 356-358

SKILLS FOR LIFE

## Checking Health Vocabulary

Number your paper from 1–19. Match each definition in Column I with the correct word or words in Column II.

### Column I

1. the body's resistance to a disease through the presence of antibodies
2. a harmful reaction of the body to a substance in the environment
3. a disease in which the sinus openings become blocked
4. a fatty substance that builds up in an artery
5. the general term for a disease that can spread
6. a cell that destroys disease germs
7. the uncontrolled growth of abnormal body cells
8. a substance that attaches to a germ and makes it harmless
9. a disease in which the body becomes unable to fight infection
10. a substance that causes an allergic response
11. a disease in which the lungs become inflamed
12. a sticky liquid that lines the mouth, nose, and windpipe
13. a medicine that destroys bacteria
14. a small dose of killed or weakened disease germs that provides immunity to a disease
15. high blood pressure
16. the general term for a disease that does not spread
17. a disease in which material builds up inside the arteries
18. a clump of useless tissue caused by the buildup of abnormal cells
19. a disease of the heart or blood vessels

### Column II

a. allergen
b. allergy
c. antibiotic
d. antibody
e. atherosclerosis
f. cancer
g. cardiovascular disease
h. communicable disease
i. AIDS
j. hypertension
k. immunity
l. mucus
m. noncommunicable disease
n. plaque
o. pneumonia
p. sinusitis
q. tumor
r. vaccine
s. white blood cell

## Reviewing Health Ideas

Number your paper from 1-17. Next to each number write the word or words that best complete the sentence.

1. Disease _____ cause communicable diseases.
2. Bacteria give off wastes that act like _____.
3. Each kind of _____ causes only one disease.
4. _____ attach themselves to disease germs and make them harmless.
5. A vaccine causes some _____ blood cells to make antibodies.
6. Antibiotics can kill only _____.
7. The respiratory system includes the nasal passages, throat, _____ , and lungs.
8. When the sinus openings into the nose and throat become blocked, _____ can result.
9. AIDS cannot be spread by _____ contact.
10. Heart disease and cancer are examples of _____ diseases.
11. When an artery leading to the brain becomes blocked, the person will likely have a _____.
12. Fairly harmless tumors grow _____ and stay in one part of the body.
13. Cancer has the best chance of being cured if it is found in the _____ stages.
14. A substance that causes an _____ is an allergen.
15. _____ grains are among the most common allergens of hay fever.
16. Regular showering or bathing keeps harmful _____ off the body.
17. Brushing and _____ prevent the growth of bacteria on the teeth.

## Understanding Health Ideas

Number your paper from 18–28. Next to each number write the word or words that best answer the question.

18. What kind of disease germ causes the most illnesses?
19. How many diseases does each kind of virus cause?
20. What is the body's second line of defense against disease germs?
21. What are two things a person with a cold can do to try to avoid a severe case of sinusitis?
22. What dietary changes can be made to reduce the chance of plaque building up in the blood vessels?
23. How does the nicotine in cigarette smoke affect the blood vessels?
24 What are the three major treatments for cancer?
25. What are two of the most common allergies?
26. What is the first step in treating an allergy?
27. What are two health benefits of regular exercise?
28. How can a person help prevent the spread of viruses from his or her hands?

## Thinking Critically

Write the answers on your paper. Use complete sentences.

1. Does having measles give you immunity to mumps? Explain your answer.
2. Cardiovascular diseases are more common in adults than in people your age. Why should you be concerned about these diseases now?

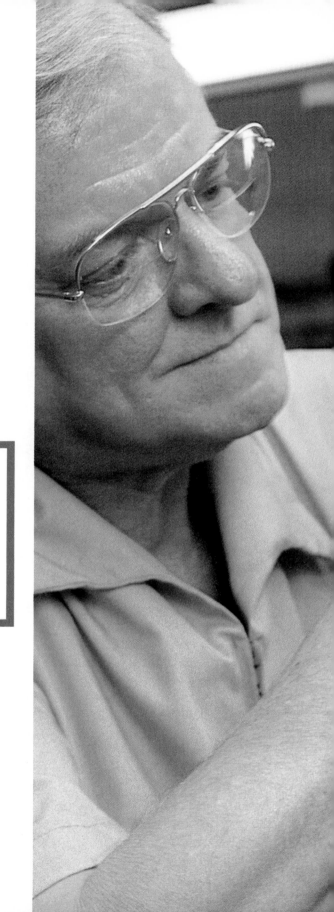

# Chapter 8

# Daily Care for Good Health

Do you like haircuts? Some people your age do. Others, like the boy in this picture, are not so sure. Taking care of your appearance can be a part of good health. There are many other things you can do to keep yourself healthy.

This chapter explains the importance of good daily health care. You will discover how you can improve your health and maintain good health every day of your life.

## Health Watch Notebook

Make a daily care collage. Look in magazines or newspapers for pictures of people doing activities that promote good health. Paste these pictures in your notebook. Under your collage, write a paragraph describing how you take care of your health each day.

1 Why Is Good Posture Important to Your Health?

2 How Can You Take Care of Your Teeth?

3 How Do Vision and Hearing Keep You Safe?

4 Why Should You Take Care of Your Skin and Hair?

5 Why Are Sleep, Rest, and Recreation Important?

234

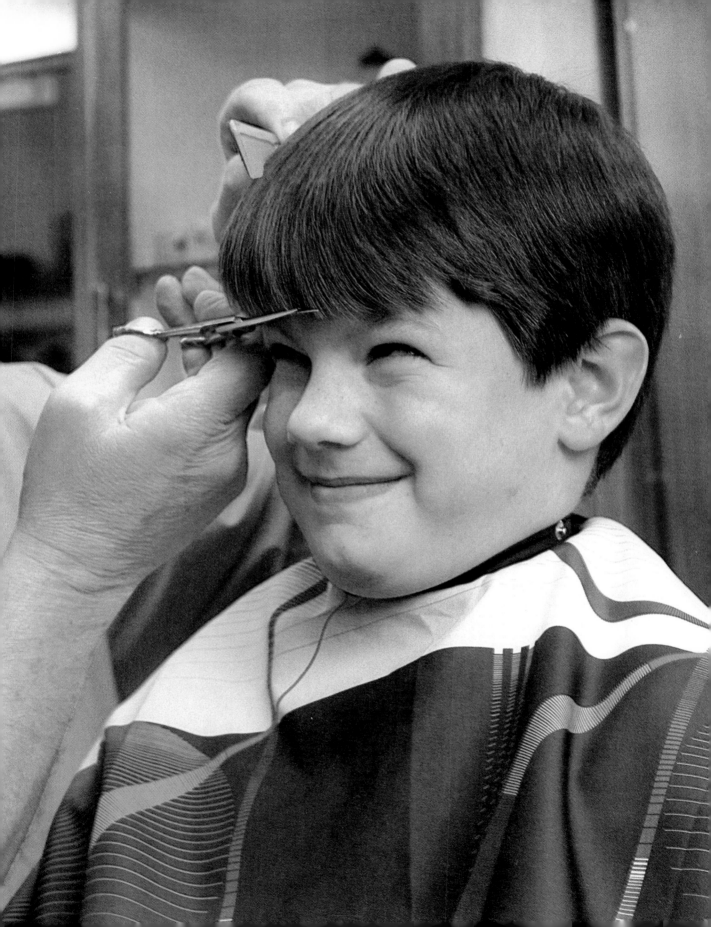

**posture** (pos′chər), the position of the body.

**Did You Know?**
Scoliosis (skō′lē ō′sis) is a condition in which the spine curves to the side, as shown in this X-ray photograph. Poor posture does not cause scoliosis. However, poor posture is sometimes a symptom of this condition. Scoliosis typically develops between the ages of eight and fifteen. Many schools have screening programs to find and help students who have developed scoliosis.

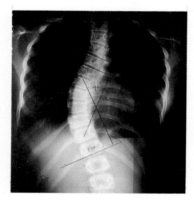

Good posture keeps the body balanced in a straight column.

# 1 Why Is Good Posture Important to Your Health?

Think of the last time you stood in one place for a long period of time. Perhaps you were waiting in line to see a movie, or presenting a report in class. Did you quickly get tired of standing? Did your neck, back, or shoulders begin to ache? Such reactions might mean you could improve your **posture**—the way you hold your body.

The drawing shows how good posture keeps various parts of the body balanced in a straight column. Bones and muscles are in position to support the body weight properly. Now notice what happens when one part of the body, such as the head, moves out of line. Other parts of the body must move out of line to balance the body. This movement puts unnecessary strain on certain bones, muscles, and other body parts. Poor posture can cause headaches, lower back pains, and other muscle soreness.

Good posture helps prevent these aches and pains. Good posture also helps you stand, sit, or move about for long periods of time without getting tired. Then you can perform activities better. In addition, good posture improves the way you look.

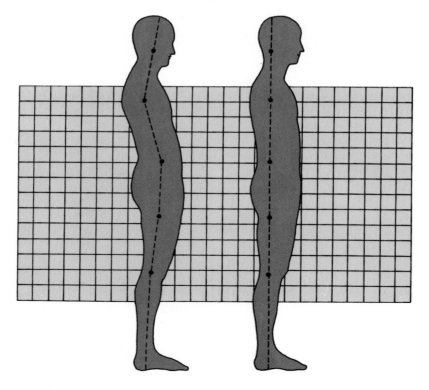

Poor posture   Good posture

## How Can You Improve Your Posture?

Your posture depends greatly upon the rest of your health. Therefore, an important way to improve your posture is to keep your body strong and healthy. Eating a balanced diet and getting plenty of exercise help build the strong bones and muscles needed for good posture. Two simple exercises for improving posture are shown here. Be sure your teacher shows you how to do them correctly. You can also help improve your posture by getting enough sleep at night. If you are rested, you will be less likely to get tired and slouch during the day.

Another way to improve your posture is to practice good posture throughout the day. While sitting, keep your body far back on the chair. When standing or walking, keep your head centered over the rest of your body. Be aware of your posture throughout the day. If you find you are slumping in your chair, make an effort to sit up straight.

The posture you develop now will likely be the posture you have throughout your life. Therefore, developing good, healthy posture is an important part of your daily health practices.

**Think Back** • *Study on your own with Study Guide page 330.*

1. How is good posture important to good health?
2. How can posture be improved?

**plaque** (plak), a sticky, colorless film, consisting largely of bacteria, that forms on teeth and gums.

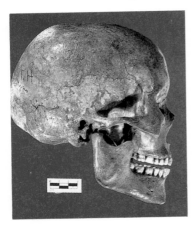

These teeth are thousands of years old.

Bacteria on a tooth

## 2 How Can You Take Care of Your Teeth?

The skull in the picture is thousands of years old. Through the years, the bone has become very fragile and brittle. Yet the teeth appear to be as strong and solid as ever. Teeth are made of very hard material. In fact, they are often the only preserved parts of prehistoric animals. However, many of the foods people eat today can damage even the strongest teeth. Your teeth need proper daily care to stay as strong and useful as possible.

### What Causes Most Dental Problems?

More than 65 percent of the young people in the United States have had some tooth decay by the time they become adults. If you have had tooth decay, you know that it can be painful. Sometimes decayed teeth need to be removed. Losing teeth can affect a person's speech, appearance, and ability to chew food.

Tooth decay is caused by **plaque**—a sticky, colorless film of bacteria. Plaque is always forming on your teeth and gums because bacteria are always present in your mouth. The picture shows a highly magnified view of plaque on a tooth. The rounded shapes are the bacteria in the plaque.

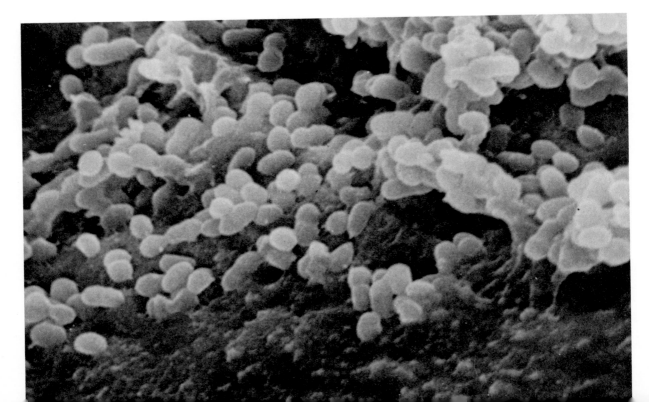

Plaque by itself does not cause tooth decay. The bacteria in plaque use the sugars in food to produce acids. The acids destroy the enamel on teeth, leading to tooth decay. The pictures show how these acids can damage a tooth.

Another common dental problem is **gum disease.** Plaque often builds up in tiny spaces between the teeth and under the gumline. If the plaque is not removed, it hardens, and is called calculus. The calculus irritates the gums. Then they might become swollen and bleed. In time, the gums pull away from the teeth as more layers of plaque build up. Pockets form in the gums and allow the bacteria to attack and weaken the bone that holds the teeth in place. Eventually, some teeth might become loose and even fall out.

**cavity** (kav′ə tē), a hole in a tooth, caused by tooth decay.

**gum disease,** a condition begun by plaque building up and hardening between the teeth and under the gumline. This buildup irritates the gums, eventually causing them to pull away from the teeth, and leaving pockets through which bacteria can attack bone.

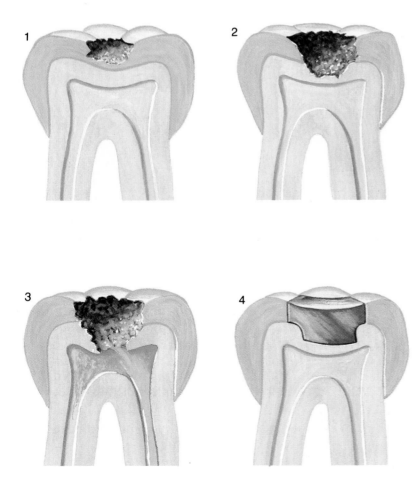

1. Acids start dissolving a tooth's smooth surface.

2. Eventually, decay spreads through the outer covering and makes a hole—**cavity**—in the tooth.

3. If the cavity is not treated, decay can spread deeper into the tooth, causing soreness and pain. Pus might form.

4. If treated in time, a dentist can clean out the decay and put in a filling. One common filling is silver amalgam—a mixture of silver, mercury, and tin. The dentist fills the cleaned cavity with this soft mixture. In a few minutes the silver amalgam hardens to form a solid filling.

239

### How Do Brushing and Flossing Help Prevent Dental Problems?

The most common dental problem of people your age is tooth decay. Gum disease is more common in adults, but people your age can also develop this problem. It often results from poor dental care during earlier years. You can help prevent both tooth decay and gum disease by cleaning your teeth daily. Brushing and flossing, shown here, are the best ways you can clean your teeth. Brushing removes plaque and bits of food from the surfaces of your teeth and gums. Flossing removes these substances from between your teeth and from under the gumline.

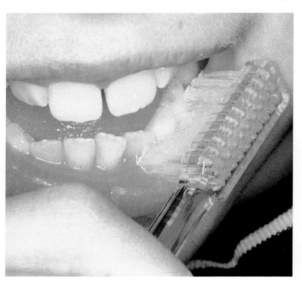

**Proper way of brushing**

Place the toothbrush bristles against the outside of the teeth, and angle the bristles against the gums. Move the brush back and forth using short, gentle strokes.

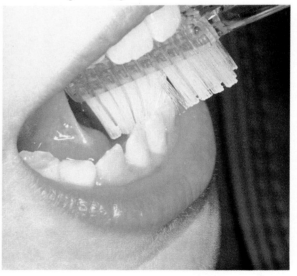

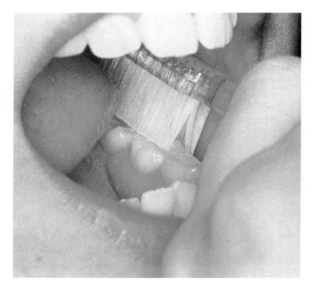

Brush the outsides and insides of all your teeth. Be sure to brush the chewing surfaces of the teeth too. Plaque and food can collect in the grooves on the chewing surfaces of teeth.

Use the front bristles to brush the insides of your front teeth.

## How Can You Help Prevent Dental Problems?

In addition to visiting the dentist regularly, you can prevent dental problems by choosing foods wisely. Many foods contain some sugar. If you eat sweet snacks or desserts, the sugar settles on your teeth and gums. The bacteria in plaque use this sugar to make acids that attack your teeth. Limit the snacks you eat, and try to brush and floss your teeth after eating to remove sugar, food, and plaque.

**Think Back** • *Study on your own with Study Guide page 330.*

1. How does the combination of plaque and sugar lead to tooth decay?
2. What do brushing and flossing remove from teeth?
3. What does correct dental care include?

### Proper way of flossing

Break off about eighteen inches of floss, and wrap most of it loosely around one of your middle fingers. Hold the floss tightly between each thumb and forefinger.

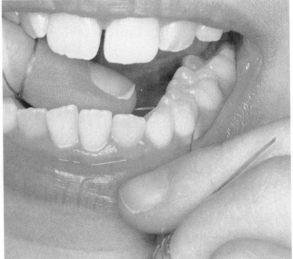

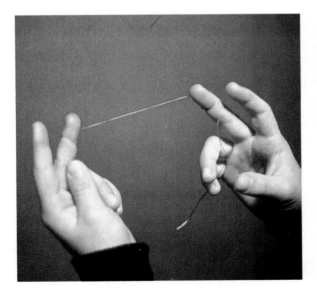

Use a sawing motion to slide the floss gently into the space between the gum and tooth. Curve the floss into a C shape after doing this.

Scrape the floss up and down gently against the side of each tooth. Use a clean part of the floss for each tooth.

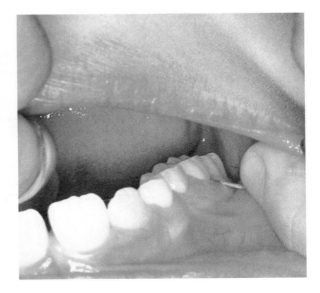

241

## 3  How Do Vision and Hearing Keep You Safe?

Your five senses—vision, hearing, touch, taste, and smell—help you every day by giving you information about the world around you. Of the senses, vision and hearing are especially important. The eyes and ears help you as you work and play and can keep you out of danger. Can you imagine crossing a busy street without being able to see and hear? Your eyes tell you when the light is green and whether there is traffic. Your ears alert you to possible dangers from oncoming cars and allow you to hear sirens and horns. Together, the two senses help keep you safe.

Because the eyes and ears are so important, you need to know how to protect them. You also need to know the signs of vision and hearing problems.

### What Are Some Common Problems with Vision?

The condition of nearsightedness is common in people your age. In this condition, a person can see objects that are close by, but objects far away appear blurred. Eyeglasses or contact lenses can correct this. A nearsighted person might need glasses to read the chalkboard at school, see a movie, or drive.

Another vision problem, more common in adults, is farsightedness. In this condition, a person can see faraway objects clearly, but close objects appear blurred. Like nearsightedness, farsightedness can be corrected with glasses. A farsighted person might need eyeglasses to read or do close work. The pictures show how objects close and far away might appear to people who are nearsighted and farsighted.

Nearsighted and farsighted people see different things clearly.

It is important for you to notify an eye doctor if you notice any change in your ability to see objects up close and far away. Often, special eyeglasses will solve the problem. However, vision changes can also indicate a more serious eye disease or infection. Soreness or itching of the eyes and headaches are also clues that you need to see an eye doctor. The chart on page 242 lists some ways that you can protect your eyes.

**What Are Some Hearing Problems?**

Your ears, like your eyes, require care. You should wash the outer part of your ears with soap and water and dry them well each day. Never place any object, even a cotton-tipped swab, into your ear. Excess earwax should only be removed by your doctor. You should also avoid loud sounds, which can permanently damage the structures in the ear that allow you to hear. If you must be near loud sounds, wear protective ear coverings or plugs to prevent hearing loss.

Sometimes hearing problems occur despite good care. One ear problem that you might be familiar with is ear infection. Ear infections occur when germs, usually from a cold, are forced into the middle ear. The germs can be forced into the ear if you blow your nose too hard or hold your nose when you sneeze. It is important to gently blow your nose and to allow both nostrils to remain open during nose-blowing and sneezing. The nerves in the ear that allow hearing can become damaged if an ear infection is not treated. If you notice pain in your ears, it is very important to see a doctor at once.

Damage to nerves in the ear can also be caused by loud noises or ear injuries. When the nerves in the ears are damaged, hearing loss is permanent. The hearing of people with damaged nerves can often be improved with the use of hearing aids.

Hearing aids can help people who have nerve damage in their ears.

**Think Back** • *Study on your own with Study Guide page 331.*

1. What are four signs that indicate the need to see an eye doctor?
2. What are some ear problems that indicate the need to see a doctor?

**sweat glands,** tiny structures in the skin that collect some body wastes and transfer them to the surface of the skin.

**perspiration** (pėr′spə rā′shən), the water, salt, heat, and other body wastes transferred by the sweat glands to the skin's surface.

## 4 Why Should You Take Care of Your Skin and Hair?

The most important way to care for your skin is to keep it clean. Tiny dirt particles and bacteria land on your skin constantly. Some of these bacteria can lead to illness when they get into your body. You can transfer the dirt and bacteria to others by shaking hands or touching an object that someone else touches. You can help prevent the transfer of bacteria to food by washing your hands before eating.

As you grow older, skin care becomes more important. Perspiration and oily skin increase your need for cleanliness.

Notice the **sweat glands** in the drawing of the skin. Sweat glands collect body wastes such as water, salt, and heat. The glands transfer these wastes, called **perspiration,** to the surface of the skin. Bacteria on your skin cause perspiration to develop an unpleasant odor, which can be most noticeable under your arms and on your feet.

Sweat glands and oil glands in skin

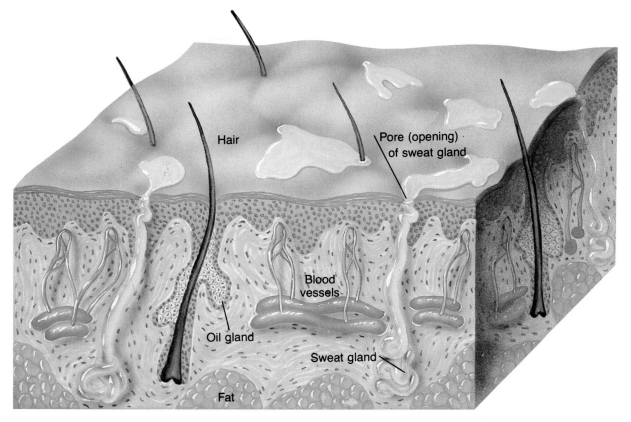

Hair

Pore (opening) of sweat gland

Blood vessels

Oil gland

Sweat gland

Fat

244

In the next few years, during puberty, your sweat glands will become more active and you will perspire more. Frequent washing removes any buildup of perspiration and bacteria. Such products as antiperspirants and deodorants can help control perspiration odor.

Notice the **oil glands** in the drawing. These glands produce an oily substance that keeps your skin soft and smooth. Like the sweat glands, your oil glands will become more active in the next few years. You might notice the skin on your face becoming more oily. The extra oil can clog some of the openings in your skin. Then pimples and other kinds of acne might form. You can help control oily skin and acne by washing your face daily with soap and warm water.

Your scalp becomes oily for the same reason your face does. Oil glands beneath your scalp become more active. Extra oil might gather on your scalp and hair and might trap dirt.

You can use a shampoo to wash away the dirt and extra oil on your hair. Shampooing also helps control dandruff. Your scalp, like the rest of your skin, sheds dead skin cells constantly as new cells grow. Oil on the scalp makes the dead cells clump into flakes of dandruff. Any shampoo will cleanse your hair and scalp of dirt, oil, and loose dandruff flakes. You might want to use a special dandruff shampoo if you have a severe dandruff problem. When you shampoo, rinse your hair thoroughly. Shampoo left on your hair can dry and flake off, looking much like dandruff.

Proper skin and hair care should be part of your daily activities. By keeping clean, you help control the buildup of dirt and bacteria on your body. You also improve your appearance. Looking your best gives you greater confidence and improves the way you feel about yourself.

**oil glands,** tiny structures in the skin that produce an oily substance and transfer it to the surface of the skin.

***Did You Know?***
The hair that you can see on your body is made of dead cells. That is why you can cut your hair without feeling any pain. You do feel pain, however, if you pull your hair because you also pull on the living part of the hair beneath your skin's surface.

**Think Back** • *Study on your own with Study Guide page 331.*

1. What will happen to people your age in the next few years that makes proper skin and hair care more important?
2. Why is it important to wash the skin and hair regularly?

245

## Investigating Practices and Products of Personal Health

1. Bring a shampoo bottle to school. List the shampoo's ingredients. Form a group with three or four classmates and compare your lists. Circle the ingredients that are on all the lists in your group. Do you think any one of the shampoos does a better job of cleaning hair than the others? Explain your answer. List some of the differences among the shampoos.

2. Observe the effectiveness of shampoo. Use a medicine dropper or straw to place a drop of cooking oil in a cup of water. Notice what happens. Mix another cup of water with a small amount of shampoo, and place a drop of oil in this cup. What happens to the oil? What does this activity tell you about how shampoo cleans your hair?

3. Working with three or four classmates, make a list of all the kinds of snack foods you recall eating. Try to include at least fifteen items. Cross out the items that can most easily help cause tooth decay and gum disease. Which items are left? What does this activity tell you about how you can help prevent dental problems?

4. The American Dental Association (ADA) approves brands of toothpaste that meet the ADA's standards of quality. The picture shows how the ADA seal of approval appears on a toothpaste label. Check several brands of toothpaste at a grocery store or drugstore to find out which ones are approved by the ADA. Record and compare the lists of ingredients to find out what the approved toothpastes have in common.

5. Use information from an encyclopedia or other book to make a poster or model of a tooth. You can use clay, cardboard, construction paper, or other materials if you make a model. Use the words *crown, root, gum, enamel, dentin, pulp, bone,* and *cementum* to label the parts of the tooth and surrounding areas.

Accepted — has been shown to be an effective decay-preventive dentifrice that can be of significant value when used in a conscientiously applied program of oral hygiene and regular professional care. Council on Dental Therapeutics — American Dental Association

## Looking at Careers

6. Looking your best helps you feel good about yourself. **Hairstylists** wash, cut, and style hair to help men and women look their best. Hairstylists keep up with current trends in hairstyles. Customers sometimes request hairstyles similar to those worn by models in magazine photographs. Hairstylists use their skills to provide the wanted look.

People who want to become hairstylists attend special schools to learn about hair care. Since many hairstylists operate their own shops, they might also take business courses in high school and college.

Hairstylists work closely with their customers. Keeping this fact in mind, write down some special qualities you think a hairstylist should have.

For more information, write to Associated Master Barbers and Beauticians of America, 219 Greenwich Rd., P.O. Box 220782, Charlotte, NC 28222.

7. Good health and good posture are important to the people in the picture. They are professional **dancers.** Dancers practice daily for many hours so that their movements express the proper feelings and are pleasant to watch. Dancers practice good posture so they will be able to move and hold their bodies in various positions during a dance routine. Dancers also learn proper breathing methods so they will not become too tired during a performance. Many dancers study the human body and how it works. They apply this information to their own body movements in dance.

People who want to become dancers often attend classes at a dance studio or at a school of fine arts.

Look in an encyclopedia to find out about the many different kinds of dance. List and describe each kind.

For more information write to the American Dance Guild, 570 7th Ave., 20th Fl., New York, NY 10018. Enclose a stamped, self-addressed envelope.

**On Your Own**

Think back to the last night you slept for a shorter period of time than is normal for you. In a paragraph, describe how you felt the next morning. Now, reread the third paragraph on this page. Do you notice any similarities between your description and the research findings described? List the similarities.

## 5 Why Are Sleep, Rest, and Recreation Important?

The boy in the picture is in a deep sleep. All appears peaceful . . . quiet . . . still. Yet, parts of his body are in a whirl of activity. His digestive system is busy breaking down the food he ate during dinner. New cells are forming to replace those worn out. Meanwhile, the feelings, sounds, and images of dreams pass through his mind.

Sleep is an important part of your life and your health. For example, your body produces most of your growth hormone while you sleep. During sleep your heart rate, breathing rate, and some of your other body processes slow down. Therefore, more energy is available to build or repair body cells. Sleep also gives some of your muscles and other body parts a chance to rest from the day's activities.

The importance of sleep is best understood when sleep is taken away. Research experiments show that people who do not sleep for a day or two often cannot perform simple tasks. They often have trouble concentrating and easily become angered. Their senses become unreliable, and sometimes they hear or see things that do not exist.

The amount of sleep a person needs depends largely on his or her age. Infants often need sixteen to twenty hours of sleep each day. Adults usually sleep seven or eight hours a night. Most people your age need nine or ten hours of sleep each night.

Sleep is an important part of your health.

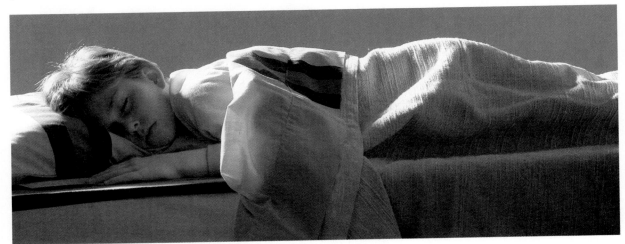

248

A healthy night's sleep includes about an hour of dreaming. Everybody dreams. You do not always remember your dreams, but sleep experiments show that people usually dream four or five times each night. Each of these dream periods lasts from a few minutes to half an hour.

The woman shown here is participating in a sleep experiment. While she sleeps, electric signals from her brain travel through wires to a machine. The machine records the signals as waves on a sheet of paper. By observing the brain waves, scientists can tell when the woman is sleeping lightly, sleeping deeply, or dreaming.

Scientists do not know why people dream, but they do know dreaming is important to health. During some sleep experiments, people were awakened whenever they started dreaming. The next day they were tired and irritable, even though they slept for their normal amount of time. Dreaming seems to be almost as important to your health as sleep itself.

### Did You Know?

Sleep experiments are helping scientists understand illnesses that used to be mysteries. For example, by observing brain waves during sleep, scientists can tell if a person has narcolepsy (när′ kə lep′ sē). This illness causes sudden attacks of deep sleep, which could occur even while a person is talking, driving, or playing. Once a person is known to have narcolepsy, that person can be helped.

Participating in a sleep experiment

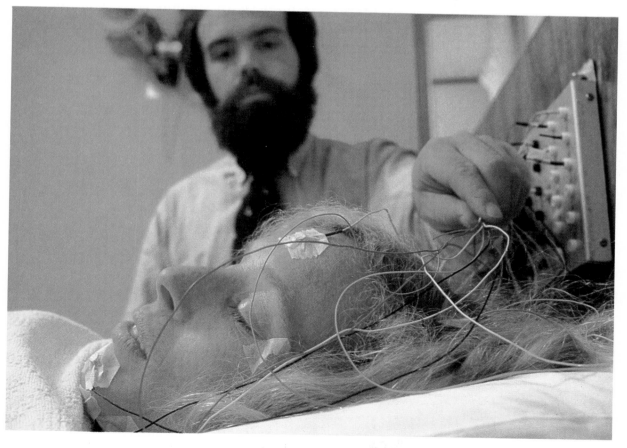

**fatigue** (fə tēg′), weariness caused by physical exercise, stress, concentration, boredom, or a lack of energy.

## How Can You Reduce Fatigue?

Several times throughout the day you might feel **fatigue**—weariness—even though you slept well the night before. Sleep does not always relieve fatigue. For example, if you skipped breakfast today, your body probably lacks energy. You might feel fatigue. Sleep will not relieve the fatigue, but food will.

Fatigue can be relieved in different ways. The kind of relief depends on the kind of fatigue. The runner shown in the picture is experiencing physical fatigue. This kind of fatigue results when muscles are used a lot. During exercise, the body produces wastes, such as carbon dioxide. After much exercise, these wastes build up in the body, making the muscles tired and sore. A rest period gives the blood a chance to remove the wastes from the muscles. Then the fatigue goes away.

You probably rest several times a day to relieve physical fatigue. After pedaling your bicycle for a while, you might rest your leg muscles by coasting. After writing sentences for spelling class, you might put your pen down for a minute to relax your hand and wrist muscles.

What kind of fatigue is this runner feeling?

250

Not all fatigue is physical. Mental fatigue often results when you concentrate on one task for a long time. For example, studying at home for two hours without a break might make you feel tired. Exercise, such as taking a walk or a bicycle ride, will help relieve this mental fatigue. The pictures show other activities you might enjoy while taking a break to relieve mental fatigue.

Stress can cause emotional fatigue. For example, you might take a test in the morning and spend the rest of the day worrying about how you did. On top of that, you might have an argument with a friend and feel angry the whole day. Such stressful situations can make you feel tired. Activities that you find relaxing or enjoyable might help relieve emotional fatigue.

Fatigue is one of your body's ways of telling you a change is needed. This change might involve rest, food, exercise, or an activity you find enjoyable.

**Think Back** • *Study on your own with Study Guide page 331.*
1. How does sleep help the body?
2. How does rest relieve physical fatigue?
3. How could someone relieve emotional fatigue?

**On Your Own**
Think of a time when strong emotions, such as anger, caused you to feel fatigue. On a sheet of paper, describe how you showed this emotional fatigue. Then, explain how you could have relieved your fatigue.

What activities do you like to do to relieve fatigue?

### Dr. Adams Keeps People Smiling

Healthy teeth are powerful cutting tools that you use every day. Because you use them so often, you might take your teeth for granted.

However, proper dental and gum care is a very important part of maintaining health according to Dr. Melba K. Adams. Dr. Adams is a periodontist—a dentist who specializes in treating gum disease. The treatment often involves cleaning the teeth below the gumline. Dr. Adams uses special tools to remove hardened plaque on the part of the teeth below the gums.

Dr. Adams also works with physicians in caring for her patients. Some of her patients take medicine for diseases such as epilepsy. Some of these medicines cause side effects, including damage to the gums. Dr. Adams talks with her patients' physicians about prescribing medicines that do not harm the mouth.

Helping patients prevent gum disease is another important part of Dr. Adams's work. She helps her patients learn how to brush and floss their teeth correctly. With Dr. Adams's help, her patients can keep their teeth as healthy as her own.

### Talk About It
1. How does Dr. Adams help her patients achieve good health?
2. If you were Dr. Adams, how would you tell your patients they could prevent gum disease?

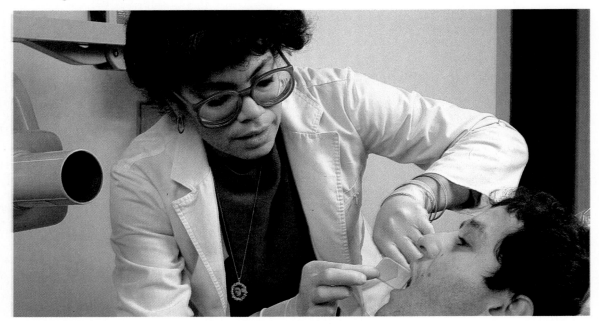

## Using the "Green Detective" to Find Plaque

Brushing and flossing help prevent the buildup of plaque on your teeth and gums. However, since plaque is colorless, you cannot always tell if you are cleaning your teeth well enough to remove all the plaque.

A small amount of green food coloring can help you discover how well you are cleaning your teeth. The food coloring stains plaque on your teeth and gums.

Clean your teeth as you usually do. Then mix two drops of green food coloring with about an inch (2.5 cm) of water in a cup, as shown. Swish the colored water in your mouth, and spit the water out into a sink. Then, examine your teeth in a mirror. Do you notice any stains from the food coloring like those in the picture? These stains show where plaque remains on the teeth and gums. Brush and floss again until all the stains are removed. The next time you clean your teeth, remember the extra brushing and flossing you needed to remove all the plaque.

Show members of your family how the "green detective" finds plaque. They might enjoy discovering how well they clean their teeth. You and your family can use food coloring every now and then to help improve your brushing and flossing skills.

## Reading at Home

*Is the Cat Dreaming Your Dream?* by Margaret O. Hyde. McGraw-Hill, 1980. Find out about the hows and whys of dreaming as you explore the world of sleep.

*Junior Body Machine* by Dr. Christian Barnard, Consulting editor. Crown, 1983. Read about how the human body works and how to keep it in the best physical health through exercise and proper diet.

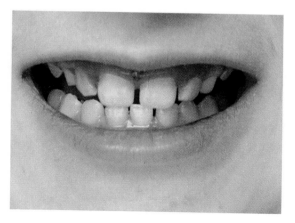

# Chapter 8 Review

## Reviewing Lesson Objectives

1. State reasons why good posture is important to good health. (pages 236–237)
2. Describe what is included in correct dental care (pages 238–241)
3. Describe symptoms of vision and hearing problems. (pages 242–243)
4. Explain why washing regularly is important for proper skin
5. and hair care. (pages 244–245)
   Explain how sleep, rest, and recreation are important for good health. (pages 248–251)

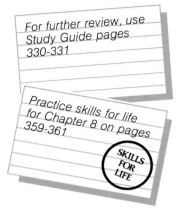

For further review, use Study Guide pages 330-331

Practice skills for life for Chapter 8 on pages 359-361

SKILLS FOR LIFE

## Checking Health Vocabulary

Number your paper from 1–8. Match each definition in Column I with the correct word or words in Column II.

### Column 1

1. a dental problem which results in gums pulling away from the teeth, leaving pockets
2. a weariness that can be caused by physical exercise
3. a hole in a tooth, caused by tooth decay
4. the water, salt, heat, and other body wastes that are transferred to the skin's surface
5. a sticky film of bacteria that forms on the teeth and gums
6. the position of the body
7. a tiny structure in the skin that collects some body wastes and transfers the wastes to the surface of the skin
8. a tiny structure in the skin that produces an oily substance and transfers the substance to the surface of the skin

### Column II

a. cavity
b. fatigue
c. gum disease
d. oil gland
e. perspiration
f. plaque
g. posture
h. sweat gland

Number your paper from 9–17. Next to each number write the word or words that correctly complete the sentences in the paragraph.

Tooth __(9)__ is the most common dental problem for young people. It is caused by the bacteria in __(10)__. The bacteria use __(11)__ in food to produce acids. The acids destroy the __(12)__ on teeth. Eventually the acids can form a hole or __(13)__ in the teeth. __(14)__ is a dental problem caused by plaque building up between the teeth and under the gum-line. As the plaque hardens it is called __(15)__. People can help prevent tooth decay and gum disease when they __(16)__ and __(17)__ their teeth.

## Reviewing Health Ideas

Number your paper from 1–15. Next to each number write the word or words that best complete the sentence.

1. Good posture enables bones and _____ to support the body weight correctly.
2. _____ posture puts unnecessary strain on other body parts.
3. Plaque is always forming because _____ are always in the mouth.
4. If pockets form in the gums, bacteria can attack the _____ that holds the teeth in place.
5. The most common dental problem of young people is _____.
6. Flossing removes plaque and bits of food from _____ the teeth.
7. To prevent dental problems, people should brush and floss their teeth at least _____ a day.
8. The longer a food stays in the mouth, the longer _____ have to form.
9. Only a dental-care professional can remove hardened _____ from teeth.
10. Frequent _____ removes the buildup of perspiration and bacteria.
11. Sweat glands and oil glands become more active during the stage of _____.
12. More _____ is available to build and repair cells when a person sleeps.
13. Experiments show that _____ is almost as important as sleep itself.
14. Physical _____ occurs when wastes such as carbon dioxide build up in the body.
15. Worrying and being angry can produce _____ fatigue.

## Understanding Health Ideas

Number your paper from 16–28. Next to each number write the word or words that best answer the question.

16. Where is a person with poor posture likely to have pain?
17. What happens when one part of the body moves out of line?
18. What do bacteria in the mouth use to produce acids?
19. What is calculus?
20. What are the two best ways to clean teeth daily?
21. What are two signs of ear problems that indicate the need to see a doctor?
22. What kinds of foods are especially harmful to the teeth?
23. What glands transfer perspiration to the skin?
24. What causes perspiration to develop an odor?
25. When should a person see an eye doctor?
26. Is most of the growth hormone produced when a person is asleep or awake?
27. How many times does a person generally dream each night?

## Thinking Critically

Write the answers on your paper. Use complete sentences.

1. Explain the meaning of the following equation: Plaque + Sugar = Decay
2. Suppose a friend seems fatigued even though he or she slept for nine hours last night. How might the friend relieve his or her fatigue?

Chapter

# 9

# Your Decisions as a Health Consumer

"Which one should I choose?" Think about a time when you might ask yourself this question. The choices you make are important, especially when they concern your health. No matter what you are choosing, some basic guidelines can help you make the wisest decisions.

This chapter will show how you can make wise decisions about the health products and services you buy and use. You will learn how to get the best products and services available at the prices you can afford. The consumer skills you learn now can be used throughout your lifetime.

## Health Watch Notebook

Collect magazine and newspaper advertisements and place them in your notebook. Under each ad, explain how it influences the consumer.

1 How Can You Become a Wise Health Consumer?
2 How Can Advertising Influence You as a Consumer?
3 What Should You Consider When Choosing Health Products?
4 How Can You Benefit Most from a Health Checkup?

# 1 How Can You Become a Wise Health Consumer?

Who is a **health consumer?** You are. In fact, everyone is. A health consumer is anyone who buys or uses products and services that contribute to health. How do the products shown here contribute to health? As you grow older, you will find yourself making more decisions on your own about what health products and services to buy and use.

Perhaps you think there is nothing much to learn about buying. You just go into a store, pick out what you want, and pay for it. Wise shopping, however, is not always that simple. For one thing, most people have to budget their money very carefully. They want to save money whenever they can. Many people have learned, too, that the most costly products are not always the best ones. Even people with a lot of money do not want to spend it needlessly.

How does each item contribute to health?

Before you make any purchase, try doing what careful shoppers do. Ask yourself if you really need what you are about to buy. In other words, do you need the product or do you just want it? Sometimes people buy a product simply because their friends use it or because they think it will make them more popular.

Unwise shoppers often buy things impulsively. That is, they see something on a shelf or counter and are attracted by it. Without any careful thought, they quickly buy the product even though they do not need it. They usually do not even realize they want the product until they see it. Products bought impulsively are often displayed at checkout counters. What are some of these products?

The chart lists some questions to ask yourself before buying a product. Use these questions as guidelines for careful shopping.

**Before-You-Buy-Guidelines**

- Do I need it or do I just want it?
- If I buy it, will I really use it?
- Am I buying on impulse?
- Do I already have other products very much like this one?
- Can I afford it?
- Could I buy something better if I take more time to look and think about it?

## What Can Help You Become a Wise Health Consumer?

When you think about a purchase before making it, you might realize that you need some help. Older members of your family are good sources of help since they probably make many of your family's health decisions. For example, your older brother or sister might have bought the toothpaste for your family. Your grandmother might have taken you to the doctor for your last examination. Your mother or father might have chosen which foods the family ate for dinner last night.

Sometimes your friends are a good source of information. Before you follow a friend's advice, however, be sure that you really need the product. You should not buy a product just because your friend has it.

The school nurse, a pharmacist, and other health care professionals can give you some advice about health care products.

The next time you go for a health checkup, you might ask the doctor about buying certain health products. You also might start looking at the library for materials that can help you be a smart shopper. A large variety of up-to-date, dependable materials are shown below. At the library, notice that some magazines on consumer advice are especially written for young people.

As you gain more experience in shopping wisely, you will find that you can make better decisions and purchases. You will also find that you can learn from your experiences. For example, suppose you buy a large can of deodorant. After using it for three days, you develop a rash. You stop using the deodorant. You also read the label. The next time you buy a deodorant, you might buy a smaller can that has slightly different ingredients. Then you will be less likely to develop a rash. Also, you will not have wasted as much money if the new deodorant causes a rash too. Judging the decisions you make will help you make wiser decisions in the future.

**Think Back** • *Study on your own with Study Guide page 332.*

1. What are six questions to keep in mind before you buy a product?
2. What are four major sources of health information?

The library has many sources of consumer information.

261

## 2 How Can Advertising Influence You as a Consumer?

You decide to buy one kind of bandage when four other kinds are on the shelf. Why? You choose one kind of suntan lotion over another. Why? You want to buy a hamburger from one restaurant instead of another. Why?

**Advertisements,** or ads, often influence your decisions to buy. An ad is a recommendation for a product or service. Radio and television commercials are forms of advertisements. Printed advertisements appear in magazines and newspapers. Every day thousands of products and services are promoted through advertising.

**Flattery**

Some ads try to convince you to buy a product by complimenting you. The message is that the product is for you because you deserve the very best.

**Free gift**

Sometimes ads offer you something "free" if you buy a certain product. A prize in a cereal box is an example. Often, though, the prize offered is worthless or its price has been added to the price of the product.

**Join the crowd**

Such ads show people using a product and indicate that "everyone" likes and uses the product. The ads urge you not to be left out.

Advertisements are sources of information. They help make people aware of different products or services. Ads help make one product stand out from other products. Some ads also give helpful information about a product or service.

Not all ads, however, give you the helpful information you need and want. Many ads are planned just to make you want to buy a product. They use various methods that have little or nothing to do with giving you worthwhile information. Six advertising methods are described and shown on these two pages. Have you noticed any of these methods in ads?

Almost every product ad uses some recognizable selling method. The product may or may not be a good choice for you. Knowing how an ad is trying to convince you will help you make better choices.

### Famous people like it
Some ads show famous people with a product. The ads want you to believe that if someone famous likes the product, you will like it too. Some people think if they use the product, they will be like the famous person.

### Scientific claims
Some ads claim that experts and scientific information back the product. These ads want people to believe that the product is good simply because an expert says it is.

### Unclear statements
Sometimes an ad includes a statement that is not explained or that can be interpreted in different ways. For example, "You can't buy a better product" might mean you could buy many products just as good.

For the No. 1 lady
"More doctors recommend"
It's my natural way to welcome morning.

### How Do Jingles, Logos, and Packaging Influence Your Decisions?

Advertisements come in many forms. Not only can you read them, watch them, and hear them—but you can sing, hum, and whistle them as well. Advertisers spend millions of dollars each year developing catchy tunes, or jingles, to sell products. Some ads involve entire songs. Other ads just have one or two lines set to music. Either way, the advertisers hope that the jingle will help you remember the product. When you are in a store, you might hum the jingle, think about the product, and automatically buy it.

Advertisers also use **logos** to sell their products. A logo is a symbol that identifies a company. Some logos are simple shapes, such as a circle or rectangle. Other logos might be detailed drawings, the initials of the company, or the full name of the company designed in a special way.

What logos have you seen?

The advertisers hope that if you are happy with one of their products, you will be happy with any product that the company makes. They hope that whenever you see the logo, you will think of the company and buy one of their products. The logos shown here might be similar to ones you have seen. How might the colors and shapes of each logo influence your decision to buy a product from that company?

Special packaging is another part of advertising. Advertisers hope that a fancy package will cause you to choose their product over another one in a plain package. For example, some shampoos come in very fancy or decorative bottles. Often the price of a shampoo is higher simply because it comes in a fancy container.

**logo,** a symbol used to identify something for advertising purposes.

### How Can You Evaluate Ads?

To be a good health consumer, you need to become aware of ads and how to analyze them. When you see or hear an ad, be sure to first identify what is being sold. A product, service, idea, or image are the things to look for. Can you identify what is being sold in each ad shown here?

Next, ask yourself how the advertiser is trying to convince you to buy something. Remember the selling methods that advertisers often use in their ads. Notice the methods used in the ads on these pages.

Finally, decide if the ad contains useful facts. The more information you have, the more likely you will be able to make a wise consumer decision. What useful information do you see in these ads?

Evaluate these ads.

"The better to see you with, my dear."

Has your vision been checked lately?
National Eye Care Week

For more information, call: 555-1234

Rule th
with Co

All the

You do not become a wise consumer overnight. It takes experience in buying, judging your purchases, and learning to evaluate ads. The more experience you get in evaluating ads, the better consumer you will become.

**Think Back** • *Study on your own with Study Guide page 332.*

1. What are six methods in which ads try to persuade people to buy a product?
2. How can jingles, logos, and packaging influence a consumer's decisions?
3. What should be kept in mind when trying to evaluate an ad?

court
t Kings

Pros do.

A Company For Your Future

## Evaluating Ads and Products

1. Make a collection of ads for health products from newspapers and magazines. Note the advertising methods used to get people to buy. Identify the useful information. Which ads are most appealing? Which of the advertised products would you consider using?

2. Think of as many advertising jingles and slogans as you can. Hum the jingles and read a list of the slogans to some of your classmates. How many products can you and your classmates identify from the jingles and slogans? Evaluate the effectiveness of each jingle and slogan.

3. Design an ad for a health product, as these students are doing. You can choose an existing product or make up one of your own. You might choose toothpaste, shampoo, or another health product that you are familiar with. Decide on a brand name. Draw a logo. Try to make your ad influence people through words and pictures. Share your ad with your classmates. Would they buy your product?

4. Think about a health product you use frequently. Do you know if you are making wise consumer choices about this product? To find out, go to the library and find a consumer publication. Look for information about the product. Be sure that the publication also contains information about competitor's products. Evaluate the different brands. Write down the benefits and drawbacks of each brand. Give reasons why you would choose one brand over another.

## Looking at Careers

5. Do you enjoy drawing and doodling? Have people ever told you that you were creative? Do your teachers ever say that you write or talk with a great deal of imagination? If you can answer yes to any of these questions, you might want to consider a career as an **advertising copywriter.**

Advertising copywriters turn ideas into effective advertisements. They write material for the ads that appear in print and on radio and television. They often have to develop the ideas for artwork and jingles as well.

The education requirements are quite varied for advertising copywriters. Most copywriters have high-school diplomas. Many also have college degrees in advertising or communications. A music or art background also is useful for this career.

Choose an ad from radio, television, or magazines and decide how you might change the ad to make it better. For example, you might think of ways the ad could be more noticeable, more humorous, or more informative.

For more information write to the American Association of Advertising Agencies, 200 Park Ave., New York, NY 10017.

# 3 What Should You Consider When Choosing Health Products?

Asking yourself if you do or do not need a health product is one way of becoming a careful health consumer. Once you decide that you need a health product, you must ask yourself which brand is the best buy. The girl shown here is examining two brands of deodorant. Both brands might be equally good at controlling body odor, yet one brand costs more. The price might be higher because the brand is advertised more often. The price might also be higher if a fancy container is used. However, the brand might cost more because it really is a better product. Consumer guides, pharmacists, and other dependable sources of information can help you find out if the brand really is better than most others.

## What Is the Unit Price of a Health Product?

Not only are store shelves stocked with many brands of the same product, but also one brand might offer several sizes of the same product. Comparing the costs of products among so many brands and sizes might seem confusing.

An easy way to find the true cost of a product is to figure out the **unit price.** The unit price is the price of a product per ounce, gram, or some other unit of measure. You can figure out the unit price by dividing the full price of a product by its **net weight**—the weight of the contents, not including the container.

Study the picture below to find the unit price of each tube of toothpaste. Which one has the lowest unit price and gives you the most for your money?

### On Your Own
Suppose you are choosing between two cans of orange juice. Both cans are the same brand. One has a net weight of 6 ounces and costs 79¢. The other can has a net weight of 12 ounces and costs $1.47. What is the unit price of each product? Which product gives you more for your money?

Which product has the lowest unit price?

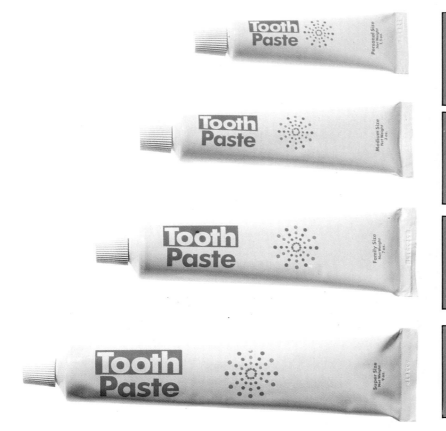

### Personal
Net weight - 1.5 oz.
Price - 69¢
69¢ ÷ 1.5 oz. = 46¢ per ounce

### Medium
Net weight - 3 oz.
Price - $1.05
$105 ÷ 3 oz. = 35¢ per ounce

### Family
Net weight - 7 oz.
Price - $1.54
$1.54 ÷ 7 oz. = 22¢ per ounce

### Super
Net weight - 9 oz.
Price - $1.89
$1.89 ÷ 9 oz. = 21¢ per ounce

## How Can Reading Labels Make You a Better Consumer?

As a consumer, you need and have the right to know what a product is made of and what it will and will not do. Laws require labels on many products. Any claims that the label makes must be truthful.

One of the first things you notice on a label is a list of ingredients. The ingredients are listed in order by weight. Therefore, the first ingredient is the one in the greatest amount by weight. What is the major ingredient of the creme rinse shown here? Checking ingredients can be very important if you know you have certain allergies.

Health care products, also give directions for use. You might not get the best results if you do not follow all of the directions. For example, if you do not follow the directions for using this creme rinse, your hair might not look clean.

As a careful consumer, you should check to see if the label carries a guarantee. A guarantee is a promise by the manufacturer to replace, repair, or give money back for a product if it proves to be unsatisfactory. The name and address of the manufacturer are also listed on the label.

Why is reading labels important?

# Creme Rinse

**Directions:** Use after every shampoo. Squeeze excess water from hair. Apply enough to cover hair from roots to ends and massage throughout hair. Rinse thoroughly.

**Contains:** Water, Cetyl Alcohol, Fragrance, Glutaral, FD&C Red #40 and FD&C Yellow #5

**Guarantee:** If you're not fully satisfied, send proof of purchase for a full cash refund to Clean Hair Company, Chicago, IL

Manufactured by Clean Hair Company, Chicago, IL

Some health care products must carry warnings by law. For example, a can of hair spray must warn the user not to let the spray get near the eyes. What other warnings are on the can of hair spray shown here?

Warnings on medicines are particularly common and helpful. Such warnings usually include information on dosage, storage, the limited usefulness of the medicine, and side effects.

As a consumer, you are responsible for reading the labels on all health products. Paying attention to the ingredients, directions, guarantees, and warnings can help you make wise consumer decisions.

What do these warnings say?

**Directions for use** – Hold can upright 10-12 inches from hair and spray evenly.

**CAUTION: Flammable. Do not use near fire or flame.**

**WARNING:** Avoid spraying in eyes. Contents under pressure. Do not puncture or incinerate. Do not store at temperatures above 120°F. Use only as directed. Intentional misuse by deliberately inhaling the contents can be harmful or fatal.

**Keep out of reach of children.**

**fad,** a product or practice that is popular only for a short time.

## What Are Fads?

Try to recall a hairstyle or an item of clothing that everyone seemed to be wearing last year. Are many people wearing it this year, or has another product become popular? Products or practices that are very popular for a short time are **fads.** Fashions, dance steps, and certain games are often fads.

Smart shoppers think carefully before they buy products that are fads. For example, a smart shopper understands that a kind of fancy jacket that is very popular this year might be out of style next year. Someone who follows that fad might soon be left with a jacket that is not worn-out but suddenly looks odd or out of date. A smart shopper might choose a plainer jacket, which is likely to be useful for several years. Which of the T-shirts shown here do you think were fads?

Following some fads is not necessarily a bad practice, but it can be limiting. Eventually you might wish you had spent your money in a different way.

**Think Back** • *Study on your own with Study Guide page 333.*

1. Why might one brand of a health product cost more than another brand?
2. How can the unit price of a product be figured?
3. What information do health product labels have?
4. Why might the purchase of fad items be unwise?

# Health Activities Workshop

## Buying Health Care Products Wisely

1. Suppose a store is having a "special" on a brand of soap. The "special" soap is packaged as two bars together and is priced at 38¢. Nearby, single bars of the same size and brand of soap are priced at 22¢ each. Is the "special" soap really a bargain? Why or why not?

2. Figure out the unit price of each can of adhesive bandages shown below. Which can gives you the most for your money?

### 100 Strips      60 Strips

# $2.60   $1.99

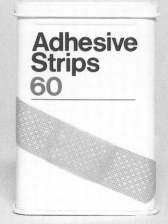

## Looking at Careers

3. Some stores employ people to work for them as **comparison shoppers.** The comparison shoppers go from store to store and check on various product prices as directed by the store manager. In this way the manager can be sure that the prices in his or her store are competitive—not much more than the prices at other stores nearby.

You might think of having a job like this as a part-time job in high school. Usually the stores train their own comparison shoppers. However, certain qualities might be helpful for such a job. What do you think some of these qualities might be? Why might a store manager want to make sure his or her prices are not much higher than prices at other stores?

For more information check with the owners or managers of stores in your neighborhood.

## 4 How Can You Benefit Most from a Health Checkup?

Besides being a consumer of health products, you are also a consumer of health services. Like the boy in the picture, you have probably used the services of a doctor during a health checkup.

How long ago was your last health checkup? Doctors think young people should have a checkup every two or three years. However, in some cases more frequent checkups are advised. For example, a young person should have a health checkup before trying out for a competitive sport, such as swimming or basketball.

When the doctor sees you regularly, he or she can check your continued growth and development. The doctor keeps a record of your health during past visits. By knowing your health history, the doctor is better able to help you if you get sick. If a doctor finds a minor problem during a checkup, the problem can be corrected before it gets worse.

During a health checkup, you get a chance to know the doctor better. You have a chance to ask any questions you might have about your health. Be open and honest with your doctor. Be sure to tell the doctor about any health problems that concern you. For example, you might have had some headaches lately. Perhaps you have had trouble seeing the writing on the chalkboard or hearing the teacher talk. The more your doctor knows about you, the easier it will be for him or her to help you.

During a health checkup, the doctor might find a problem that needs further study. For example, you might have a temperature of 101°F (38.3°C). Normal body temperature is about 98.6°F (37°C). Your higher temperature might indicate the beginning of some illness or the presence of an infection. The doctor might ask that someone take your temperature the next day and call him or her. Also, the doctor might instruct you to stay home from school and rest and drink plenty of fluids. If the doctor's instructions sound complicated, you might write them down.

Suppose the doctor prescribes some medicine, but after a couple of days of taking the medicine, you get no relief. Be sure you or someone else calls your doctor. You should also make sure someone calls your doctor if you get any unpleasant or unexpected side effects from the medicine. Do not wait for your next checkup.

As a wise health consumer, you should talk with your doctor about any treatment plans that are suggested. You have the right to know what is going to be done for you and why.

How often should you have a health checkup?

## What Happens During a Health Checkup?

The pictures on these two pages show some of the common procedures a doctor follows during a health checkup. You might recognize some of these procedures from your own checkups. When you go for a checkup, be sure to ask the doctor about any procedure you wonder about.

The doctor or nurse checks height and weight to determine whether you are growing in the way that is right for you.

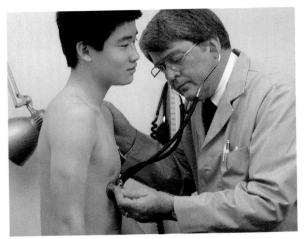

Using a stethoscope, the doctor listens to the heart to make sure its beat is steady. The doctor can also tell if the valves of the heart are opening and closing properly.

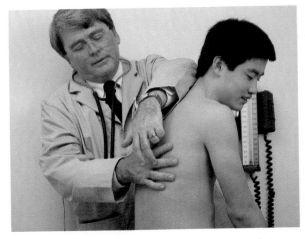

The doctor also uses the stethoscope to listen to the sounds the air makes in the lungs. The doctor can then tell if air is getting to all parts of the lungs. Tapping the back is another method the doctor uses to listen to the sounds in the lungs.

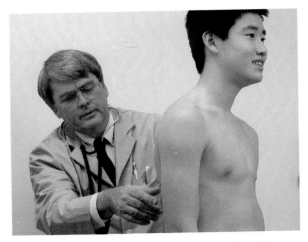

The doctor or nurse notes posture, since it gives some clues about general health. He or she searches, in the event of poor posture, for possible causes such as poor nutrition, lack of proper sleep or exercise, or bone deformities.

278

1. About how often do young people your age need a health checkup?
2. What are your responsibilities as a wise consumer of a doctor's health care services?
3. List eight procedures that a doctor follows in a checkup.

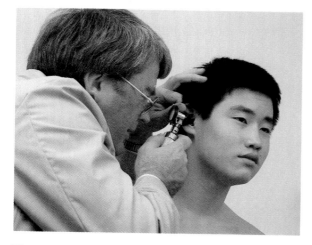

The doctor looks for signs of disease or infection in the eyes, ears, nose, and throat. He or she also checks to see if the eardrums are unbroken and to see if any accumulations of wax need to be removed.

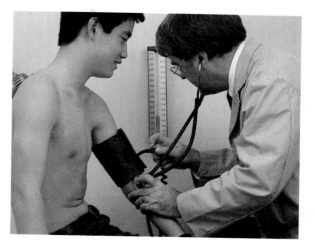

The doctor or nurse checks the blood pressure at full force of the heart's beating and at the time the heart is filling up with blood to see if these pressures are within normal ranges.

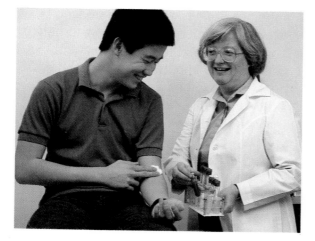

The doctor or nurse takes a blood sample and sends it to a laboratory for tests. One of the tests reveals if a sufficient number of red blood cells are in the blood. A sample of urine is also sent to a laboratory. From the urine test results, the doctor notes how well the kidneys are working.

The doctor checks your vaccination record to be sure you are properly protected against such diseases as tetanus, polio, measles, mumps, German measles, and diphtheria.

## Esther Peterson: Protecting the Consumer

Esther Peterson used to have a lot of complaints when she came home from shopping for her family. At the supermarket she had to decide between "giant" pint packages and just plain pint packages. She had to figure out whether to buy king-sized boxes or jumbo-sized boxes. "Cents off" sales caught her eye, but she could not tell how much money she was saving.

Esther Peterson complained that a person needed to be an expert in mathematics to figure out the best buys.

She complained that advertisements and packages were designed to confuse the consumer. However, Esther Peterson was an adviser on consumer affairs to both President Johnson and President Carter. Therefore, perhaps more than others, she was able to do something about problems that plagued shoppers.

Working for laws that ensured fair packaging and labeling was one way Esther Peterson helped make shopping easier. These laws require simple, direct information about a product to appear clearly on each container. The shape of a container must not mislead shoppers as to the product's size. The label must not give false or useless information.

Esther Peterson has also advised different companies about how to help consumers. Next time you go shopping, notice all the information given on food packages, clothes labels, and even on signs on shelves in the stores. Thanks to the work of Esther Peterson and others, you have the information you need to become a wise consumer.

### Talk About It
1. How has Esther Peterson helped consumers?
2. How have you used information on packages or labels to decide which product to buy?

## Becoming a Careful Health Consumer

You can help all the members of your family become better health consumers. Just practice some of the ideas and suggestions you have learned in this chapter.

The next time your family goes shopping, ask to go along. Offer to help make the shopping list. At the store be a smart shopper. Read the labels and find out the unit prices of the items that you want to buy. Some stores post the unit price of an item right on the shelf.

Be sure to read the labels on all health products carefully. Examine the ingredients. Be sure that your family needs the product. Remember not to be fooled by advertising techniques and special packaging.

When you follow some of these practices, you and your family members are being careful health consumers. You can save money and feel good about yourself as well.

## Reading at Home

*Body Sense, Body Nonsense* by Seymour Simon. Lippincott, 1981. Find out about human health through folk sayings about the human body.

*Health Care for the Wongs: Health Insurance, Choosing a Doctor* by Marilyn Thypin and Lynn Glasner. EMC, 1980. Learn how one particular family found out about medical clinics, how to obtain health insurance, and how to select a family doctor.

# Chapter 9 Review

## Reviewing Lesson Objectives

1. List some guidelines that can help people become wise consumers of health products. (pages 258–261)
2. List several methods that advertisers use to promote the sale and use of products. Explain what to keep in mind when evaluating an ad before selecting a health product. (pages 262–267)
3. Explain why a consumer should compare unit prices, read labels, and be aware of fads when choosing health products. (pages 270–274)
4. State the responsibilities that consumers have in getting the most out of their health checkups. Describe some of the procedures a doctor follows during a health checkup. (pages 276–279)

For further review, use Study Guide pages 332-333

Practice skills for life for Chapter 9 on pages 362-364

SKILLS FOR LIFE

## Checking Health Vocabulary

Number your paper from 1–6. Match each definition in Column I with the correct word or words in Column II.

### Column I

1. the cost of a product per ounce, gram, or some other unit of measurement
2. a public notice or announcement recommending a product or service
3. the weight of the contents of a product, not including the container
4. a person who buys or uses a health product
5. a symbol used to identify something for advertising purposes
6. a product or practice that is popular only for a short time

### Column II

a. advertisement
b. fad
c. health consumer
d. logo
e. net weight
f. unit price

Number your paper from 7–15. Next to each number write a sentence using each word or group of words.

7. consumer guide
8. guarantee
9. health checkup
10. health service
11. impulse
12. label
13. selling method
14. smart shopper
15. stethoscope

## Reviewing Health Ideas

Number your paper from 1–13. Next to each number write the word that best completes the sentence.

1. A health _____ buys or uses health products or services.
2. A basic question to ask before buying a product is "Do I _____ it or do I just want it?"
3. Advertisements can be sources of useful _____.
4. Some ads try to convince people to buy a product by showing a _____ person who uses it.
5. A catchy jingle helps consumers to _____ a certain product.
6. A _____ is a symbol that identifies a company.
7. A product in a fancy package will probably cost _____ than the same kind of product in a simple package.
8. A product's net weight includes the weight of the product but not the weight of the _____.
9. Ingredients on labels are listed in order by _____.
10. A _____ is a promise by the manufacturer to replace, repair, or give money back for a product that is unsatisfactory to the consumer.
11. A person should tell a doctor about any unexpected side _____ from a prescribed medicine.
12. Noting posture gives a doctor some clues about a patient's general _____.
13. The results from a urine test let a doctor know how well a patient's _____ are performing their work of removing wastes from the body.

## Understanding Health Ideas

Number your paper from 14–22. Next to each number write the word or words that best answer the question.

14. What are three possible sources of information about health products?
15. How is the statement, "You can't buy a better product" an example of an unclear statement in ads?
16. What is a logo?
17. How can a person figure out the unit price of a product?
18. What are four kinds of information found on the labels of health products?
19. What is a fad?
20. How often do doctors recommend that young people have health checkups?
21. What does a doctor usually check for when he or she looks in a patient's ears during a checkup?
22. What are three diseases for which people usually get vaccinations?

## Thinking Critically

Write the answers on your paper. Use complete sentences.

1. How can you benefit most from a health checkup?
2. What would you conclude about a product whose ads do not seem to give any useful information?
3. Why might a wise consumer decide to buy a product that has a higher unit price than a similar product with a lower unit price?

283

# 10

# Working for a Healthy Community

Have you ever seen a building like the large, flat one in the picture? It is a water treatment plant. Here, water is cleaned and made safer to drink for the community. Providing clean water is an important health service. This chapter describes the many health services the people in your community share. You will also discover ways you can help improve your community's health now and in the future.

## Health Watch Notebook

Contact your local health officials, recreation department, or department of sanitation to find out about the services they offer your community. Report your findings in your notebook.

1  What Health Services Do People Provide for the Community?
2  How Do People Help Provide a Clean Environment?
3  How Can People Dispose of Garbage More Safely?
4  How Does a Community Reduce Noise?
5  What Recreational Opportunities Does a Community Provide?
6  How Can You Help Keep Your Community Healthy?

**epidemiologist**
(ep′ə dē′mē ol′ə jist), a physician or research scientist who studies the occurrence and causes of diseases.

**sanitarian** (san′ə ter′ē ən), an environmental health specialist who works to ensure the safe quality of food, water, or air for the public health.

## 1 What Health Services Do People Provide for the Community?

Every time you wash your hands or bandage a cut, you are performing a health service for yourself. You can provide for some of your own health needs. Your family and your doctor provide for other health needs. Some of your health needs, however, require the services of other people in the community.

### How Do Health Departments Serve the Community?

People in the health department perform very different jobs. However, they all work together for the public health, especially when a health problem occurs. For example, suppose an outbreak of food poisoning occurs in a community. The pictures show how some people in the health department might respond to solve this problem.

Epidemiologists search for the source of the food poisoning.

The contaminated food is found to all come from one restaurant. Sanitarians close the restaurant and inspect it.

Laboratory technicians test samples of the victims' blood or leftover food and discover that a harmful kind of bacteria contaminated the food.

After discovering how the bacteria got into the food, a sanitarian shows the restaurant owner how to prevent the problem from happening again.

A local health department serves the community in many other ways. The goal of these services is to protect the community from disease. Some sanitarians check the quality of the water in a community, as shown. They might test drinking water to make sure it is safe to use. They might also test water from lakes, rivers, and swimming pools.

Public health nurses make home visits to help families learn how to take care of sick family members. The nurses might also advise families about nutrition and child care. Some health departments operate clinics that provide vaccinations against diseases. Other clinics provide care for people with high blood pressure and other health problems.

Some health department workers help control the spread of disease by spraying insect killer where certain insects are likely to breed. The workers also help control the populations of rats and other pests that spread disease.

Health departments keep records of all births, deaths, marriages, and cases of certain communicable diseases in the community. This information is valuable when planning for new health facilities or when trying to find the cause of certain epidemics.

### Did You Know?

A sanitarian checks the cleanliness of forks, spoons, and other eating utensils in restaurants. First, the sanitarian rubs a cotton swab over the utensil. Then, the cotton swab is placed in a germ-free container and sent to a laboratory. There, workers can determine the number of bacteria on the swab. A high bacteria count indicates that the utensil was not properly cleaned.

How is this public health worker serving the community?

### How Do Hospitals Serve the Community?

If someone asked you to describe what happens in a hospital, you might reply "Doctors and nurses help sick people get well." This answer is true, but incomplete. The following pictures will help you answer this question more completely. They show some of the people who helped Ann while she was in the hospital. Ann had a bad fall and broke her leg. Notice the variety of health professionals who work at a hospital to serve the community's health needs.

Emergency medical technicians gave Ann first aid and brought her and her parents to the emergency room of the hospital.

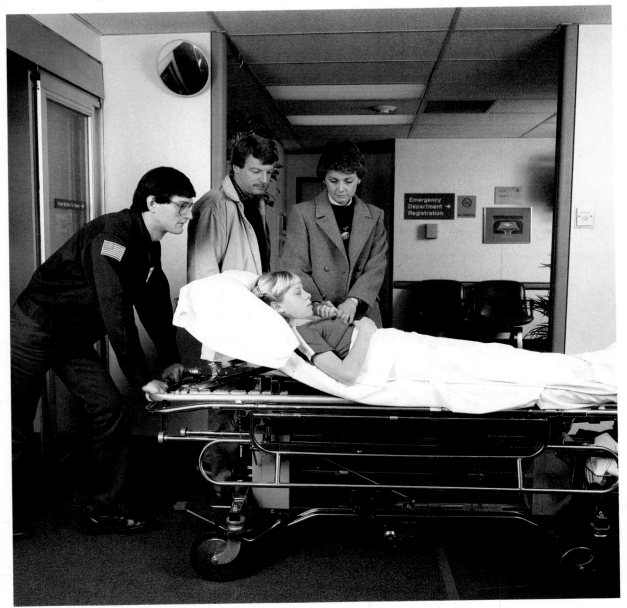

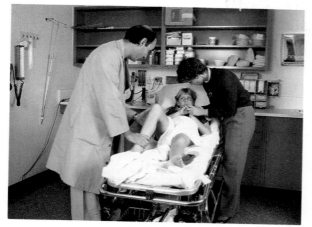

A doctor examined her injury.

One of Ann's parents stopped at the admissions office to give some information for the records.

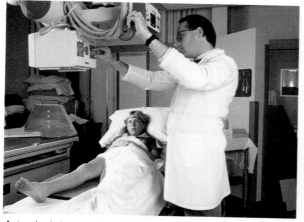

A technician took X-ray pictures of Ann's leg. The pictures showed bits of broken bone in her leg. She needed surgery to remove the bits of bone and repair torn muscles.

A laboratory technician tested samples of Ann's blood to check for the presence of certain diseases. The results helped doctors plan for the surgery.

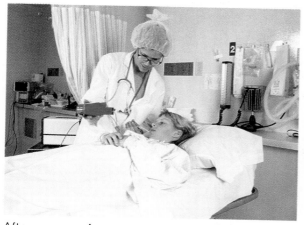

After surgery Ann was taken to the recovery room. Nurses watched her closely in case any problems resulted from the surgery.

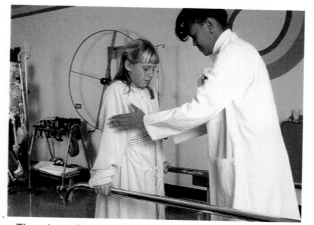

The day after surgery, Ann worked with a physical therapist to learn how to use crutches.

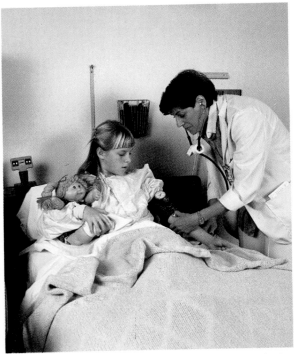

Ann had to spend several days in the hospital. Nurses provided the day-to-day care and emotional support that she needed. Nurses also performed treatments and gave Ann medications that the doctor ordered.

Ann did not see all the people in the hospital who helped her get well. Some of these people were the pharmacists. They prepared the medicine she needed.

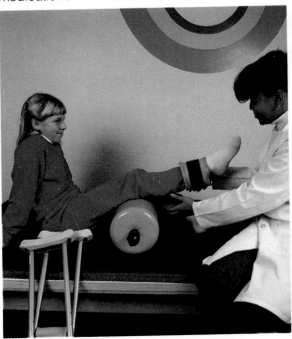

Ann left the hospital about a week after surgery. However, she needed to return for more physical therapy about two months later to regain strength in her leg.

All the health services that helped Ann were the responsibility of the hospital administrators. They plan and direct hospital services based on the community's needs.

## How Do Volunteers Serve the Community?

Some people work in communities as volunteers. They offer their time and services without getting paid. The picture shows a volunteer called a candy striper. This person helps hospital patients under the direction of a nurse or other staff member. Other volunteers work in a hospital at the information desk.

Volunteers might help ill people at home by shopping or housecleaning for them. They also deliver hot meals to people who live alone and cannot shop or cook for themselves. Other volunteers might drive handicapped people to and from work. The work of volunteers is an important part of a community's health.

**Think Back** • *Study on your own with Study Guide page 334.*

1. How does a local health department improve the health of a community?
2. How do doctors, nurses, laboratory technicians, and pharmacists in hospitals each contribute to the health of patients?
3. In what ways do volunteers serve a community?

Some volunteers work in hospitals.

291

**environment**
(en vī′rən mənt), all the living and nonliving surroundings that affect living things.

**pollution** (pə lü′shən), a change in the environment that is harmful or undesirable to living things.

## 2 How Do People Help Provide a Clean Environment?

Look around you. Notice everything you see, indoors and outdoors. Listen closely for any sounds. Do you detect any odors? All of the sights, sounds, and odors are part of your **environment.** Your environment is all of the living and nonliving things that surround and affect you. The water you drink, the air you breathe, the sounds you hear, and the ground you walk on are all part of your environment.

The actions of people often cause harmful or undesirable changes in the environment. Any such change is **pollution.** Most pollution comes from wastes that people add to the environment. Sewage, engine exhaust, and garbage are some wastes that pollute the water, air, and land. Many people in your community work to reduce the problems of pollution. They try to provide a clean, healthy environment for everyone.

### What Is Sewage?

Sewage, or wastewater, from factories, houses, and other buildings threatens the safety of the drinking water supply. Sewage from your home might include human wastes, bits of food that go down the kitchen drain, and water you use to wash your hands. Factory sewage, like that shown in the river, often includes oil, grease, and poisonous chemicals. All sewage usually contains bacteria and viruses, which can cause disease. Sewage also contains sticks, rags, and other large objects that drain into sewers from city streets.

What does sewage contain?

292

## How Do Treatment Plants Improve a Community's Water?

To reduce the amount of water pollution, most communities in the United States pipe their sewage to wastewater treatment plants, commonly called sewage treatment plants. Many factories have their own sewage treatment plants. The drawing shows how some harmful substances are removed from sewage at such a plant, although not all plants use all these processes. First, sewage is piped through screens that remove sticks and other large objects. Next, the sewage moves into settling tanks where small, solid materials settle out. The remaining sewage then might go to aeration tanks. Bacteria in the tanks feed on the sewage. Air is pumped into the aeration tanks to keep the bacteria alive. In another settling tank, the bacteria clump together and settle out. Next, chlorine gas is added to kill harmful bacteria and some viruses. Finally, the treated sewage is pumped to a nearby river, lake, or other body of water.

Notice the difference between the sewage that enters the treatment plant and the sewage that leaves it. The treated wastewater is clean enough to send to a river or lake, but, of course, the water is still not safe to drink. Many harmful substances remain, even if you cannot see them. Also, the water might have an unpleasant color, taste, and smell.

To make water safe and pleasant for drinking, communities use water treatment plants. These plants help to clean water from rivers or lakes. The water passes through a series of screens, settling tanks, and filters. Chlorine is added to kill harmful bacteria. In some communities, the water is then sprayed into the air. This process adds oxygen to the water to make it taste better. The clean water then is piped to homes and other places in the community.

Sewage after and before treatment

Sewage is cleaned at a sewage treatment plant

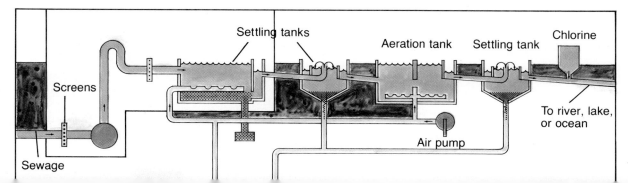

Settling tanks

Aeration tank    Settling tank

Chlorine

Screens

To river, lake, or ocean

Air pump

Sewage

## Why Is Groundwater Pollution Dangerous?

One of the greatest dangers that faces the environment is groundwater pollution. About half the people in the United States get their drinking water from the ground. The drawing shows how wastes and other substances can leak from underground pipes and from storage tanks and drums. Notice how this pollution can spread throughout the groundwater and enter wells and streams.

Perhaps the most dangerous sources of groundwater pollution are the billions of gallons of poisonous chemical wastes produced in the United States each year. Some of these wastes are made harmless by burning them at high temperatures or changing them in other ways. Most poisonous—or toxic—wastes, however, are stored in drums and left in open dumps or buried. People in some communities have had to move because chemicals from leaking drums have contaminated the water supply.

New laws, improved storage, and clean-up efforts have helped prevent or improve some cases of groundwater pollution. However, much remains to be done to solve this problem.

What causes groundwater pollution?

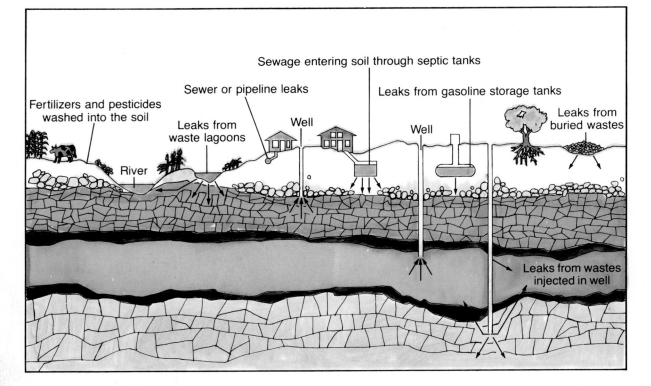

### What Are Some Problems Caused by Air Pollution?

No matter where you live, the air is probably polluted to some amount. Most air pollution results from the burning of such materials as coal, oil, and gasoline. This burning produces waste gases and particles.

The pie graph shows that cars cause most of the air pollution in the United States. Car exhaust contains many harmful gases. One gas is **carbon monoxide.** It deprives the body of oxygen and can cause dizziness and headaches. Sunlight causes other gases in car exhaust to combine and form **smog.** You can imagine how the smog in the picture irritates the eyes and throat. Smog can also make breathing difficult, especially for babies, older people, and people with respiratory problems.

Notice the other sources of air pollution on the pie graph. Factories and power plants burn great amounts of coal and oil, producing smoke. The smoke contains harmful gases and tiny bits of coal, oil, lead, and other substances. The smoke irritates the eyes and respiratory system.

However, air pollution can be more than just irritating. In the last forty years, thousands of people have become ill or died from unusually heavy levels of air pollution. For example, in 1948 an industrial town in Pennsylvania experienced three windless days of heavy, deadly pollution. Smoke hung over the valley town, turning the sky dark gray. Twenty people died and thousands became ill. A similar incident killed four thousand people in London in 1952. These and other disasters have increased people's efforts to develop ways to reduce air pollution.

**carbon monoxide** (kär'bən mo nok'sīd), a colorless, odorless, and poisonous gas in the exhausts of motor vehicles.

**smog** (smog), pollution caused by engine exhaust gases reacting with other gases in the presence of sunlight.

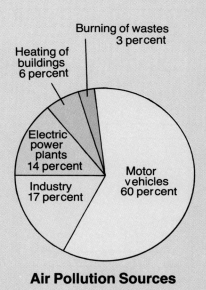

Burning of wastes
3 percent

Heating of buildings
6 percent

Electric power plants
14 percent

Industry
17 percent

Motor vehicles
60 percent

**Air Pollution Sources**

**acid rain,** rain that contains a higher than normal amount of acids. These acids are caused by certain gases released into the air.

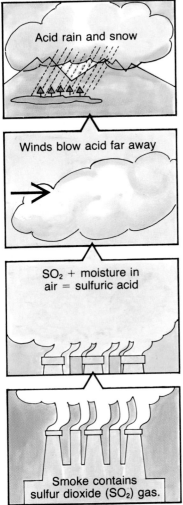

Formation of acid rain

## What Are the Effects of Acid Rain?

Sometimes the solution to one problem causes another problem. For example, some power plants use extremely tall smokestacks to release smoke high enough into the air so that it does not cause air pollution for the towns nearby. While winds carry the smoke away, certain gases in the smoke react with moisture in the air to make tiny drops of acids. Raindrops mix with these acids and fall to the ground as **acid rain.**

Acid rain is caused largely by the burning of coal and oil that contain much sulfur. The drawing shows how the burning of fuels with sulfur leads to acid rain. Notice that acid rain often falls on rivers, lakes, and forests hundreds of miles from the cities or factories that caused it.

Although acid rain does not seem to hurt humans directly, it can be very harmful to crops, trees, and fish. This pollution destroys millions of dollars of crops in the United States each year. Some lakes in the northeastern United States, as well as in Norway and Sweden, are almost lifeless due to the acid rain. Some of these lakes are being restored by adding lime to the water, as shown. The lime cancels the effect of the acid. Then the lake can be restocked with fish. Many people think, however, that the best solution is to reduce the amount of air pollution that causes acid rain in the first place.

Lakes damaged by acid rain can sometimes be restored.

## How Are People Reducing Air Pollution?

In recent years much progress has been made in reducing some kinds of air pollution. Antipollution devices on cars have greatly reduced the amount of carbon monoxide in automobile exhaust. Aircraft also use antipollution devices. Many factories use machines, such as the ones shown to the right, that remove most of the particles from smoke before it goes up the smokestack. Other devices, called **scrubbers,** remove much harmful gas, as well as particles, from smoke. These devices are expensive, but they work.

People are reducing air pollution by using fuels that burn more cleanly. Newer cars use lead-free gasoline. These cars do not pollute the air with bits of lead. In addition, engineers are improving engines that use electricity and other energy sources instead of gasoline. Some industries use coal that contains less sulfur. Low-sulfur coal burns more cleanly than high-sulfur coal and reduces acid rain. Scientists have developed ways to remove up to 40 percent of the sulfur from coal.

Perhaps the simplest way to reduce air pollution is to cut down on the use of cars and other machines that burn fuel. Some communities encourage car pooling, in which people share rides to work. Using public transportation also cuts down on the number of cars on the road. In some large cities, cars are not allowed in the downtown areas. How does this practice reduce pollution?

**scrubber,** a device attached to a factory smokestack that removes much of the harmful gas and most of the particles from smoke.

Special machines remove most particles from smoke.

---

*Did You Know?*

Acid rain slowly eats away at rock and metal, damaging buildings and statues, including the Statue of Liberty and other famous monuments. For example, acid rain and other kinds of pollution have caused more damage to the famous Greek Parthenon in the last fifty years than all causes did in its first two thousand years.

---

**Think Back** • *Study on your own with Study Guide page 334.*

1. What harmful substances are found in sewage?
2. How do sewage treatment plants reduce water pollution?
3. What is one way groundwater can become polluted?
4. How does acid rain form?
5. What are some ways people are reducing air pollution?

**sanitary landfill,** an area of land where garbage is buried in such a way as to minimize water pollution, air pollution, and the spread of disease.

**recycling,** changing a waste product so that it can be used again.

Glass can be recycled.

How is garbage buried at a sanitary landfill?

## 3 How Can People Dispose of Garbage More Safely?

Disposing of garbage is a major problem for many large cities. Garbage has to go somewhere. In the past, "somewhere" was usually a street, river, or open dump on the edge of town. These methods of garbage disposal were extremely unhealthy. The garbage attracted rats and other animals that carried diseases. The trash was often burned at the dump, but this burning caused much air pollution.

Today many communities dispose of garbage in ways that pollute as little as possible. One way is by using a **sanitary landfill.** Bulldozers smash the garbage together, as shown. Then a tractor covers the garbage with a layer of dirt. The next day, another layer of garbage is compacted and covered with dirt. This process is repeated with each day's garbage. Sanitary landfills reduce some kinds of pollution, but they must be checked constantly for leaks. Some landfills leak dangerous chemicals into the soil and groundwater. Another problem with sanitary landfills is that they use up a lot of land, and many communities are running out of land for them.

Another way to deal with the garbage problem is by **recycling**—changing waste products so they can be used again. The glass bottles in the picture, for example, will be separated according to their color. The glass will be crushed, melted, and made into new bottles. Paper, aluminum, and rubber are some other materials that can be recycled.

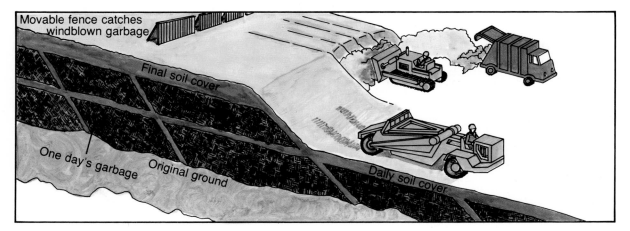

Movable fence catches windblown garbage

Final soil cover

One day's garbage

Original ground

Daily soil cover

Some communities burn garbage in large furnaces called incinerators. Trucks empty the garbage into a huge pit, like the one shown. A crane lifts the garbage and drops it down a chute that leads to an incinerator. Many incinerators have scrubbers or other devices to remove many of the materials from the smoke.

Disposing of wastes without polluting improves the quality of life in a community. Clean water, air, and land provide what a community needs for good health.

**Think Back** • *Study on your own with Study Guide page 335.*
1. What are the advantages and disadvantages of using sanitary landfills to dispose of garbage?
2. How do recycling and incineration help communities deal with garbage disposal?

*Did You Know?*
Some hospitals and large apartment buildings in Sweden use one of the most advanced garbage-disposal systems in the world. Trash is dumped into chutes and is sucked through a vacuum-powered pipeline to a central incinerator. The heat from the burning garbage generates electricity, warms buildings, and melts ice on roads during the winter.

Some communities burn garbage in large incinerators.

## Discovering How Your Community Fights Pollution

1. You can get an idea of how part of the water treatment process works by making a water filter. First, mix some dirt in a small jar of water to make the water dirty. Then, cut off the bottom of a plastic bottle and cover any sharp edges with tape. Close the narrow opening of the bottle with cotton. Next, arrange layers of pebbles and sand in the bottle, as shown. Now, hold the filter over a jar and pour the dirty water into the filter. The water will take a few minutes to go through the filter.

Compare the dirty water with the filtered water. Remove some of the cotton and examine it. What could you do to get the filtered water cleaner? *CAUTION: Do not drink the filtered water at any time. It is still not clean enough to be safe.*

2. Use an earth science textbook or an encyclopedia to find out how a condition called a temperature inversion can affect air pollution.

3. Find out what happens to garbage after it is picked up from your home. You might find the information you need by talking with an adult at home. You could also talk with someone at the local Department of Streets and Sanitation, health department, or the company that collects your garbage. Write a report on how the garbage is disposed of and share the information with the class.

4. Talk with an older adult, such as a grandparent or family friend, about pollution problems in the past. How did pollution affect life in the past? Have different kinds of pollution increased or decreased over the years?

## Looking at Careers

5. Many people use their education and skills to help fight pollution. Some **sanitary engineers,** for example, work with architects to design sewage treatment plants, water treatment plants, incineration plants, or sanitary landfills. They make sure the plant or landfill is being built properly so that it will serve its purpose safely.

Once the structure is built, other kinds of sanitary engineers, sometimes called operation engineers or control engineers, oversee the day-to-day operation of the plant or landfill. Like all engineers, sanitary engineers need at least four years of college education.

Find the nearest sewage or water treatment plant or incineration plant in your area. Then call or write to see if group tours are available.

For more information write to the Engineer's Council for Professional Development, 345 E. 47th St., New York, NY 10017.

6. If you enjoy the beauty of the outdoors and want others to enjoy it, you might consider a career as a **landscape architect.** These architects design outdoor open areas such as parks, community gardens, tree-lined medians along highways, and the parklike property around office buildings.

Before designing any property, a landscape architect needs to consider the purpose of the property. For example, is the space supposed to be used for playing sports, for picnicking, or for just walking through? Often a large park is supposed to provide all these and other kinds of spaces.

Keeping the purpose in mind, the architect looks at the land—its shape, the way sunlight hits it, the kind of plants on it, the makeup of the soil, and the buildings or land around it. Then the architect is ready to draw up plans. The plans might include ideas of where to plant certain trees, flowers, and shrubs; where to enlarge or make a pond; where to put sidewalks, fountains, and benches; and what materials to use.

Many colleges across the country offer four- or five-year programs for people wanting to be landscape architects.

Look around your home, school, or neighborhood for a place you think could be improved by a landscape architect. Describe the improvements you would make.

For more information write to the American Society of Landscape Architecture, Inc., 1900 M St. NW, Washington, DC 20036.

## 4 How Does a Community Reduce Noise?

How is the jet in the picture polluting the environment? Fumes from the engines certainly pollute the air. The engines of this jet cause another harmful or undesirable change in the environment—noise.

Noise pollution is nothing new. In the 1700s Benjamin Franklin moved across Philadelphia to escape the noise of a nearby market. In 1906 a woman led a campaign to ban tugboat whistles at night in the New York harbor. Today, however, noise pollution is a much more serious problem. Machines—from hair dryers to jets—cause noise that can have harmful effects on people's health.

Too much noise can be annoying and interrupt activities. It makes some people nervous or tired. Continuous loud noise narrows blood vessels, making the heart work harder. Blood pressure might increase. In addition, loud noise over a period of time causes hearing loss. About twenty million people in the United States suffer some permanent hearing loss because of too much noise in their environment. Such hearing loss often comes from loud, continuous noise at factories and other work places. Increasingly common causes of hearing loss include the use of stereo headphones and the loud, continuous sounds from radios held too close to the ear.

How is the jet polluting the environment?

The chart shows some of the noise levels that people experience. Notice that noise is measured in units called **decibels.** Over a period of time, noise levels of eighty decibels or more can cause ear damage. Think about the noises that you experience. Compare them to the examples in the chart.

Since the early 1970s, laws have led to the design of quieter motors and engines. Trucks, airplanes, factories, and some appliances are less noisy than they once were. Subway trains in some cities use rubberized wheels. These wheels do not screech as steel wheels do. In Europe, construction workers sometimes work inside small sheds or tents to reduce noise for the community.

The picture shows one way people protect themselves from noise pollution in a noisy environment. What other kinds of workers might wear headsets to shield out noise?

**Think Back** • *Study on your own with Study Guide page 335.*
1. How does noise pollution affect people in a community?
2. What are some sources of noise that can be unhealthy?
3. How can noise pollution be reduced?

**decibel** (des′ə bəl), a unit for measuring the loudness of sound.

*Did You Know?*
Studies have shown that people who live in quiet places for a long time generally have better hearing than those who live in noisy places.

Some workers have to protect their hearing.

| Decibels | Source | Effect on hearing |
|---|---|---|
| 150 | Jet take-off less than 100 feet away | Possible eardrum rupture |
| 140 | Shotgun blast, aircraft carrier deck | |
| 130 Painful | Jet take-off 300 feet away, earphone at loud level | |
| 120 | Firecrackers, loud thunder, siren nearby | |
| 110 Uncomfortable | Radio held close to ear, steel mill, car horn at 3 feet | |
| 100 | Subway train, power lawn mower, jackhammer | Permanent hearing damage (8 hours of continuous exposure) |
| 90 Loud | Heavy city traffic, food blender | Temporary hearing damage |
| 80 | Garbage disposal, freight train 60 feet away | Possible temporary hearing damage |
| 70 Annoying | Automobile at 50 mph 50 feet away, party | |
| 60 | Typewriter, window air conditioner | |
| 50 Quiet | Singing birds, normal conversation | |
| 40 | Library, refrigerator, soft background music | |
| 30 | Dripping faucet, rural area at night | |
| 20 Very quiet | Light rainfall, rustling leaves, whisper | |
| 10 Just able to be heard | Breathing | |

## 5  What Recreational Opportunities Does a Community Provide?

In the mid-1850s the poet William Cullen Bryant was concerned about the rapid growth of New York City. He feared that buildings and streets would soon replace all the fields and wooded areas on Manhattan Island. Bryant called for ". . . a range of parks and public gardens along the central part of the island . . . for the refreshment and recreation of the citizens. . . " A few years later, the city established one of the largest city parks in the world—Central Park.

Communities provide parks of all kinds. Some, like Central Park shown here, have places where people can play sports, row a boat, have a picnic, or stroll along paths. All these activities are forms of recreation. Other forms of recreation include attending a concert, visiting a zoo, drawing, and other activities you might enjoy in your spare time. Recreation gives you a chance to relax, exercise, and relieve stress. Some amount of recreation is important for good mental and physical health. A community can provide places for all kinds of recreation.

Central Park—an important recreational area for New York

Many people enjoy visiting a museum to relax, have fun, and learn about the world around them. Museums are exciting and fascinating places to explore. The museum in the picture has a collection of famous aircraft and spacecraft. Here you can see these machines and learn about the people who flew them. You might find some similar items at a museum of science and technology, where you can discover the wonders and uses of science through displays and activities. Art museums contain masterpieces from famous artists all over the world. Museums of natural history let you explore ancient civilizations or look at dinosaur fossils. Historical museums offer glimpses of your community's past.

Other recreational facilities include planetariums and aquariums. Notice the round roof of the planetarium in the picture. Inside, the ceiling becomes a night sky, showing you images of stars and planets. You can take an imaginary journey through space.

An aquarium takes you on a different journey—to the depths of streams, lakes, and oceans. At the aquarium shown, visitors can observe the rich, colorful variety of life that inhabits the waters of the world. Which of these facilities have you visited?

Planetarium

Aquarium

Museums are exciting places to explore.

**On Your Own**
Parks and forested areas provide places for recreation. Write a paragraph explaining why else these areas are important to a community.

## What Outdoor Areas Do Communities Provide?

Most communities—whether they be towns, cities, or counties—have set aside large areas of land where people can enjoy nature. Such areas might be called parks, woods, groves, or forest preserves. These places usually have picnic facilities as well as hiking and biking trails.

Many cities and towns have nature centers located nearby. Nature centers give people the opportunity to learn about wildlife while enjoying the outdoors. Wildlife managers talk to visitors about the kinds of animals they might see on the trails.

Another kind of outdoor recreational area is an arboretum. An arboretum is actually a living tree museum. The arboretum in the picture is beautifully landscaped with trees from all over the world. Each kind of tree is identified so that visitors can learn more about nature as they walk along the paths.

## What Other Recreational Opportunities Do Communities Offer?

Playgrounds, beaches, swimming pools, and gymnasiums are a few other places of recreation your community might have. In addition, many organizations in your community probably offer a wide range of activities. The Girl Scouts, Boy Scouts, YWCA, YMCA, local park districts, and other community organizations have programs that include sports, exercise classes, art classes, camping, field trips, and many other activities.

Your community might provide many opportunities for you and others to relax, explore, learn, and have fun. Recreation is an important part of good health.

**Think Back** • *Study on your own with Study Guide page 335.*

1. How is recreation important to good health?
2. What are some opportunities for recreation that communities might provide?
3. What would be found in a planetarium? in an aquarium? in an arboretum?

## 6 How Can You Help Keep Your Community Healthy?

So far, you have read about how people in the community help improve your health. You can help improve the community's health too.

One of the best ways to help your community is to fight pollution. Notice the litter in the picture. This pollution was not caused by car exhaust or factory sewage. It was caused by individuals who did not bother to use the trash cans. Such land pollution makes a community unhealthy and unsightly. Try not to litter. Even gum wrappers pollute the landscape. Parks and sidewalks often have trash cans. Use them. If a trash can is not nearby, save the trash until you can throw it away properly.

Recycling helps reduce the amount of garbage your community must deal with. Many communities have recycling centers where aluminum, paper, glass, and other materials are collected. The materials are then made into new products. Recycling makes a lot of sense. It saves much of the energy, money, and natural resources that would have gone into making a totally new product. Recycling also reduces some of the air, water, and noise pollution that would have resulted from making a new product.

Everybody can help fight pollution.

People can further reduce air pollution by using cars less often. Think about the times you asked someone to drive you somewhere. Could you have walked or ridden a bicycle instead?

You can help reduce noise pollution by lowering the volume of radios, televisions, and record players. Loud music from radios outdoors can be especially annoying to others in the community.

A problem cannot be solved unless people know the problem exists. Make an effort to find out about local health problems by reading newspapers and listening to newscasts. What health problem is this girl reading about?

All of these suggestions show how your actions can affect the health of others. Perhaps you can think of other ways you could help keep your community healthy. You are an important part of your community. Try to make it as healthy and pleasant a place as possible.

**Think Back** • *Study on your own with Study Guide page 335.*

1. How can people help keep their community healthy?
2. What are the advantages of recycling certain materials instead of throwing them away?

Learning about health problems is the first step to solving them.

## A Community Grows a Paradise

In any city or town, a building might be torn down from time to time. Often the resulting empty lot becomes a temporary parking lot or junkyard. It also might become an unsafe place for children to play.

Empty lots, however, do not need to become eyesores. In fact, in one neighborhood in Chicago, community members have turned an empty lot into a place of enchantment.

After a corner building was torn down, some people got permission to make a garden that everyone in the community could enjoy. They cleared the land of rubble and garbage, put up a fence, and began to plan the garden. Part of their garden was to be planted with flowers. People could sit on benches in this part of the garden and talk, rest, and just enjoy their surroundings. The other part of the garden was used to grow vegetables. Here, members of the community could grow their own food.

With the plans set, the gardeners of the neighborhood got to work. They laid down woodchip paths, prepared the soil, planted flowers, shrubs, and vegetables, and painted a sign. People in the neighborhood and local businesses donated plants and materials. Adults and children worked together to keep the garden growing.

The garden was so beautiful, the community named it "El Paraiso," which means The Paradise. People in this Chicago neighborhood are proud of their planted paradise.

### Talk About It
1. What is included in "El Paraiso?"
2. What are some community benefits of fixing up empty lots?

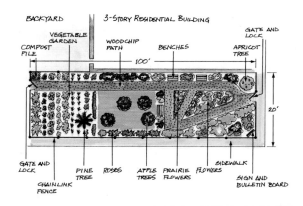

# Health at Home

## Improving Your Home Environment

In this chapter, you have learned about different kinds of pollution and how you can reduce pollution in your community. Below are some additional ways to keep your home environment as healthy and pleasant as possible.

Cooperate with members of your family to reduce noise pollution at home. For example, suppose someone is watching television in the living room and it is interfering with the music from your radio in the bedroom. Instead of turning up the volume on the radio, ask the person to turn down the volume on the television. Look for other sources of noise at home. Talk with your family about ways to reduce the noise.

The family members shown here are working together to improve their home's appearance. Take a look around the outside of your home and decide how you could improve it. Every day pick up litter that might have blown near your home. Encourage the rest of your family to do the same.

## Reading at Home

*The Hospital Book* by James Howe. Crown, 1981. Learn more about what happens in the various parts of a hospital.

*Safeguarding the Land* by Gloria Skurznski. Harcourt, 1981. Read about careers in public land management, such as ranger and conservationist.

# Chapter 10 Review

## Reviewing Lesson Objectives

1. Describe how health departments, hospitals, and volunteers each contribute to meet the needs of the community. (pages 286–291)
2. State some causes of water pollution and air pollution. Describe how communities reduce water and air pollution. (pages 292–297)
3. Describe how communities can dispose of solid wastes more safely. (pages 298–299)
4. Explain how noise pollution affects the people in a community. Describe how noise levels can be reduced. (pages 302–303)
5. List and describe some recreational facilities and activities that a community provides for its members and explain how they meet the health needs of people. (pages 304–307)
6. List several ways an individual can help improve the environment and health of a community. (pages 308–309)

For further review, use Study Guide pages 334-335

Practice skills for life for Chapter 10 on pages 365-367

SKILLS FOR LIFE

## Checking Health Vocabulary

Number your paper from 1–11. Match each definition in Column I with the correct word or words in Column II.

### Column I

1. a person who works to ensure the quality of food, water, and air for the public health
2. an area of land where garbage is buried in such a way as to minimize pollution
3. a unit for measuring the loudness of sound
4. all the living and nonliving surroundings that affect living things
5. a device attached to factory smokestacks that removes harmful gases and particles from smoke
6. a change in the environment that is harmful or undesirable to living things
7. changing a waste product so that it can be used again
8. a colorless, odorless, and poisonous gas that is part of motor vehicle exhaust
9. a physician or research scientist who studies the occurrence and causes of disease
10. pollution caused by engine exhaust gases reacting with other gases in the presence of sunlight
11. a kind of pollution caused when certain gases mix with moisture in the air

### Column II

a. acid rain
b. carbon monoxide
c. decibel
d. environment
e. epidemiologist
f. pollution
g. recycling
h. sanitarian
i. sanitary landfill
j. scrubber
k. smog

## Reviewing Health Ideas
Number your paper from 1–15. Next to each number write the missing word or words that complete the sentence.

1. A _____ inspects restaurants and other places to make sure food is safe to eat.
2. The medicines that people use in a hospital are prepared by _____.
3. Most pollution comes from _____ that people add to the environment.
4. Water is made safe to drink at a _____ treatment plant.
5. Chlorine is added to sewage or drinking water to kill harmful _____.
6. In some places, toxic wastes have leaked into the ground and contaminated the _____.
7. Most air pollution results from the _____ of coal, oil, and gasoline.
8. Carbon monoxide, which is part of car exhaust, deprives the body of _____.
9. Some gases in factory smoke react with moisture in the air to make _____ rain.
10. Scrubbers remove much of the harmful gas and many of the _____ from smoke.
11. Many factories reduce air pollution by using coal that contains less _____.
12. Glass, paper, aluminum, and rubber are materials that can be _____ and used again.
13. Loud continuous noise narrows blood _____.
14. An arboretum is a living _____ museum.
15. A person must know about a health problem before helping to _____ that problem.

## Understanding Health Ideas
Number your paper from 16–25. Next to each number write the word or words that best answer the question.

16. What is the purpose of a recovery room in a hospital?
17. What kind of information do local health departments keep on record?
18. What might sewage contain?
19. What are settling tanks used for at sewage and water treatment plants?
20. What is one source of groundwater pollution?
21. What is one effect of acid rain?
22. How is garbage disposed of at a sanitary landfill?
23. What is one source of noise that can damage hearing permanently?
24. What could be seen at a museum of natural history?
25. What is one way a person can improve the health of the community?

## Thinking Critically
Write the answers on your paper. Use complete sentences.

1. Describe an example of a community health problem in which epidemiologists, public health nurses, and sanitarians help solve the problem.
2. Suppose a company wants to build a large factory in your community. What questions would you ask the company before they build the factory?
3. How could air pollution or water pollution in one part of the country affect people in other parts of the country?

313

# Using Metric

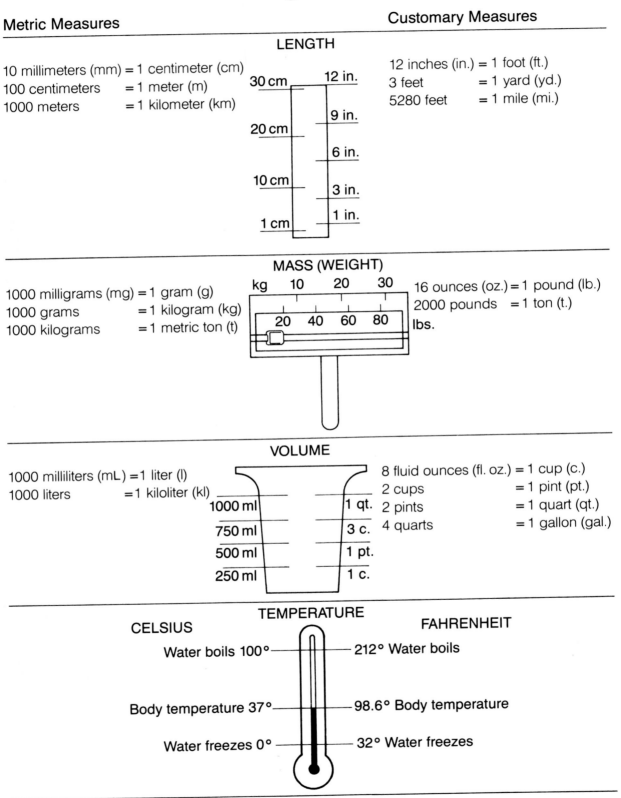

**Metric Measures**

**Customary Measures**

## LENGTH

10 millimeters (mm) = 1 centimeter (cm)
100 centimeters    = 1 meter (m)
1000 meters        = 1 kilometer (km)

30 cm — 12 in.

20 cm — 9 in.

— 6 in.

10 cm — 3 in.

1 cm — 1 in.

12 inches (in.) = 1 foot (ft.)
3 feet          = 1 yard (yd.)
5280 feet       = 1 mile (mi.)

## MASS (WEIGHT)

1000 milligrams (mg) = 1 gram (g)
1000 grams        = 1 kilogram (kg)
1000 kilograms    = 1 metric ton (t)

kg   10    20    30

20   40   60   80

lbs.

16 ounces (oz.) = 1 pound (lb.)
2000 pounds     = 1 ton (t.)

## VOLUME

1000 milliliters (mL) = 1 liter (l)
1000 liters      = 1 kiloliter (kl)

1000 ml — 1 qt.
750 ml — 3 c.
500 ml — 1 pt.
250 ml — 1 c.

8 fluid ounces (fl. oz.) = 1 cup (c.)
2 cups       = 1 pint (pt.)
2 pints      = 1 quart (qt.)
4 quarts     = 1 gallon (gal.)

## TEMPERATURE

CELSIUS

FAHRENHEIT

Water boils 100° —— 212° Water boils

Body temperature 37° —— 98.6° Body temperature

Water freezes 0° —— 32° Water freezes

# Independent Study Guide

Use the *Independent Study Guide* to review the lessons
in each chapter. After you read each lesson, answer
the questions to find out what you remember.
Answering the questions will help you learn the
important ideas in each lesson. You can also use the
study guide to help you review for the chapter test.

# Chapter 1 Study Guide

On a separate sheet of paper write the word or words that best complete the sentence or answer the question.

Lesson
**1**
pages
20–23

1. _____ is the way a person feels about herself or himself.
2. People who have a _____ self-image generally feel good about themselves.
3. Having _____ is a characteristic of someone with a good self-image.
4. People can often get along with others when they _____ differences in other people.
5. What is an attitude?
6. Everyone is special because _____ is exactly like anyone else.
7. People should recognize and accept their _____ but not dwell on them.
8. People can help to overcome their weaknesses if they think more about their _____.
9. Making _____ is a part of life.
10. When a person makes a mistake, he or she should try to _____ from it.
11. The way a person reacts to a disappointment can either _____ or hurt the person's self-image.

Lesson
**2**
pages
26–29

1. A _____ is a connection between persons or groups.
2. Getting _____ with others does not mean always doing what other people do.
3. How should people treat other people?
4. Friends can talk to each other about their _____.
5. What do friends usually share?
6. Many people feel _____ when they think they have been treated unfairly, or notice other people being treated unfairly.
7. Keeping angry feelings inside can make a person feel _____.
8. People can deal with anger when they first _____ that they are angry.
9. Why is it important to get rid of angry feelings?
10. Keeping the mind busy can often help a person get rid of _____.
11. What are two ways to work off angry feelings?
12. Whom might a person talk to if feelings of anger will not go away?

1. _____ is the body's physical and mental reactions to demanding situations.
2. _____ events as well as upsetting or dangerous events can cause stress.
3. What are seven common effects of stress?
4. When first dealing with problems that cause stress, people should realize that they are _____.
5. When several problems are bothering someone, it is best to work on _____ at a time.
6. Some problems cannot be solved and must simply be _____.
7. Describe a breathing exercise that helps a person relax.
8. Besides doing breathing exercises, how else might a person relax?
9. Getting the mind off a problem is not the same as _____ a problem.
10. What are the five basic steps of decision-making?

1. How is a long-term goal different from a short-term goal?
2. People can set _____ goals when they have abilities that help them reach their goals.
3. A realistic goal is not too hard and not too _____.
4. What do people gain as they reach their goals?
5. When people try new activities, they often discover that they have _____ that they did not know they had.
6. What should a plan for reaching a goal include?
7. Why is it important to check your progress while trying to reach a goal?
8. Goals are easier to reach when they are divided into _____ parts.
9. People often have an easier time reaching a goal when they set aside a special _____ to work on that goal.

# Chapter 2 Study Guide

On a separate sheet of paper write the word or words that best complete the sentence or answer the question.

**Lesson 1**

pages 50–52

1. The stage of rapid growth that usually begins between the ages of nine and fifteen is called the growth _____.
2. How long does the growth spurt usually last?
3. Who usually begins their growth spurts first, girls or boys?
4. At what ages do girls usually begin their growth spurt?
5. When do boys usually experience rapid changes in growth?
6. Different parts of the body grow at _____ rates during the growth spurt.
7. The timing of the growth spurt does not affect _____ size.

**Lesson 2**

pages 54–55

1. Endocrine glands make chemicals called _____.
2. Which pea-sized gland produces the growth hormone?
3. What happens when the pituitary gland stops making a lot of growth hormone?
4. Which gland produces hormones that cause the reproductive glands to become more active?
5. The _____ produce sperm cells.
6. Egg cells are produced in the _____.
7. _____ from the ovaries and testes cause the body to develop adultlike features.
8. What is puberty?

**Lesson 3**

pages 56–61

1. A mother and a father share in giving a child _____ traits.
2. Traits are passed on from one _____ to the next.
3. Where are chromosomes found?
4. What does the structure of DNA look like?
5. The chemical structure of _____ determines a person's heredity.
6. What is a gene?
7. How many chromosomes are in each body cell?
8. How many chromosomes are in each reproductive cell?
9. Chromosomes that determine a person's sex are called _____ chromosomes.
10. An _____ cell always contains an X chromosome.
11. A sperm cell can have an X or _____ chromosome.
12. Children in a family received forty-six chromosomes from their parents, but not the _____ forty-six chromosomes.
13. What influences how fast a person grows during the growth spurt?

**Lesson 4**

pages
64–65

1. Heredity, endocrine glands, and health _____ affect a person's growth.
2. People cannot control the actions of their _____ and their endocrine glands.
3. Heredity sets _____ for a person's growth.
4. People can give themselves the materials they need for growth by eating a _____ of foods.
5. What can give a person control over weight, body shape, and muscle development?
6. Strong muscles can help a person hold the body correctly, giving the person good _____.
7. Muscles can develop only if a person _____ them.
8. How many hours of sleep do eleven- to twelve-year-olds need each night?
9. When does the body usually build new cells?
10. What hormone is produced mainly when a person sleeps?
11. List three wise health decisions that can help a person grow properly.

**Lesson 5**

pages
66–67

1. How might changes during the growth spurt make a person feel?
2. Changes in height and weight can lead to _____ changes.
3. Mood swings, unhappy feelings, and worrying about the way you look are a normal part of _____.
4. During the growth spurt, friendships with people of the same _____ often become more important.
5. Friendships often change as people develop new _____.

**Lesson 6**

pages
68–69

1. If you have a good self-image, you will probably have a greater _____ in yourself.
2. Accepting _____ can help a person develop a strong self-image.
3. New responsibilities come with new _____.
4. List four people a person could talk to about feelings concerning growth.
5. During the growth spurt, your friends might grow slower or _____ than you grow.
6. Your own pattern of growth makes you a _____ person.

319

# Chapter 3 Study Guide

On a separate sheet of paper write the word or words that best complete the sentence or answer the question.

Lesson
**1**
pages
76–81

1. People get their energy from _____.
2. List three major kinds of carbohydrates.
3. Which two carbohydrates provide most of the energy that the body uses?
4. _____ provides almost no energy but helps to move materials through the body.
5. Eating too much _____ can lead to tooth decay and overweight.
6. Which group of nutrients supplies energy and carries important nutrients to the body cells?
7. List three problems that too much fat in the diet can lead to.
8. Which group of nutrients builds and repairs cells?
9. Dried beans, peas, eggs, and fish are good sources of _____.
10. List four parts of the body that are made mainly of proteins.
11. Most animal sources of food contain more _____ than protein.
12. People generally do not need to take vitamin pills if they eat a _____ of food.
13. Which food is a good source of calcium and phosphorus?
14. How do the minerals iron and copper help the body?
15. The body is mainly made up of the nutrient called _____.

Lesson
**2**
pages
82–87

1. No single food can supply all the _____ that the body needs every day.
2. How many daily servings do children need from the milk-cheese group?
3. _____ daily servings are recommended from the meat-fish-poultry-bean group.
4. People should eat foods from each food group every _____.
5. Which four foods do nutrition experts think that people should limit?
6. Most sweetened breakfast cereals contain one _____ sugar.
7. Fried foods should be limited because they contain a lot of _____.
8. Too much cholesterol can lead to diseases of the _____ and blood vessels.
9. Too much salt can lead to _____ blood pressure.

1. State one reason why grocery stores have a greater variety of foods today than they did one hundred years ago.
2. Washing, cutting, mixing, cooking, drying, canning, and freezing foods are examples of food _____.
3. Drying removes water from food so that _____ cannot grow in the food and spoil it.
4. List two foods that have been dried.
5. How is freeze-drying different from drying?
6. Which two food-processing methods reduce the size and weight of food?
7. How are canned and frozen foods convenient?
8. Canned foods are sealed airtight to prevent _____ from entering them.
9. How does freezing foods prevent bacterial growth?
10. Many processed foods are high in _____.
11. Fresh foods lose some of their _____ between the time they are picked and the time they are eaten.
12. _____ foods keep nearly all their nutrients unless they have been completely precooked.
13. A food labeled *fortified* or *enriched* has _____ added to it.
14. What is milk usually fortified with?
15. Any substance added to food is called an _____.
16. What is a preservative?
17. What does the Food and Drug Administration do if it discovers a harmful additive?
18. Vegetables that are cooked until _____ have lost much of their vitamins.

1. A wise consumer reads and compares food _____ to find foods with the most nutrition at the best price.
2. If a food label lists the ingredients "sugar, barley, dried skim milk, and honey," then that food contains mostly _____.
3. List three kinds of nutrition information that might be found on a food label.
4. How might the name of the food manufacturer be important to a food consumer?
5. Many restaurants serve foods that are high in _____, sugar, and salt.
6. A person can avoid _____ at a restaurant by taking leftover food home.

# Chapter 4 Study Guide

On a separate sheet of paper write the word or words that best complete the sentence or answer the question.

Lesson
**1**
pages
106–111

1. How can exercise improve mental health?
2. What two important social skills do team sports help develop?
3. What substances does the cardiovascular system carry to the cells and away from the cells?
4. A strong heart _____ longer between beats than a weaker heart.
5. Why is a fit heart important when a person exercises?
6. Regular exercise helps keep the _____ clear of fatty material.
7. How does the breathing of a fit person differ from the breathing of an unfit person?
8. Exercise can improve muscular strength, flexibility, and _____.
9. Muscular strength and flexibility are two parts of physical fitness called _____ fitness.

Lesson
**2**
pages
112–115

1. Body fatness is a part of _____ fitness.
2. Body fat is stored _____.
3. Where is body fat found?
4. What tool can be used to measure body fat?
5. How much body fat should an eleven- to twelve-year-old have?
6. A _____ is the unit used to measure the energy in food.
7. Generally, how many Calories does an eleven- to twelve-year-old need to take in every day?
8. People gain weight if they take in _____ Calories than they use.
9. What is the best way to take in the right amount of Calories and nutrients every day?
10. The number of Calories a person uses depends on how much a person _____ and how long an activity is done without stopping.

Lesson
**3**
pages
116–117

1. _____ fitness is the ability to perform well in activities that require certain skills.
2. What is agility?
3. What part of skills fitness is the ability to quickly do activities that require strength?
4. The amount of time it takes a person to move once he or she observes the need to move is called _____ time.

**Lesson 4**

pages 120–125

1. People can build fitness by setting fitness _____.
2. It is important to determine a person's needs, interests, and _____ before setting fitness goals.
3. Some people have a body type that makes it easy for them to gain body _____.
4. Running in place can help a person measure _____ fitness.
5. What part of health fitness can push-ups measure?
6. What test can a person do to measure his or her flexibility?
7. The backward hop can be used to test the part of skills fitness called _____.
8. What test can measure coordination?
9. A good way to test speed is to _____ in place.

**Lesson 5**

pages 126–129

1. Choosing activities that improve certain parts of fitness can help a person achieve fitness _____.
2. People should not stop doing an _____ just because it does not improve a certain part of fitness.
3. What parts of health fitness is soccer excellent for developing?
4. What parts of skills fitness is baseball excellent for developing?
5. To build and maintain fitness, a person should exercise at least _____ times a week.
6. While a person is exercising, the heart should beat at a rate of _____ beats per minutes.
7. How can a person keep track of how hard the heart is working while exercising?
8. Why is it important to warm up before exercising?
9. List three exercises that are good for warming up.
10. Why are comfortable shoes and loose clothing important for exercising?
11. After doing highly active exercise, a person should do _____ exercises.
12. How do cooling down exercises help the body?
13. A person who has not exercised for a long time should start slowly and _____ build up the amount of exercise done.

# Chapter 5 Study Guide

On a separate sheet of paper write the word or words that best complete the sentence or answer the question.

Lesson

**1**

pages
142–143

1. Accidents do not just happen; they are _____.
2. Many people cause accidents because they take unnecessary _____.
3. People should cross streets only at _____.
4. What are two safety rules that help protect people from harm?
5. It is important to wear a _____ belt while riding in a car.

Lesson

**2**

pages
144–149

1. _____ are the most common kind of accident in the home.
2. What can people put on the back of a rug to prevent others from slipping?
3. What is a poison?
4. List three common household items that are poisonous.
5. All poisons, including medicines, should be kept out of reach of young _____.
6. Poisonous substances bought in a store have _____ written on their labels.
7. Plugging too many appliances into one outlet can cause a _____.
8. Unused outlets should be _____, especially if young children are around.
9. People should never use electrical appliances in or near _____.
10. How can putting a screen around a fireplace prevent a fire?
11. Unlike a fall or poisoning, a _____ often harms more than one person.
12. Before throwing away a burnt-out match, it should be _____.
13. If a stranger asks to see or talk to someone who is not home, what should a person do?
14. A person should never let a stranger know he or she is home _____.
15. Rather than giving directions to a stranger, a young person could tell a stranger to ask an _____.
16. If a person chooses to give directions to a stranger, he or she should stay _____ feet away from the car.

1. What is an emergency?
2. People can have the best chances of reacting correctly and safely to an emergency if they are _____.
3. List three kinds of telephone numbers that should be listed near the telephone.
4. Some communities use the number _____ as a special emergency telephone number.
5. A smoke _____ makes a loud, shrill noise when smoke reaches it.
6. What can a person use to put out a small fire?
7. If a large fire occurs, a person should leave the building _____.
8. List four items that a home first-aid kit should contain.

1. Immediate medical care is called _____.
2. First aid requires _____ thinking and quick actions.
3. What should a person do as quickly as possible if an emergency occurs?
4. Moving an injured person can often make the injury _____.
5. When giving first aid, a person should not do more than he or she _____ how to do.
6. What should a person do if someone is trying to cough up an object?
7. First aid for a person who has stopped breathing is called artificial _____.
8. Most people suffer brain damage or die after four to _____ minutes without oxygen.
9. What position should the victim be in for artificial respiration?
10. What is the general treatment for a first-degree or second-degree burn?
11. What is the correct first-aid procedure for a third-degree burn?
12. Shock occurs when the heart, lungs, brain, and other organs do not get enough _____.
13. What can cause a person to go into shock?
14. First aid for shock includes laying the person down and keeping the person _____.
15. If a person has a leg, chest, or _____ injury, do not raise the legs to improve circulation.

# Chapter 6 Study Guide

On a separate sheet of paper write the word or words that best complete the sentence or answer the question.

Lesson
**1**
pages
168–169

1. A _____ is a chemical that changes the way the body works.
2. Certain teas, coffees, and soft drinks contain _____, which can increase the activity of the nervous system.
3. How does alcohol affect the nervous system?
4. Tobacco and tobacco smoke contain the drug _____.
5. List three products that can produce harmful fumes.

Lesson
**2**
pages
170–173

1. List three ways medicines can get into the body.
2. What kind of health professional can prepare a prescription medicine?
3. An over-the-counter medicine can be bought without a _____.
4. List four kinds of information that can be found on a prescription label.
5. What are two common side effects that might be listed on the label of an OTC medicine?
6. Taking two or more medicines at the same time without a doctor's permission is called drug _____.

Lesson
**3**
pages
174–179

1. What is drug abuse?
2. _____ occurs when a drug user must use more and more of a drug to get the same effect.
3. How is mental dependence different from physical dependence?
4. When does withdrawal occur?
5. What are the five main groups of drugs?
6. Which group of drugs speeds up the nervous system?
7. Taking cocaine can cause _____—seeing or hearing things that are not really there.
8. Which group of drugs slows down the nervous system?
9. Tranquilizers and barbiturates are _____ without a prescription.
10. _____ are drugs made from opium or opiumlike substances.
11. _____ is a narcotic that is illegal and not used medically in the United States.
12. _____ are drugs that change the messages carried by the nerves to the brain.
13. How can inhalants cause death?
14. Drug abuse affects _____ by causing an increase in crime.
15. More than _____ of all motor vehicle accidents involve someone who has abused a drug.

**Lesson 4**

pages 180–181

1. Marijuana contains about _____ chemicals.
2. Which main mind-altering chemical easily builds up in the body of a marijuana user?
3. The THC from one marijuana cigarette can stay in the body for a _____.
4. The most damaging effects of marijuana occur in the _____.
5. What are two driving skills that the use of marijuana weakens?
6. Marijuana is especially dangerous to young people because it can interfere with their physical, _____, and mental growth.
7. It is _____ to grow, buy, sell, or use marijuana.

**Lesson 5**

pages 182–185

1. Alcohol is a _____ drug.
2. How quickly can alcohol enter the bloodstream?
3. If a large person and a smaller person drink the same amount of alcohol, which person has the higher blood alcohol level?
4. What are two effects of drinking a large amount of alcohol?
5. _____ is a disease of the liver which can be caused by the long-term use of alcohol.
6. Physical and mental dependence on alcohol is called _____.
7. Alcoholism can be controlled with proper help only if the alcoholic _____ the help.
8. List three special branches of Alcoholics Anonymous and state which part of the family each branch helps.

**Lesson 6**

pages 186–189

1. Smokers have to breathe faster than others because of the carbon _____ in cigarette smoke.
2. When _____ from cigarette smoke cool on a smoker's lungs, they form a brown, sticky mass.
3. A cigarette smoker becomes _____ on the nicotine in tobacco.
4. What are three diseases that smoking can cause?
5. _____ smoke comes from someone else's cigarette.
6. How is sidestream smoke different from mainstream smoke?
7. How is snuff different from chewing tobacco?
8. List three harmful effects from using chewing tobacco or snuff.

**Lesson 7**

pages 192–193

1. _____ pressure leads some people to abuse drugs.
2. What can a person say if she or he is pressured to use drugs?
3. State an activity that a person can do to resist the pressure of abusing drugs.
4. What are five important steps in making a decision?

# Chapter 7 Study Guide

On a separate sheet of paper write the word or words that best complete the sentence or answer the question.

Lesson
**1**

pages
200–203

1. Disease germs cause _____ diseases.
2. What are the most numerous kinds of organisms?
3. Describe the kind of place in which bacteria grow best.
4. Name three other diseases that can be caused by the bacteria that cause pneumonia.
5. Viruses harm the body by entering and _____ body cells.
6. How can viruses be seen?

Lesson
**2**

pages
204–209

1. The body's first-line defenses work to keep disease germs out of the body's tissues and _____.
2. List three first-line defenses against disease.
3. _____ _____ cells surround and destroy disease germs.
4. How do stomach acids play a role in the body's first line of defense against disease germs?
5. What is the third line of defense against disease germs?
6. How many kinds of disease germs can each kind of antibody attack?
7. List three diseases each of which provides lifelong immunity once a person has had the disease.
8. How can a person build immunity to certain diseases without getting those diseases?
9. The AIDS virus does not spread by _____ contact.
10. What are two ways people can become infected with the AIDS virus?

Lesson
**3**

pages
210–215

1. What is the most common disease in the United States?
2. What causes a runny nose during the early stage of a cold?
3. During what stage of a cold can a person pass the cold viruses to others?
4. What are sinuses?
5. How can antibiotics help a person with sinusitis?
6. When a person has pneumonia, thick mucus collects in the lungs and interferes with _____.
7. Disease germs can make the _____ red and swollen, causing a sore throat.
8. A severe sore throat might mean that the person has a disease called _____ throat.

**Lesson 4**

pages 218–223

1. Why are communicable diseases less dangerous today than they were in the beginning of this century?
2. Disease germs do not cause _____ diseases.
3. _____ involves the passing of genes from parents to children.
4. Cigarette smoking greatly increases the chances of getting cardiovascular diseases and lung _____.
5. Heredity and _____ usually act together to cause a noncommunicable disease.
6. Cardiovascular diseases are diseases of the _____ and blood vessels.
7. How can hypertension affect the artery walls?
8. What happens when an artery that supplies blood to the heart becomes blocked?
9. What are two causes of strokes?
10. How does exercise reduce the risks of heart disease?
11. How does stress affect the blood vessels?
12. What are three environmental factors that increase the chances of getting cancer?

**Lesson 5**

pages 224–227

1. An _____ is a harmful reaction in some people's bodies to certain substances.
2. What disease does an allergic reaction often resemble?
3. Why can breathing be difficult for a person with asthma?
4. What are two symptoms that might result from an allergic reaction to an insect sting?
5. Other than avoiding allergens, how can allergies be treated?

**Lesson 6**

pages 228–229

1. Why is it important to have a healthy lifestyle?
2. The body's _____ against disease work best if the body is in good physical condition.
3. A healthy lifestyle includes eating foods low in fat, sugar, salt, and _____.
4. A healthy lifestyle includes making wise decisions about tobacco, alcohol, and other harmful _____.
5. How does bathing regularly help prevent diseases?
6. The body's defenses work better when a person deals with _____ in healthy ways.

# Chapter 8 Study Guide

On a separate sheet of paper write the word or words that best complete the sentence or answer the question.

Lesson
**1**

pages
236–237

1. Good posture helps a person move about for long periods of time without getting _____ .
2. Good posture keeps parts of the body _____ in a straight column.
3. List three problems that poor posture can cause.
4. Posture depends on the rest of a person's _____ .
5. What is the correct way to sit in a chair?
6. When people stand or walk, the _____ should be centered over the body.
7. How does the posture people have as adults usually compare to the posture they had as young people?

Lesson
**2**

pages
238–241

1. What percentage of young people have tooth decay by the time they become adults?
2. List three things that the loss of teeth can affect.
3. What is plaque?
4. The bacteria in plaque use sugar in food to produce _____ .
5. Acids destroy _____ on teeth and lead to tooth decay.
6. What can happen if a cavity is not treated?
7. Hardened plaque is called _____ .
8. What happens to gums in gum disease?
9. The most common dental problem of eleven- to twelve-year-olds is tooth _____ .
10. How can people remove plaque and bits of food between their teeth and under their gumline?
11. How often do people need to brush and floss?
12. Why are sticky sweets especially harmful to teeth?

Lesson
**3**

pages
242–243

1. If a person is _____ , he or she can see objects close by, but objects far away appear blurred.
2. A vision problem that is more common in adults than children is _____ .
3. Whom should you notify if you have eye pain, itching, headaches, or trouble seeing?
4. Ear infections occur when _____ get into the middle ear.
5. What are two things that can damage a person's hearing?

1. What is the most important way to care for the skin?
2. Tiny dirt particles and _____ land on the skin constantly.
3. How can people prevent the transfer of bacteria to food?
4. Oily skin and _____ increase the need for cleanliness.
5. What are three body wastes the sweat glands collect?
6. What causes perspiration to change to an unpleasant odor?
7. At what stage in life do sweat glands get more active?
8. What products can people use to control perspiration and body odor?
9. Which glands help to keep the skin soft and smooth?
10. Extra oil on the skin can clog openings and produce _____ and other forms of acne.
11. How can people control oily skin and acne?
12. What is dandruff?
13. What can look like dandruff if it is not rinsed completely out of the hair?

1. What kind of hormone is produced mainly when people sleep?
2. List two body functions that slow down during sleep.
3. During sleep, more _____ is available to build and repair cells.
4. List three problems that can occur when people miss a day or two of sleep.
5. _____ often need sixteen to twenty hours of sleep each day.
6. How many hours of sleep does a typical eleven- to twelve-year-old need each night?
7. How long does a person usually dream during a healthy night's sleep?
8. How long does a typical period of dreaming last?
9. During sleep experiments, how can scientists tell if a person is sleeping lightly, deeply, or dreaming?
10. Sleep does not always relieve _____.
11. What are three kinds of fatigue?
12. What is the best way to relieve physical fatigue?
13. What can cause emotional fatigue?
14. Fatigue is a sign that the body needs a _____.

# Chapter 9 Study Guide

On a separate sheet of paper write the word or words that best complete the sentence or answer the question.

Lesson
**1**
pages
258–261

1. What is a health consumer?
2. A wise shopper knows that the most costly products are not always the _____ products.
3. What do careful shoppers ask themselves before they buy a product?
4. _____ shoppers quickly buy a product when they see it even though they do not need it.
5. _____ members are often good sources of information when it comes to making health decisions.
6. What should a person remember before he or she follows a friend's recommendation?
7. The _____ has good, dependable materials about becoming a wise health consumer.
8. As people gain _____ in shopping wisely, they often find that they can make better decisions and purchases.
9. When people _____ the decisions they make, they can make wiser decisions in the future.

Lesson
**2**
pages
262–267

1. What is an advertisement?
2. List two forms of advertisements.
3. Some ads are planned just to make a person buy a product, and offer little or no helpful _____.
4. List two reasons why the advertising method that uses free gifts is often deceiving.
5. How are jingles effective forms of advertisements?
6. Advertisers use _____ to identify their company.
7. The cost of a product in a fancy package is often _____ than another product in a simpler package.
8. Evaluating advertisements can sometimes be tricky because advertisers often use several _____ in one ad.

**Lesson 3**

pages 270–274

1. List three reasons why one brand of a product might cost more than another brand.
2. The _____ price of a product is the cost of the product divided by the net weight.
3. The net weight is the weight of the contents, not including the _____.
4. Any claim that a label makes must be _____.
5. How are the ingredients listed on a label?
6. What is a guarantee?
7. Some health products, such as hair spray, must carry _____ by law.
8. When people follow _____, they often wish they had spent their money in a different way.

**Lesson 4**

pages 276–279

1. How often do doctors think young people should generally have health checkups?
2. It is very important to be _____ with the doctor.
3. The more the doctor knows about a person, the more she or he can _____ the person.
4. What might a temperature higher than 98.6°F (37°C) indicate?
5. What should a person do if the doctor's instructions seem very complicated?
6. What should a person do if he or she has an unpleasant side effect from a medicine?
7. What does a doctor check to determine if a person is growing in a way that is correct for that person?
8. What instrument does the doctor use to check the heart and lungs?
9. What might poor posture indicate?
10. The doctor tests the blood _____ to see if it is in the normal ranges.
11. What is one thing that can be learned from a blood test?
12. A _____ test can help a doctor determine how well the kidneys are working.
13. List five diseases that people get vaccinations for.

# Chapter 10 Study Guide

On a separate sheet of paper write the word or words that best complete the sentence or answer the question.

**Lesson 1**

pages 286–291

1. People in a health department perform different jobs but work together for _____ health.
2. What kind of health worker would inspect a restaurant to check on safety methods?
3. What is the goal of the public health department?
4. What kind of health worker makes home visits and instructs families on health, child care, and nutrition?
5. To which hospital area would a person be brought if he or she has suffered an injury?
6. What kind of hospital worker would help a patient learn to walk with crutches?
7. People called _____ offer their time and services without getting paid.

**Lesson 2**

pages 292–297

1. The living and nonliving things that surround and affect you make up your _____.
2. What is pollution?
3. To prevent some water pollution, sewage is partly cleaned at a _____ treatment plant.
4. What kind of gas is added to sewage to kill harmful bacteria and some viruses?
5. To make water safe for drinking, communities use _____ treatment plants.
6. What are three sources of groundwater pollution?
7. What is the most dangerous source of groundwater pollution?
8. Most air pollution results from the _____ of coal, oil, and gasoline.
9. What causes most air pollution in the United States?
10. How does carbon monoxide affect the body?
11. Smoke and smog irritate the _____ system.
12. Acid rain is caused largely by burning coal and oil that contain large amounts of _____.
13. What are three things toward which acid rain is directly harmful?
14. Devices called scrubbers remove much harmful _____ as well as particles from factory smoke.
15. List two ways people can cut down on the use of cars.

**Lesson 3**

pages 298–299

1. In the past, what kinds of problems were caused when people threw their garbage in the street, river, or in an open dump?
2. Garbage is compacted, layered, and covered with dirt at a sanitary _____.
3. List two disadvantages of a sanitary landfill.
4. What are four kinds of materials that can be recycled?
5. Some communities burn their garbage in large furnaces called _____.

**Lesson 4**

pages 302–303

1. What are three health effects of too much noise?
2. How many people in the United States suffer permanent hearing loss because of too much noise in the environment?
3. Noise is measured in units called _____.
4. A noise level of _____ decibels or more can cause ear damage over a period of time.
5. Motors and engines are _____ than they once were.
6. Some subway trains use _____ wheels to reduce noise.

**Lesson 5**

pages 304–307

1. Recreation can give people a chance to relax, exercise, and relieve _____.
2. What kind of museum would likely contain fossils and other signs of the past?
3. What would a person see in a planetarium?
4. What can people learn about at an aquarium?
5. What is one place people can learn about wildlife as they enjoy the outdoors?
6. List three community organizations that might offer recreational activities.

**Lesson 6**

pages 308–309

1. What is one of the best ways people can help their community?
2. What should people do with litter when a trash can is unavailable?
3. List three things that recycling can save.
4. When people walk or ride a bicycle, they can reduce _____ pollution.
5. How can people find out about local health problems?

# Skills for Life Handbook

Use the activities in this handbook to develop skills for life—skills that will help you deal with events in your life in positive, healthful ways. Read stories about how people your age deal with some difficult situations. Then answer the questions to tell what these people should do or to evaluate what they have done.

**Deciding What to Do**   You will learn how to use the 5-step process and how to evaluate choices to make responsible decisions.

**Feeling Good About Yourself**   You will learn how people develop self-esteem by thinking positive thoughts about themselves.

**Dealing with Problems**   You will learn how to cope with difficult, sad, or other stressful situations and how to deal with strong emotions.

**Setting Goals**   You will learn how to set realistic goals and then how to achieve them.

SKILLS FOR LIFE

## Learning When and How to Say No
You will learn when it is important to resist peer pressure to avoid doing things that may be harmful or wrong. You will develop techniques for saying no in such situations.

## Evaluating Ads and Choosing the Best Product
You will learn how advertising can influence choices and how to use ads and labels to evaluate products in order to choose the best.

## Getting Along and Communicating with Others
You will learn ways to get along better with others, including ways to resolve conflicts as well as improve communication.

# Deciding What to Do

Sylvia and her friend Jeannette made plans to meet for lunch on Saturday at a local fast-food restaurant. When they arrive, they each order their meals and sit at a table. Sylvia notices that Jeannette has ordered only a soft drink, and comments on this to her friend. Jeannette confides that she has not been hungry since her sister gave her some diet pills that she obtained from her doctor. Jeannette points out that Sylvia, too, could avoid being hungry. She offers to share her diet pills with Sylvia.

Sylvia knows that it is dangerous to use medicines prescribed for someone else. She also knows that diet pills can be harmful. She points out to Jeannette that the best way to lose weight is to follow a sensible diet and exercise more. Jeannette continues to urge Sylvia to take the diet pills.

On a separate sheet of paper or the *Health for Life* decision-making chart, examine this situation. Use the five-step decision-making process to decide the choices that Sylvia has and the possible outcome of each choice. Ask yourself whether each choice fits the following guidelines for a good decision:
• The choice is safe and promotes good health.
• The choice is legal.
• Sylvia's parents would approve of the choice.
• The choice shows respect for Sylvia and others.

What would you advise Sylvia to do? Why?

# Feeling Good About Yourself

While leaving the lunch line, Lucy tripped and spilled her tray on the cafeteria floor. Students nearby clapped, and Lucy felt very embarrassed.

Like everyone, Lucy has a "voice" inside her head that tells her about herself. This "voice" is really positive or negative thoughts that Lucy has about herself. Often, Lucy finds herself having negative thoughts when she could substitute more positive thinking. These thoughts make Lucy feel bad about herself. After tripping in the cafeteria, Lucy finds herself thinking negative thoughts about herself, even though she knows that spilling her tray does not make her a bad person. She is uncomfortable with this negative thinking, but is also embarrassed that she spilled her lunch tray.

Answer the following questions on a separate sheet of paper.

1. What negative thoughts might Lucy have after tripping? Write at least five negative things that Lucy might think.
2. For every negative thought that Lucy might have about herself, what is one positive thing that she could substitute? Write one positive thought for each negative thought that Lucy could have.

# Dealing with Problems

Jackie has been feeling a lot of stress lately. She has overslept almost every day this week, and has had to rush to catch the school bus every morning. She has not had time to eat a healthy breakfast all week, and has forgotten her lunch three times. She also has forgotten her books and homework several times. Jackie's mother is annoyed with her because she needs constant reminders to get out of bed in the morning. She also is not doing her morning chores.

Jackie knows that she has a problem that she needs to work on. She realizes that several factors are causing her to feel stress. She would like to identify these problem areas and decide what to do about them to relieve her stress.

Divide a sheet of paper into three columns. Label the columns *Causes, Solutions,* and *Consequences.* Write your answers to the following questions on this sheet of paper.

1. What factors are causing stress in Jackie's life? List as many as you can in the *Causes* column.
2. How could Jackie deal with each problem? List as many solutions as you can in the *Solutions* column.
3. What are some possible consequences of each suggestion? List as many as you can in the *Consequences* column.
4. What do you think is the best solution for each problem? For each cause, circle the solution that you would advise Jackie to use.

# Deciding What to Do

Paul has just finished reading Chapter 2, "Growing and Changing." He knows that both heredity and good health decisions affect his growth. He has been invited to go on a weekend campout with his best friend's family. Having just gotten over a bout with the flu, Paul still does not feel completely well. He is still quite tired, and needs more rest than usual. Paul also has a lot of schoolwork to catch up on. He has a test on Monday morning that he needs to study for. He also knows that next week will be especially busy.

Paul knows that he needs rest in order to recover from his illness and remain healthy. He does not want to put his health in danger. On the other hand, he very much wants to go camping with his friend's family. He knows that they would have a good time fishing, hiking, and sleeping in tents. Paul also knows that he will not have a chance to go camping again until next year.

On a separate sheet of paper or the *Health for Life* decision-making chart, examine this situation. Use the five-step decision-making process and what you learned in Chapter 2 to decide what Paul should do.

# Learning When and How to Say No

While spending the afternoon with her friends at the shopping mall, Sarah is offered a cigarette by Lisa. Sarah knows that smoking can affect her growth and health, but does not want to lose her friends.

Sarah has learned that when her friends try to get her to do something, it is called *peer pressure.* She knows that peer pressure can be positive, such as when her friends encouraged her to try out for the school play. She also knows that peer pressure can be negative. When her friends encourage her to smoke cigarettes, it is negative peer pressure.

Learning how to say no to negative peer pressure is an important part of growing up. There are several ways to say no without losing friends. These methods include:

1. Just saying no.
2. Ignoring the friend's suggestions.
3. Changing the subject or suggesting another activity.
4. Explaining that true friends do not push each other to do things that they don't want to do.
5. Leaving the situation.

Divide a sheet of paper into two columns. On the left side of the paper, list five different ways that Sarah could say no to Lisa. Use the five methods above as a guide. In the right-hand column, write the possible consequences of each method. Which suggestion would you advise Sarah to follow?

# Dealing with Problems

Jorge is upset with his family. His parents always expect Jorge to participate in family activities, even though Jorge would rather be with his friends. His older sister often embarrasses Jorge by telling his friends stories about what Jorge did when he was little. Worst of all, Jorge has to share a bedroom with Felipe, his little brother, who is always trying to tag along whenever Jorge is with his friends. Jorge is at his wit's end. He loves his family, but he feels pressured to spend too much time with them. He would like to have more time for himself and his friends. He feels that he has no privacy. He wishes that he did not have to share a room with Felipe. He finds himself getting angry with his family members easily, and this makes him uncomfortable.

Answer the following questions on a separate sheet of paper.
1. Why is Jorge upset?
2. What would you advise Jorge to do to help him cope with his feelings?
3. How will your suggestion in question #2 help Jorge?

# Deciding What to Do

Susan's mother is concerned because Susan has been very tired lately. The doctor has told Susan that she is below the average weight for her height. He is concerned that she is not taking in enough nutrients to stay healthy. Susan thinks that she looks fine at her current weight. She is very active and does not eat many Calories each day. Susan is not certain that she wants to gain weight. She really does not want to become overweight, but she knows that the doctor would like her to gain 5 to 10 pounds. She admits to herself, though, that she *has* been unusually tired lately.

On a separate sheet of paper, list the choices Susan has in this situation. Evaluate each choice by asking the following questions.

1. Is Susan's choice safe? Does it promote good health?
2. Would Susan's parents and doctor approve of her decision?
3. Does the choice show respect for Susan and others?

What would you advise Susan to do?

# Getting Along with Others

Mary Ann's best friend, Jane, is overweight for her height. Mary Ann knows that Jane is self-conscious about her weight and is trying to lose a few pounds. The other girls in Mary Ann's group, though, often make fun of Jane's weight, even when she can hear them. Mary Ann does not join in when her friends criticize Jane, but she does not say anything to stop them from being hurtful. Mary Ann knows that Jane is very discouraged and feels left out by the group. She feels bad for her friend, and she does not want her feelings to be hurt any more.

On a separate sheet of paper, write your answers to the following questions.

1. What could Mary Ann tell Jane to show that she respects her feelings?
2. What are three things that Mary Ann could say to her friends to discourage them from making fun of Jane?
3. What might be the consequences of each suggestion in question 2?
4. Which suggestion would you choose?

# Choosing the Best Products

Steven's health class has just finished reading Chapter 3 in his health book. Steven is eager to share what he has learned with his family. After discussing good nutrition with his parents and sister, Steven asks if he can plan and prepare a meal for them. His parents agree to help him select a menu, make a shopping list, and shop for and prepare a healthy dinner. Together, they decide to have spaghetti with meat sauce, salad, bread, milk, and fruit.

On a separate sheet of paper, write your answers to the following questions.

1. Using the menu for their dinner, what items will be on Steven's shopping list? (List as many as you can.)
2. When shopping for the items on his list, what should Steven keep in mind? Use what you learned in Chapter 3 to list as many factors as you can to help Steven choose the most nutritious foods.
3. How can reading food labels help Steven evaluate products and decide which brands to buy?

# Deciding What to Do

While practicing the shuttle run for the President's Physical Fitness Test, Jim twisted his ankle. It is not bruised, but it is swollen and does hurt a little to walk or run. The school nurse gave Jim an ice pack and told him to rest the ankle for a day to allow the swelling to go down. She advised him to notify his doctor if the pain increased or the swelling did not improve within a day.

Jim is disappointed because he had planned to play in an important Little League game tonight. He knows that his teammates are depending on him to pitch, and he does not want to let them down. He also is scheduled to be tested on the shuttle run tomorrow during PE class. He has been practicing this event and is impatient to be tested. On the other hand, Jim knows that an injury can get worse if it is not taken care of. If this were to occur, he knows that he might be prevented from participating in his favorite activities for longer than a day.

On a separate sheet of paper or the *Health for Life* decision-making chart, examine this situation. Use the five-step decision-making process and what you learned in Chapter 4 to determine what choices Jim has and which he should choose.

SKILLS FOR LIFE

# Feeling Good About Yourself

Laura is very discouraged. Every time a team captain chooses players in PE class, she is the last to be chosen. She knows that she is not the best athlete in the class, but she has become more skillful and coordinated this year.

Like everyone else, Laura has a "voice" in her head telling her about herself. When Laura has negative thoughts, she hears the voice telling her negative things about herself. When she has positive thoughts, she tells herself good things. When teams are being chosen in PE class, Laura finds herself having negative thoughts. She doubts her skills and abilities, and wonders whether she will have friends if she does not play ball well.

Divide a sheet of paper into two columns by folding it in half lengthwise. On the left side of the paper, list five examples of negative thinking that Laura might have when teams are being chosen. In the right-hand column, write a positive thought that Laura could substitute for each negative thought.

# Setting Goals

An important part of growing up and learning about yourself is developing the ability to recognize what you are good at and in what areas you need improvement. When you have identified these areas, it becomes possible to form goals for yourself and work to achieve your goals.

Physical fitness is essential to overall health. Exercise can improve both physical and mental well-being. Because of this, it is important for you to include exercise in your daily activities. You can develop an exercise plan by identifying your fitness strengths and weaknesses. You can then develop goals for yourself.

On a separate sheet of paper, use what you learned in Chapter 4 to answer the following questions.

1. What are your fitness strengths? In what areas would you like to improve?
2. What are three fitness goals that you would like to achieve?
3. How will you measure whether you have reached your fitness goals? If you cannot measure one of your goals, revise it so that it becomes measurable.

# Deciding What to Do

Because both of his parents have to work today, Jake is home alone with his six-year-old sister, Laura. His parents have left instructions not to have any visitors or allow anyone into the house while they are gone. They have also left telephone numbers where they can be reached and the telephone numbers of the neighbors, police department, and fire department.

The day is passing smoothly. As Jake works on a science project, Laura plays with her building set. Later, both Laura and Jake hear a knock at the door. As he checks through the peephole, Jake asks, "Who is it?" A man answers that he needs to use the phone for an emergency. Jake does not know the man, but recognizes him from the neighborhood. Jake knows that he is not supposed to open the door for strangers, but wants to help the man.

On a separate sheet of paper or the *Health for Life* decision-making chart, examine this situation. Use the five-step decision-making process and what you learned in Chapter 5 to determine Jake's choices. Evaluate each choice by asking whether it is safe and whether Jake's parents would approve of his decision. What would you advise Jake to do?

# Learning When and How to Say No

Carlos and his neighbor Kurt have spent the afternoon ice skating. The sun is beginning to go down, and the temperature is dropping. Both boys are supposed to be home before it is dark. Although Carlos and Kurt only live a few blocks away from the skating rink, they are too tired and cold to walk home. They also know that they will not make it home before it is dark. Both boys' parents are still at work, so they cannot call home for a ride. None of their friends are at the rink, either, so they cannot get a ride home with someone they know. Kurt suggests that he and Carlos hitch-hike home. He urges that there is no need to worry since they live so close to the skating rink. Carlos knows that hitch-hiking can be very dangerous. He decides that he would rather be cold and tired and arrive home late than put himself in a dangerous situation. He does not want to go along with Kurt's plan to hitch-hike home.

Fold a piece of paper in half lengthwise to make two columns. In the left column, list five ways that Carlos could say no to Kurt. In the right-hand column, write the possible consequences of each method. Which suggestion do you think is best?

# Communicating Well

Katy and Robert were riding their bicycles in the park when Robert fell off his bike. He landed hard, striking his elbow on the pavement. His shirt was torn and his elbow was scraped. Small pieces of gravel were on Robert's skin, and he was bleeding a little. The elbow appeared to be very bruised, and it hurt Robert to bend it. Katy told Robert that he should go home to wash the elbow, apply ice, and have an adult check the injury. Robert protested that he was not hurt. Katy pointed out that he might need to see a doctor, but Robert argued that he was not injured badly enough to cut their bicycle ride short. He cradled his elbow in his other hand, and winced when he moved his arm.

On a separate sheet of paper, write your answers to the following questions.

1. In what ways are Robert's words different from his actions?
2. How can Katy tell if Robert is hurt or not?
3. How is communication confused in this situation?
4. What can Katy say to Robert to convince him to get first aid?

# Deciding What to Do

SKILLS FOR LIFE

It is Saturday, and Erin is home alone for the day. Her mother had to go to work, and her father went to visit Erin's uncle, who is in a hospital several miles away. When Erin's mother calls, she suggests that Erin ask Patty, her fourteen-year-old cousin, to come over for the afternoon.

Shortly after Patty arrives, she and Erin decide to make lunch. While Erin is making sandwiches, Patty removes a pack of cigarettes from her purse and lights one. After taking a puff, she offers the lit cigarette to Erin and encourages her to share it.

Erin knows that cigarettes contain many harmful substances, and that they are habit-forming. She does not want to harm her body or develop a dangerous habit. She also thinks that smoking is an ugly habit. She does not want to smell like smoke or have stained teeth. On the other hand, Erin is grateful that Patty has come to keep her company. She does not want her older cousin to think that she is a baby. She wonders if smoking just once would really be a problem.

On a separate sheet of paper, list the choices that Erin has. Evaluate each choice by asking the following questions.
1. Is the choice safe? Does it promote good health?
2. Is the choice legal?
3. Would Erin's parents approve of her choice?
4. Does the choice show respect for Erin and others?

Which choice would you advise Erin to make? Why?

# Learning When and How to Say No

Gerald and Larry are neighbors and have been close friends since they were very young. Because they live so close to each other and enjoy being with each other, they often walk home from school together.

One day while walking home from school, Larry pulls a bottle of liquor from his backpack. He tells Gerald that he took it from his older brother, and that no one will ever know that it is missing. After taking a drink from the bottle, he offers it to Gerald and encourages his friend to share it with him.

Gerald knows that alcohol is illegal and dangerous for him to use. He does not want to use anything that will harm his body or cause a dangerous habit to form. He is certain that he does not want to drink any of Larry's liquor. Larry continues to insist that he try the liquor.

On a separate sheet of paper, write five ways that Gerald can say no to Larry.

# Dealing with Problems

SKILLS FOR LIFE

Danny has always been taught that smoking is harmful to the body. Neither of his parents smoke, nor do his friends. Danny knows that tobacco contains nicotine, an addictive drug. Lately, some of his friends have been encouraging Danny to try smokeless tobacco. They say that it is not harmful like smoking because it does not cause lung cancer. Danny knows that smokeless tobacco can cause a number of serious health problems, including oral cancer, and he will not try it. He does not want to develop a destructive addiction, and firmly tells his friends that he is not interested in trying smokeless tobacco. His friends, though, tell Danny that if he will not chew with them, he cannot do anything with them. This does not change Danny's mind about using smokeless tobacco, but going against his friends' wishes does make him uncomfortable. He feels sad and hurt to be left out of his group.

On a separate sheet of paper, write five suggestions to help Danny cope with the feelings created by peer pressure. Which suggestion would you encourage Danny to follow?

# Deciding What to Do

Wendy has been invited to a slumber party for her friend's birthday, and she has been looking forward to it all week. The morning of the party, Wendy's throat feels scratchy. She does not feel too ill, but knows that her mother would not let her go to the party if she knew about Wendy's sore throat. Although she does not want to miss the party, Wendy is worried that her sore throat will get worse during the night, and that one of her friends will catch it from her.

On a separate sheet of paper or your *Health For Life* decision-making chart, examine this situation. Use the five decision-making steps and what you learned in the chapter on fighting disease to determine what Wendy should do. Evaluate her options by asking:

1. Is the choice safe? Does it promote good health?
2. Would Wendy's parents and friends approve of her decision?
3. Does the choice show respect for herself and others?

What decision would you make?

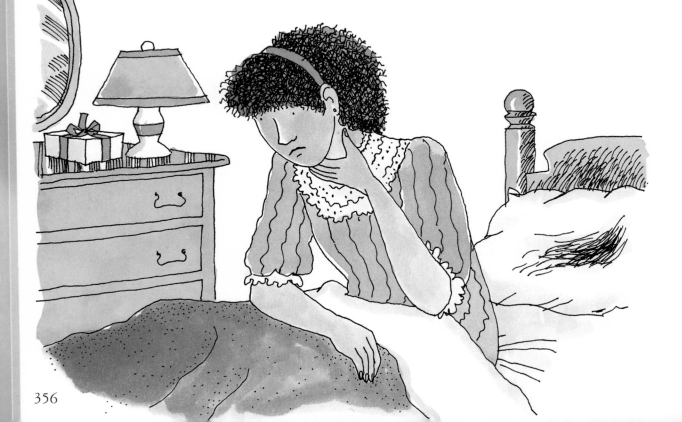

# Choosing the Best Advertisement

The job of advertisers is to influence consumers to buy their products. Advertisers know that people who do not feel well are especially likely to purchase health products that promise to help them feel better. Their advertisements aim to convince consumers that their products will relieve the symptoms of illness better than the competitors' products. Consumers spend a great deal of money on health products, many of which are not effective.

Divide a sheet of paper into three columns by folding it into thirds lengthwise. Label the columns A, B, and C. Along the left margin, number from 1 to 6. Look at the advertisements for products A, B, and C shown below. Use what you learned in Chapter 7 to compare the products by answering the following questions for each. Write your answers in the appropriate column on your paper.

1. What product is the advertisement trying to sell?
2. What symptoms does the advertisement claim that the product will help?
3. What does the advertisement promise the consumer?
4. How does the advertisement attempt to draw the consumer away from the competitors?
5. What helpful information does the advertisement give?
6. Which product would you be most likely to buy?

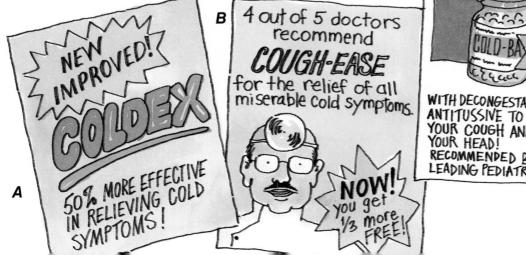

# Communicating Well

Wallace has stayed home from school because he has a bad headache and sore throat. His mother was unable to take the day off from work, but has made an appointment for him at the doctor's office. A neighbor will take Wallace to the doctor on her way to the store and will give him a ride home. For the first time, however, Wallace must see the doctor alone. He is a little nervous that he might forget to tell the doctor something important, and he wants to communicate clearly during his appointment. Wallace decides that it would be a good idea to make a list of things that he would like to remember to tell the doctor. He writes his symptoms and some questions he has for the doctor in a notebook.

On a separate sheet of paper, write your answers to the following questions.
1. What information will the doctor need to know?
2. How can Wallace be sure that he gives the doctor the necessary information?
3. How can Wallace make certain that he understands the doctor's instructions?
4. How can Wallace be sure that he remembers what the doctor instructs him to do?

# Deciding What to Do

After wearing them for three years, Abigail has just had her braces removed. The orthodontist has given her a retainer, a device to keep her teeth in the proper position. Abigail is supposed to wear her retainer all day and night. Abigail is relieved to have her braces off after waiting for so long, and she enjoys the compliments that people give her new smile. She is also glad that no one can call her names like "Metal Mouth" any more.

Abigail does not like to wear her retainer because she finds it to be uncomfortable. The retainer also makes her feel self-conscious because she lisps a little when wearing it. Because she is uncomfortable with it, Abigail would prefer not to wear her retainer all of the time. On the other hand, she wants her teeth to remain in the correct position so that she does not have to wear braces again.

On a separate sheet of paper or the *Health for Life* decision-making chart, evaluate this situation. Use the five-step decision-making process and what you learned in this chapter to determine the options that Abigail has. What would you advise Abigail to do?

# Feeling Good About Yourself

Josie has just found out that she has scoliosis, a condition that causes her spine to bend to the side. Her doctor has explained that Josie must wear a special brace for several months to straighten her spine and improve the condition. The brace is bulky, and shows through Josie's clothes. It also prevents Josie from moving in certain ways. She is self-conscious because she appears different from her classmates and cannot always participate in their activities. Sometimes, other kids make fun of Josie, which makes her feel even more uncomfortable around everyone else.

Fold a sheet of paper in half lengthwise to divide it into two columns. Label one column *Negative Thoughts* and the other *Positive Thoughts*. Write your answers to the following questions on this sheet of paper.

1. What negative thoughts might Josie have as a result of having scoliosis? Write your answers in the *Negative Thoughts* column.

2. For each negative thought that Josie might have about herself, write a positive thought that she could substitute in the *Positive Thoughts* column.

# Dealing with Problems

SKILLS FOR LIFE

William is feeling very anxious. His parents are getting divorced, and his mother expects him to look after his little sister after school and start dinner for the family each evening. William misses being able to play with his friends. He does not like the responsibility of caring for his sister. His schoolwork is suffering because his chores often prevent him from finishing his homework until late in the evening. He is often very tired during the school day and has even fallen asleep during class. He only sees his father on weekends and his mother is very tired at the end of the day. Therefore, no one is available to help William with his homework.

William knows that he is under stress. He realizes that a lack of rest and recreation can affect his health. He wants to identify the problem areas and determine what to do about them.

Divide a sheet of paper into three columns. Label the columns *Causes, Solutions,* and *Consequences.*

1. What factors in William's life are causing him to feel stress? List as many problems as you can in the *Causes* column.
2. How could William deal with each problem? List as many options as you can in the *Solutions* column.
3. What are some possible outcomes of each solution? List each outcome in the *Consequences* column next to the solution.
4. For each problem, circle the solution that you would advise William to use to reduce his stress.

# Deciding What to Do

Olivia stayed home from school today because she has a cold, sore throat, and cough. Because both of her parents work, she is home alone. As the day goes on, she finds that her sore throat is getting worse. Olivia finds a cough medicine and a cold remedy in the medicine cabinet. One bottle tells her that the product will relieve the symptoms of a cold and sore throat but does not mention anything about a cough. The other product promises to relieve the symptoms of a sore throat and cough. Both bottles list warnings about using the medicine.

Olivia is not certain which, if any, medicine she should take. She is not sure if the warnings on the labels apply to her. She does not want to harm her body. She decides to not take any medicine until her mother comes home.

On a separate sheet of paper or the *Health for Life* decision-making chart, examine this situation. Use the five-step decision-making process to evaluate why Olivia made the right decision. Evaluate each choice by asking whether it fits the guidelines for a good decision.

# Choosing the Best Advertisement

Larry and his younger brother, Steven, are watching television on Saturday morning. Larry notices that every time a commercial comes on the screen, his brother says, "I want that." He knows that television advertisers try to influence consumers to purchase their products by making promises about the products. Larry also knows that these commercials often do not present accurate or useful information to consumers, especially young viewers like Steven.

Larry decides to analyze the cereal ads that he and his brother see that morning and to observe the influence of these commercials on Steven. The advertisement for one cereal, Super Crunchees, features a cowboy who promises "the best crunch in the west." Another cereal, Sweet Nuggets, offers a golden ring in each box and promises the sweetest taste. A third brand of cereal, Oat Toasties, promises 100% of the United States RDA for the essential vitamins and minerals. Larry noted that his brother responded most to the advertisement for Sweet Nuggets.

On a separate sheet of paper, write your answers to the following questions.
1. What did each cereal advertisement promise the consumer?
2. What useful information about the product did each advertisement give the viewer?
3. Why do you think that the Sweet Nuggets commercial appealed the most to Steven?
4. Using what you learned in Chapter 9, which cereal would you choose, and why?

# Communicating Well

Hector has recently learned that he has diabetes, a disease in which the body is not able to absorb the proper amount of sugar and starch. He has found out that people with diabetes must carefully monitor their diet and exercise so that they do not become ill. Hector will need to follow a special food and activity plan each day. In addition, many people with diabetes must take a medicine called *insulin*. The doctor is explaining to Hector that he must take a certain amount of insulin at specific times each day. Hector becomes a little confused, because the doctor is giving him a lot of instructions. He is not sure that he understands everything that he is being told, nor is he certain that he will remember everything that he needs to do to stay healthy.

On a separate sheet of paper, write your answers to the following questions.
1. What should Hector do as he listens to the doctor?
2. How can Hector be certain that he understands what the doctor is saying?
3. How can Hector be sure that he remembers the information that the doctor gives him?

# Deciding What to Do

Leroy's mother has asked him to go to the grocery store to buy a large container of laundry detergent. She instructed him to select the brand with the best price. Once there, Leroy finds four brands that cost the same amount. One brand, packaged in a plastic jug, contains phosphates, an ingredient that Leroy has heard is unhealthy for the environment. Another brand, in a cardboard box, contains artificial colors. A third brand, in a cardboard box, is labeled *biodegradable,* a term that tells Leroy that the detergent breaks down into a harmless form in the environment. A fourth brand, in a plastic jug, is also labeled *biodegradable.* Leroy knows that he must select one of these detergents, but he is not sure which to choose. He decides to make his choice by evaluating each detergent's effects on the environment.

On a separate sheet of paper or the *Health for Life* decision-making chart, examine this situation. Use the five-step decision-making process and what you learned in Chapter 10 to determine Leroy's choices. Evaluate each choice by asking whether it shows respect for the environment. What decision would you advise Leroy to make, and why?

# Setting Goals

Lisa's class is trying to earn enough money to buy three new microscopes for their science lab. When investigating money-making activities, they discover that they can collect money from the local recycling center by turning in used aluminum cans and old newspapers. They are excited that they can earn money while improving their community, and decide to collect these items from their neighbors. Their goal is for each student to collect one bag of cans and twenty newspapers each week. Every Saturday, their science teacher will take two volunteers from the class to the recycling center to turn in their cans and papers. The class determines that by the end of two months, they will have enough money to buy the microscopes.

For the first few weeks, the project goes smoothly. The class is eager, and each student contributes at least one bag of cans and twenty newspapers each week. Soon, however, the students begin to lose interest, and fewer contributions are made. The students become discouraged.

On a separate sheet of paper, list five ways to help the class continue to work toward their goal.

# Choosing the Best Place to Live

People choose the places where they live for a variety of reasons. These reasons may include what the community has to offer each resident. Many people consider parks, beaches, other recreation facilities, schools, and hospitals to be very important factors in their choice of a place to live.

SKILLS FOR LIFE

Pretend that you are planning to buy a house in a new town. On a separate sheet of paper, write the factors that would be important to you in choosing a place to live. List as many factors as you can think of. Then write your answers to the following questions.

1. Which factors are most important to you as a consumer?
2. If you were buying a home, would the community in which you now live meet your requirements?
3. If your community does not meet your requirements, what changes would need to be made before you would choose to buy a home there?
4. How could you help make the necessary changes in your community?

# Glossary

**Pronunciation Key**

The pronunciation of each word is shown just after the word, in this way: **ab bre vi ate** (ə brē′vē āt). The letters and signs used are pronounced as in the words below. The mark ′ is placed after a syllable with primary or heavy accent, as in the example above. The mark ′ after a syllable shows a secondary or lighter accent, as in **ab bre vi a tion** (ə brē′vē ā′shən).

| | | | | |
|---|---|---|---|---|
| **a** | hat, cap | | **o** | hot, rock |
| **ā** | age, face | | **ō** | open, go |
| **ä** | father, far | | **ô** | order, all |
| | | | **oi** | oil, voice |
| **b** | bad, rob | | **ou** | house, out |
| **ch** | child, much | | | |
| **d** | did, red | | **p** | paper, cup |
| | | | **r** | run, try |
| **e** | let, best | | **s** | say, yes |
| **ē** | equal, be | | **sh** | she, rush |
| **ėr** | term, learn | | **t** | tell, it |
| | | | **th** | thin, both |
| **f** | fat, if | | **ŦH** | then, smooth |
| **g** | go, bag | | **u** | cup, butter |
| **h** | he, how | | **u̇** | full, put |
| | | | **ü** | rule, move |
| **i** | it, pin | | | |
| **ī** | ice, five | | **v** | very, save |
| | | | **w** | will, woman |
| **j** | jam, enjoy | | **y** | young, yet |
| | | | **z** | zero, breeze |
| **k** | kind, seek | | **zh** | measure, seizure |
| **l** | land, coal | | | |
| **m** | me, am | | **ə** | represents: |
| **n** | no, in | | **a** | in about |
| **ng** | long, bring | | **e** | in taken |
| | | | **i** | in pencil |
| | | | **o** | in lemon |
| | | | **u** | in circus |

# A

**abdomen** (ab′dō mən), the lower part of the body of humans and other mammals, containing the digestive organs, such as the stomach and intestines.

**acid rain,** rain that contains a higher than normal amount of acids. These acids are caused by certain gases released into the air.

**acne** (ak′nē), a skin disease in which the oil glands become clogged and inflamed, often causing pimples.

**additive** (ad′ə tiv), any substance added to food for a particular purpose.

**advertisement,** a public notice or announcement recommending a product or service.

**agility** (ə jil′ə tē), the ability to change the position of the body quickly and to control body movements.

**alcoholism** (al′kə hô liz′əm), a disease in which a person cannot control his or her use of alcohol.

**allergen** (al′ər jən), a substance in the environment that causes an allergy.

**allergy** (al′ər jē), a harmful reaction of the body to a substance in the environment.

**antibiotic** (an′ti bī ot′ik), a medicine that destroys or weakens bacteria.

**antibody** (an′ti bod′ē), a tiny substance made by the white blood cells that attaches to a disease germ, making it harmless.

**antiperspirant** (an′ti per′spər ənt), a chemical preparation that controls body odor by closing the pores of sweat glands.

**aquarium** (ə kwer′ē əm), a place where living fish and water plants are collected and shown.

**arboretum** (är′bə rē′təm), a place where trees and shrubs are grown and exhibited for scientific and educational purposes.

**artery** (är′tər ē), a blood vessel that carries blood from the heart to other parts of the body.

**artificial respiration** (är′tə fish′əl res′pə rā′shən), a method of first aid that forces air into the lungs.

**atherosclerosis** (ath′ər ō sklə rō′sis), a cardiovascular disease in which material builds up inside the arteries.

**attitude** (at′ə tüd), a way of thinking about a particular idea, situation, or person.

# B

**bacteria** (bak tir′ē ə), a group of organisms that can usually be seen only with a microscope. Some bacteria are harmful, causing disease and tooth decay.

**blood alcohol level,** the percentage of fluids in the bloodstream that is alcohol.

**body fatness,** the amount of a person's weight that is body fat.

# C

**caffeine** (ka fēn′), a mild stimulant drug found in some coffees, teas, soft drinks, and chocolate.

**calipers** (kal′ə pərz), an instrument used to measure the thickness of something. Calipers can be used to measure the thickness of body fat under the skin.

**Calorie** (kal′ər ē), a unit used to measure the amount of energy a food can produce in the body and the amount of energy the body uses during activity.

**cancer** (kan′sər), the uncontrolled growth of abnormal body cells.

**carbohydrates** (kär′bō hī′drātz), a group of nutrients that supplies energy and includes sugar, starch, and fiber.

**carbon dioxide** (dī ok′sīd), a colorless, odorless gas produced as a body waste in humans and other animals.

**carbon monoxide** (kär′bən mo nok′sīd), a colorless, odorless, and poisonous gas in the exhausts of motor vehicles.

**cardiovascular** (kär′dē ō vas′kyə lər) **disease,** a disease of the heart or blood vessels.

**cardiovascular** (kär′dē ō vas′kyə lər) **system,** the body system made up of the heart, blood, and blood vessels. This system moves oxygen and nutrients to body cells and removes cell wastes.

**cavity** (kav′ə tē), a hole in a tooth, caused by tooth decay.

**cell** (sel), the basic unit of living matter.

**chlorine** (klôr′ēn′), a chemical added to sewage and to drinking water to kill bacteria.

**cholesterol** (kə les′tə rol′), a fatlike substance that is made naturally in the body and is present in foods from animal sources.

**chromosome** (krō′mə sōm), a strand of matter in the nucleus of a cell that contains the information for a person's heredity.

**cilia** (sil′ē ə), hairlike projections that line parts of the respiratory system.

**circulation** (sėr′kyə lā′shən), the flow of the blood from the heart through the arteries and veins back to the heart.

**cirrhosis** (sə rō′sis), a disease of the liver that is often caused by heavy, long-term use of alcohol.

**clinic** (klin′ik), a place where people can receive medical treatment, often free or at low cost.

**communicable** (kə myü′nə kə bəl) **disease,** a disease that can spread, usually from one person to another.

**community** (kə myü′nə tē), a group of people living in the same area.

**contagious** (kən tā′jəs), able to be spread from one person to another.

**coordination** (kō ôrd′n ā′shən), the ability to use the senses together with body parts or to use two or more body parts together.

# D

**dandruff,** clumps of dead skin cells that form on the scalp.

**decibel** (des′ə bəl), a unit for measuring the loudness of sound.

**deodorant** (dē ō′dər ənt), a chemical preparation that controls body odor by slowing the growth of bacteria on the skin.

**dependence,** the need for a drug. This need might be mental, physical, or both.

**depressant** (di pres′nt), a drug that slows down the work of the nervous system.

**diet,** a general term for the kind of food and drink a person consumes daily.

**dietitian** (dī′ə tish′ən), an expert on how the body uses nutrients and what nutrients are necessary for good health.

**disease germ,** an organism or substance that causes a communicable disease.

**DNA,** a chemical substance that makes up chromosomes and determines inherited traits.

**drug,** any chemical substance that changes the way the body works. The physical changes might cause changes in emotions and behavior.

**drug abuse,** the intentional use of drugs for reasons other than health.

**drug misuse,** incorrect use of a medicine in a way that can harm health.

# E

**egg cell,** the female reproductive cell.

**electron microscope,** an instrument that enables people to view viruses and other tiny substances up to two million times their actual sizes.

**emergency,** a sudden need for quick action.

**enamel** (i nam′əl), the smooth, hard, outer layer of a tooth.

**endocrine** (en′dō krən) **gland,** an organ that produces chemicals and releases them directly into the blood.

**energy,** the ability to do work. The body gets energy from food to do all the work that keeps the body alive and healthy.

**enriched,** having had nutrients, such as vitamins and minerals, added.

**environment** (en vī′rən mənt), all the living and nonliving surroundings that affect living things.

**epidemiologist** (ep′ə dē′mē ol′ə jist), a physician or research scientist who studies the occurrence and causes of diseases.

# F

**fad,** a product or practice that is popular only for a short time.

**fatigue** (fə tēg′), weariness caused by physical exercise, stress, concentration, boredom, or a lack of energy.

**fats,** a group of nutrients that provides energy and carries certain vitamins through the body.

**fiber** (fī′bər), a carbohydrate that helps move food and wastes through the body.

**first aid,** immediate medical care given to someone who is injured or suddenly ill.

**flexibility** (flek′sə bil′ə tē), the ability to move the joints fully and to move body parts easily.

**food consumer,** a person who buys or uses food. Everyone is a food consumer.

**food processing,** the changing of food before it is eaten.

**fortified** (fôr′tə fīd), enriched with vitamins and minerals.

# G

**gene** (jēn), a small part of a chromosome that influences a specific inherited trait.

**goal** (gōl), something a person wants to do or achieve.

**groundwater,** water in the ground, near the earth's surface. Groundwater is usually located in the soil and in the cracks of rock beneath the surface.

**growth spurt,** a period of rapid growth. A growth spurt usually begins between the ages of nine and fifteen.

**guarantee** (gar′ən tē′), a promise by a manufacturer to replace, repair, or give money back for a product if it proves to be unsatisfactory.

**gum disease,** a condition begun by plaque building up and hardening between the teeth and under the gumline. This buildup irritates the gums, eventually causing them to pull away from the teeth, and leaving pockets through which bacteria can attack bone.

# H

**hallucinogen** (hə lü′sn ə jen), a drug that causes changes in the senses, often making a person see, hear, smell, or feel things that are not really there.

**health consumer,** a person who buys or uses health products or services.

**health fitness,** the kind of fitness that helps a person look and feel his or her best and reduces the risk of disease.

**heredity** (hə red′ə tē), the passing of traits from parents to children.

**hormone** (hôr′mōn), a chemical, made by an endocrine gland, that affects how body cells work.

**hypertension** (hī′pər ten′shən), high blood pressure.

# I

**immunity** (i myü′nə tē), the body's resistance to a disease through the presence of antibodies.

**infection** (in fek′shən), the presence of disease germs in the body.

**inhalant** (in hā′lənt), a substance that gives off fumes, which could produce druglike effects when breathed deeply into the body.

# L

**lifestyle,** the way a person lives his or her life. A person's lifestyle includes that person's daily or usual actions that affect his or her health.

**logo** (lō′gō), a symbol used to identify something for advertising purposes.

# M

**mainstream smoke,** smoke that is exhaled by the smoker.

**marijuana** (mar′ə wä′nə), the dried leaves and stems of a hemp plant used illegally as a mind-altering drug.

**medicine,** a drug that produces changes in the body to prevent, treat, or cure an illness.

**minerals,** a group of nutrients needed to provide healthy teeth, bones, muscles, and blood cells.

**mucus** (myü′kəs), a watery and somewhat sticky liquid that lines the mouth, nose, throat, windpipe, and lungs.

**muscular endurance** (en dyür′əns), the ability of muscles to work for long periods of time without getting tired.

# N

**narcotic** (när kot′ik), a legal term for a drug made from opium or from a substance like opium that is produced artificially.

**net weight,** the weight of the contents of a product, not including the container.

**nicotine** (nik′ə tēn′), a stimulant drug found in cigarette smoke.

**noncommunicable** (non′kə myü′nə kə bəl) **disease,** a disease that is not caused by germs and that does not spread.

**nucleus** (nü′klē əs), the part of a cell that controls the cell's activities.

**nutrient** (nü′trē ənt), a substance found in food that your body needs to stay healthy.

**nutrition** (nü trish′ən), the study of nutrients and how the body uses them. Also, food or nourishment.

# O

**oil glands,** tiny structures in the skin that produce an oily substance and transfer it to the surface of the skin.

**organ,** a structure made of living tissues that perform a specific function. For example, each endocrine gland is an organ.

**organism** (ôr′gə niz′əm), an individual living thing.

**ovaries** (ō′vər ēz), female reproductive glands.

**overdose,** an amount of a drug that is too large for the body and can cause a dangerous reaction.

**over-the-counter medicine,** a drug that can be purchased without a doctor's order.

**oxygen** (ok′sə jən), a colorless, odorless, and tasteless gas that humans, other animals, and plants need to live.

# P

**penicillin** (pen′ə sil′ən), an antibiotic that cures many bacterial diseases.

**perspiration** (pėr′spə rā′shən), the water, salt, heat, and other body wastes transferred by the sweat glands to the skin's surface.

**pharmacist** (fär′mə sist), a person licensed to fill prescriptions.

**physical fitness,** the ability to exercise, play, and work without tiring easily and without a high risk of injury.

**pituitary** (pə tü′ə ter′ē) **gland,** the endocrine gland that makes growth hormone and other hormones that control the activities of other endocrine glands.

**planetarium** (plan′ə tər′ē əm), a building or room where the movements of the sun, moon, planets, and stars can be shown on the inside of a dome.

**plaque** (plak), a fatty substance that builds up along the inside walls of an artery. Also, a thin, sticky, colorless film, consisting largely of bacteria, that forms on teeth and gums.

**pneumonia** (nü mō′nyə), a respiratory disease in which a lung becomes inflamed, often accompanied by chills, a pain in the chest, cough, and fever.

**poison,** a substance that is harmful if it gets inside the body.

**pollution** (pə lü′shən), a change in the environment that is harmful or unpleasant to living things.

**posture** (pos′chər), the position of the body.

**prescription** (pri skrip′shən) **medicine,** a drug that can be purchased only with an order from a doctor.

**preservative** (pri zėr′və tiv), an additive that helps keep food from spoiling.

**proteins** (prō′tēnz′), the group of nutrients that builds, repairs, and maintains body cells.

**puberty** (pyü′bər tē), a period of time when the body develops more adultlike qualities, including the ability to reproduce.

# R

**recreation** (rek′rē ā′shən), activity, such as exercise or a hobby, that provides relaxation during leisure time.

**recycling,** changing a waste product so that it can be used again.

**reflexes,** automatic body reactions.

**relationship** (ri lā′shən ship), a connection or condition that exists between two or more people.

**reproduce** (rē′prə düs′), produce offspring.

**reproductive cell,** a cell that gives a male or female the ability to reproduce. The male reproductive cells are sperm cells, and the female reproductive cells are egg cells.

**reproductive gland,** a gland that develops reproductive cells, giving a male or female the ability to reproduce. The male reproductive glands are testes, and the female reproductive glands are ovaries.

**respiratory** (res′pər ə tôr′ē) **system,** the body system that includes the nose, air passages, and lungs. This system helps bring oxygen to the body and remove carbon dioxide from the body.

**rickets** (rik′its), a childhood disease in which the bones do not develop properly; caused by a lack of vitamin D and calcium.

# S

**sanitarian** (san′ə ter′ē ən), an environmental health specialist who works to ensure the safe quality of food, water, or air for the public health.

**sanitary landfill,** an area of land where garbage is buried in such a way as to minimize water pollution, air pollution, and the spread of disease.

**scoliosis** (skō′lē ō′sis), a condition in which the spine curves to the side.

**scrubber,** a device attached to a factory smokestack that removes much of the harmful gas and most of the particles from smoke.

**scurvy** (skėr′vē), a disease characterized by bleeding gums, bruises on the skin, and extreme weakness; caused by a lack of vitamin C.

**self-image,** the way a person feels about himself or herself.

**sewage** (sü′ij), the waste material carried through sewers and drains, also called wastewater.

**sewage treatment plant,** a facility where sewage is partially cleaned before being sent to a river, lake, or ocean; also called wastewater treatment plant.

**shock,** a condition that occurs when the body fails to circulate blood adequately, causing body functions to slow down.

**sidestream smoke,** smoke that comes from the end of a burning cigarette.

**sinusitis** (sī′nə sī′tis), a disease in which the sinus openings become blocked.

**skills fitness,** the kind of fitness that helps a person perform physical skills.

**smog** (smog), pollution caused by engine exhaust gases reacting with other gases in the presence of sunlight.

**snuff,** a powder made from grinding tobacco leaves and stems. It is usually sniffed through the nose.

**sodium** (sō′dē əm), a soft silver-white element, which is the main component of salt.

**sperm** (spėrm) **cell,** the male reproductive cell.

**stimulant** (stim′yə lənt), a drug that speeds up the work of the nervous system.

**stress,** the body's physical and mental reactions to demanding situations.

**sulfur dioxide** (sul′fər dī ok′sīd), a major component of air pollution. Sulfur dioxide reacts with moisture in the air to form acid rain.

**sweat glands,** tiny structures in the skin that collect some body wastes and transfer them to the surface of the skin.

**symptom** (simp′təm), a sign or indication of a disease.

# T

**tar,** a yellow or brown substance in the smoke of cigarettes. Tars form a brown, sticky mass in smokers' lungs.

**testes** (tes′tēz) *sing.* **testis** (tes′tis), male reproductive glands.

**THC,** the main mind-altering chemical in marijuana.

**tolerance,** a condition in which the body gets used to the presence of a drug and needs larger amounts of that drug to produce the same effects.

**tooth decay,** a condition in which acids destroy the enamel of teeth.

**toxic,** poisonous.

**trait** (trāt), a feature or quality of a person or thing.

**tumor** (tü′mər), a clump of useless tissue caused by the buildup of abnormal cells.

# U

**unit price,** the price of a product per ounce, gram, or other unit of measure.

**unnecessary risk,** an action that is not necessary to perform and that greatly increases the threat to a person's safety.

# V

**vaccine** (vak′sēn), a small dose of killed or weakened disease germs that prevents a person from getting a disease.

**vein** (vān), a blood vessel that carries blood back to the heart.

**virus** (vī′rəs), a group of tiny, disease-causing substances.

**vitamins** (vī′tə mənz), a group of nutrients needed in small amounts to keep the body working properly.

**volunteer** (vol′ən tir′), a person who offers services without pay.

# W

**water treatment plant,** a facility where water from a river or lake is cleaned to make it safe and pleasant for drinking; also called water purification plant.

**white blood cell,** a blood cell that destroys disease germs.

**withdrawal,** the symptoms that occur when a person who is physically dependent on a drug stops taking it.

# Index

*A **bold-faced** number indicates a page with a picture about the topic.*

# G

# H

# Acknowledgments

**Page 162:** From "She Knew What to Do" from CHILD LIFE magazine. Copyright © 1981 by Benjamin Franklin Literary & Medical Society, Inc., Indianapolis, Indiana. Adapted by permission of the publisher.

**Page 310:** Figure by Josephine Bellalta-Moriarty from "Local Garden Helps Pilsen Bloom" by Rebecca Severson, THE NEIGHBORHOOD WORKS, April 1985. Reprinted by permission of Josephine Bellalta-Moriarty.

# Picture Credits

**Page 18–19:** © Photri/Marilyn Gartman Agency

**Page 26(l):** © Donald Smetzer/Click/Chicago

**Page 27(l):** © Donald Dietz/Stock Boston

**Page 31:** Courtesy Daniel L. Feicht/Cedar Point, Inc.

**Page 44:** Photo courtesy of WTTW, Chicago

**Page 58:** © Ed Reschke

**Page 59: (b)** Courtesy of Genetics Department, Children's Memorial Hospital, Chicago, IL.

**Page 63:** © Plantek 1985/Photo Researchers

**Page 74–75:** © 1983 Mark Wexler

**Page 76:** © Rice Sumner Wagner

**Page 81:** Jim and Mary Whitmer

**Page 90:** Courtesy The Manning Brothers Historical Collection

**Page 91:** Jim and Mary Whitmer

**Page 92:** Edith G. Haun/Stock Boston

**Page 100:** Courtesy Parke-Davis, Division of Warner Lambert Company

**Page 104–105:** © David Brownell 1983

**Page 106:** Jim Whitmer/Nawrocki Stock Photo

**Page 110(l):** © Joseph Nettis 1983/Photo Researchers **(r):** Focus West

**Page 111:** Bill Ross/West Light

**Page 116(l):** Jim Whitmer/Nawrocki Stock Photo **(c):** Joseph A. DiChello, Jr.

**Page 117(c):** Click/Chicago

**Page 119:** John J. Lopinot

**Page 120(r):** © Dave Black 1986

**Page 136:** John J. Lopinot

**Page 143(tr):** Courtesy Speciality Vehicle Institute of America

**Page 162:** Reprinted with permission from THE SATURDAY EVENING POST Company © 1981

**Page 166–167:** Warshaw Collection. Smithsonian Institution.

**Page 172:** © University Museum. University of Pennsylvania

**Page 174:** Larry Mulvehill/Photo Researchers

**Page 179:** © Russ Kinne 1978/Photo Researchers

**Page 180(t,b):** Courtesy Dr. Donald T. Tashkin, M.D., University of California Los Angeles

**Page 183:** Ira Kirschenbaum/Stock Boston

**Page 184(l):** Martin K. Rotker/Taurus **(r):** © 1985 James E. Eisman/Journalism Services/Nawrocki Stock Photo

**Page 191:** Cameramann International

**Page 198–199:** Lou Lainey/© DISCOVER PUBLICATIONS, INC.

**Page 200(l):** Jonathon D. Eisenback/Phototake **(c):** Eric Gravé/Phototake **(r):** L.J. LeBeau, University of Illinois Hospital/Biological Photo Service

**Page 201(l,r):** Gene Cox/Micro Colour, England

**Page 203(tl):** Omikron/Photo Researchers **(cl):** Dr. R. Dourmashkin/SPL/Photo Researchers **(bl):** T. R. Broker/Phototake **(r):** Dick Luria/Photo Researchers

**Page 204–205:** Lennart Nilsson, from *Behold Man*, Courtesy Little, Brown and Company, Boston. Used with permission.

**Page 208(t):** Courtesy Centers for Disease Control

**Page 209:** Prof. Luc Montagnier/Institut Pasteur/CNRI/Science Photo Laboratory/Photo Res.

**Page 211(t):** Dr. R. Dourmashkin/SPL/Photo Researchers **(b):** T. R. Broker/Phototake

**Page 213(t):** Ray Simon/Photo Researchers

**Page 215(r):** © 1985 Martin M. Rotker/Taurus

**Page 217:** Dr. Rob Stepney/SPL/Photo Researchers

**Page 218(l):** Lennart Nilsson, from *Behold Man*, Courtesy Little, Brown and Company, Boston. Used with permission.

**Page 218(r):** Photograph by Dr. Lennart Nilsson

**Page 219(l):** Photograph by Dr. Lennart Nilsson

**Page 219(r):** Lou Lainey/© DISCOVER PUBLICATIONS, INC.

**Page 220(l):** Warren Uzzle/© DISCOVER PUBLICATIONS, INC.

**Page 224:** Marty Cooper/Peter Arnold Inc.

**Page 226:** Hans Pfletschinger/Peter Arnold Inc.

**Page 230:** Courtesy Parke-Davis, Division of Warner-Lambert Company

**Page 236:** Susan Leavines/Photo Researchers

**Page 238(t):** Courtesy Cleveland Museum of Natural History **(b):** Z. Skobe, Forsyth Dental Center/Biological Photo Service

**Page 240–241:** Copyright by the American Dental Association. Reprinted by permission.

**Page 247:** Robert Lightfoot/Nawrocki Stock Photo

**Page 249:** © 1986 Christopher Springman. All rights reserved.

**Page 250:** Joseph A. DiChello, Jr.

**Page 252:** Photo by John E. Gilmore for Scott, Foresman

**Page 280:** Courtesy National Archives

**Page 284–285:** Cameramann International

**Page 286(tl):** © Ed Bock 1985 **(tr):** Tom Pantages

**Page 287:** Ann McQueen/Stock Boston

**Page 291:** Brent Jones

**Page 292:** © Michael Philip Manheim/Marilyn Gartman Agency

**Page 295:** Cameramann International/Marilyn Gartman Agency

**Page 296:** Ted Spiegel/Black Star

**Page 296:** Ted Spiegel/Black Star

**Page 299:** © Ovak Arslanian

**Page 302:** Ray Hillstrom/Hillstrom Stock Photo

**Page 303:** Coco McCoy/Rainbow

**Page 304:** Tom Hollyman/Photo Researchers

**Page 305(t):** Courtesy Adler Planetarium, Chicago **(c):** Gerald Corsi/Tom Stack **(b):** Nathan Benn/Woodfin Camp & Assoc.

**Page 310:** Rebecca Severson/Chicago Botanic Garden

All photographs not credited are the property of Scott, Foresman and Company. These include photographs taken by the following photographers:

James L. Ballard: Pages 20–21, 28–29 (all), 30, 32–33, 36, 42, 48–49, 50–51, 53, 64–65 (all), 66–67 (all), 68, 69, 70, 71, 92 (b), 107, 116 (r), 137, 143 (l), 145, 148 (all), 149, 150, 152, 156, 163, 175, 178, 185, 195, 228 234–235, 256–257, 260–261, 264–265 (all), 266 (l), 267 (r), 268, 272, 277–279 (all), 281, 286 (br), 306–307, 311

Ralph Cowan: Pages 130–135 (all)

Michael Goss: Pages 24–25, 77, 78, 79, 83 (all), 84–85, 86–87, 95, 153, 154–155 (b), 170 (all), 171, 192 (all), 229

Edward Hughes: Pages 181, 188, 189

Glen D. Phelan: Pages 61 (b), 297

Diana O. Rasche: Pages 143 (br), 288–290 (all)

Ryan Roessler: Pages 96–97 (b), 140–141, 157 (all), 158–159 (all), 169, 190, 258–259, 269, 273, 298 (l)